HIGHER EDUCATION FOR AFRICAN AMERICANS BEFORE THE CIVIL RIGHTS ERA, 1900-1964

On the Cover:
Students Studying in Reading Room of Howard University Library,
by Alfred Eisenstaedt

HIGHER EDUCATION FOR AFRICAN AMERICANS BEFORE THE CIVIL RIGHTS ERA, 1900-1964

MARYBETH GASMAN AND ROGER L. GEIGER, EDITORS

PERSPECTIVES ON THE HISTORY OF HIGHER EDUCATION

VOLUME TWENTY-NINE, 2012

TRANSACTION PUBLISHERS
RUTGERS, THE STATE UNIVERSITY OF NEW JERSEY
NEW BRUNSWICK AND LONDON

Library of Congress Catalog Number: 2012006831
ISBN: 978-1-4128-4771-1
Printed in the United States of America

Library of Congress Cataloging-in-Publication Data

Higher education for African Americans before the Civil Rights era, 1900-1964 / Marybeth Gasman and Roger L. Geiger, editors.
    p. cm. — (Perspectives on the history of higher education ; v. 29)
    ISBN 978-1-4128-4771-1
    1. African Americans—Education (Higher)—History—20th century.
2. African American college students—History—20th century. 3. African American universities and colleges—History—20th century. 4. Discrimination in higher education—United States—History—20th century. I. Gasman, Marybeth. II. Geiger, Roger L., 1943-
  LC2781.H547 2012
  378.1'982996073—dc23
                                                        2012006831

Contents

Introduction: Higher Education for African-Americans before the Civil Rights Era, 1900–1964

Marybeth Gasman and Roger L. Geiger

On May 29–30, 1900, W. E. B. Du Bois convened the Fifth Conference for the Study of the Negro Problems at Atlanta University. His subject that year was *The College-Bred Negro*. For the conference, Du Bois had conducted a survey of American colleges and universities to identify African-American graduates. He obtained the names of some 2,500 individuals and managed to elicit responses from half of them. An extraordinary piece of sociological research for any era, the Atlanta study documents the higher educational attainments of African-Americans thirty-seven years after Emancipation, but also in the midst of the Jim Crow era in the South. Given systematic oppression and persecution, there can be little wonder at the meagerness of graduate numbers or the weaknesses of educational opportunities up to and including the "Negro Colleges." However, the conclusions of the study are on balance hopeful, as are the attitudes of most respondents. Individual African-Americans and their institutions had overcome great difficulties to attain this level of accomplishment. And Du Bois's purpose was to point the way for further progress.

This volume considers the next phase in the gradual expansion and elevation of African-American higher education, the long march from Jim Crow conditions to the Civil Rights Act of 1964. Such progress as was possible was made against heavy odds—the "separate but (un)equal" policies of the segregated South, less overt but pervasive racist attitudes in the North, and formidable legal obstacles to obtaining equal rights. These facts speak for themselves. But the story is nevertheless one of hope prevailing despite formidable obstacles. The studies that follow examine important aspects of these developments. This introduction provides an overview and context of the principal episodes in this protracted saga.

The Landscape of African-American Higher Education, 1900–1910

When Du Bois focused the Atlanta Conference on higher education for African-Americans, the issue was both a timely and a personal one. Booker T. Washington, the "Wizard of Tuskegee," had emerged as the spokesman for this subject and, indeed, for the "Negro Question" in the South. In frequent speeches, Washington lauded the kind of industrial education that he had instituted at Tuskegee Normal and Industrial Institute as the answer to self-improvement for African-Americans and racial harmony in a segregated society. This message was gratifying for White philanthropists who wished to address some of the glaring educational deficiencies of southern African-Americans, but could only do so without challenging White hegemony. At this juncture, Du Bois had little quarrel with industrial education per se; he even taught summer school at Tuskegee in 1903. But this was not the kind of education that he had received and that he wished to provide others as a professor at Atlanta University. He had graduated from Fisk University and entered Harvard as a junior. He graduated with honors, pursued postgraduate studies at the University of Berlin, and earned a Harvard PhD (1895).[1] Other African-Americans needed to obtain a liberal or academic education to provide the cultural and professional leadership that could scarcely emerge from industrial schools. A case had to be made for "Negro Colleges" (now called Historically Black Colleges and Universities, or HBCUs). Du Bois did this in the way he knew best at this stage of his long career—with an empirical sociological study.

His 1900 study of the *College-Bred Negro* marshaled evidence for several strong recommendations. He noted the great need for "common schools and manual training," as well as a "growing demand for industrial and technical training." However, he emphasized the "distinct demand for the higher training of . . . leaders of thought and missionaries of culture among the masses." Du Bois backed this conclusion with responses from prominent northern educators, a few of whom clearly sympathized with Booker T. Washington. But Harvard president Charles Eliot supported Du Bois's most crucial recommendations: "teachers, preachers, lawyers, engineers, and superior mechanics, the leaders of industry, throughout the Negro communities of the South, should be trained in superior institutions." Du Bois also polled HBCU graduates, who reported overwhelmingly that college training had been beneficial for them, more so than any alternative could have been. Here was unambiguous endorsement of the connection between HBCUs and the emerging concept of the Talented Tenth. Du Bois's study of *The Philadelphia Negro* and the Atlanta University Studies gave him an unrivaled knowledge of the American Black community. From Du Bois's perspective, Washington's disregard for college-educated African-Americans when pandering to White audiences threatened to undermine this possibility. Hence, the defense of the College-Bred Negro presaged Du Bois's imminent estrangement.[2]

Du Bois also recommended that "34 Negro colleges are entirely too many," and that "eight, or at most, ten colleges" could accommodate the current number of qualified students. He identified the strongest candidates in each of eight states, plus Howard in Washington and Lincoln and Wilberforce in Pennsylvania and Ohio, respectively. At first glance, such shrinkage seems inconsistent with his powerful advocacy for college education. Actually, Du Bois was in line with contemporary thinking on this issue. University of Chicago president William Rainey Harper wrote that same year that "the problem of the small college" was one of the two most pressing issues in American education. Soon afterward, both the General Education Board and the Carnegie Foundation for the Advancement of Teaching addressed this issue by supporting the stronger (White) colleges. All agreed that small colleges with inadequate resources should focus on lower levels of education. For Du Bois, elimination or demotion of those struggling institutions, and strengthening the remaining HBCUs, would allow them to "escape some of the deserved criticisms that have been aimed at [them.]"[3] In keeping with this goal, much of the *College-Bred Negro* documents the differences in quality among these institutions.

In 1910, Du Bois revisited this subject with a second, more extensive, Atlanta University Study—*The College-Bred Negro American*. Together, these volumes present an incomparable portrait of higher education for African-Americans in the first decade of the twentieth century. The conclusions were essentially the same, but presented now as "resolutions" endorsed by the presidents of the principal HBCUs. The "demotion" of the weaker HBCUs is only implied in this volume, accompanied by more extensive data on qualitative differences among the schools.[4]

Du Bois grouped the HBCUs according to five waves of foundings. Before the Civil War, Lincoln and Wilberforce universities were established by northern abolitionist church groups. Thirteen colleges were founded in the late 1860s under the auspices of the Freedman's Bureau, including Howard, Fisk, and Atlanta universities. In the 1870s, nine colleges were established by Northern church groups, mostly Methodists; and in the next decade African-American Baptist and Methodist churches established five more colleges. Finally, under state colleges, Du Bois listed only four institutions. Although the 1890 Morrill Act required land-grant funds in segregated states to be shared with a Black institution, most of these 1890s land-grants did not teach at the collegiate level for another two decades.[5] The eight to ten colleges he sought to promote dated from the earlier, Freedman's Bureau era, but a few of the church-related colleges qualified as well. All HBCUs in the South began as multipurpose educational institutions. As of 1899, just six counted more than twenty collegiate students and they were heavily outnumbered by secondary and often primary school students. To evaluate their work, he compared them to the "smaller New England colleges." Only Howard was judged "nearly equal"; Fisk, Atlanta, Wilberforce, Leland, and Paul Quinn were "from 1 to 2 years behind"; and the others (mostly unnamed) were either "2 to 3 years behind" or "little above an ordinary New England High School." The variability in college quality was perceived to be a general problem across American higher education. The Bureau of Education had divided female colleges into "A" and "B" divisions in 1887, and the Harvard Law School felt compelled to rate colleges in 1893 according to the fitness of their graduates for admission. Du Bois sought to be objective by examining curricula and library holdings. Above all, and unlike many critics who came after him, he wished to accurately identify these weaknesses so that they might be remedied.[6]

The first decade of the twentieth century was a critical time for American colleges. The academic revolution of the 1890s had displaced the old classical college with a discipline-based curriculum, which had undermined older notions of a liberal education. To adapt, colleges needed additional resources to hire more teachers with modern disciplinary training. For the HBCUs, however, the meager support from churches and missionary organizations was drying up. The enormous pools of capital now marshaled by northern philanthropists were deliberately directed to Hampton and Tuskegee—the industrial/normal schools that had been so adroitly promoted by Samuel Chapman Armstrong and Booker T. Washington.[7] Moreover, the worsening subjugation of African-Americans in the Jim Crow South made educational progress especially difficult. For the decade, enrollments in American higher education increased by 50 percent, but the HBCUs that Du Bois tracked grew by just 40 percent. Only one of his prescriptions seemed to be validated: enrollments became increasingly concentrated in the strongest institutions. Howard, Fisk, Atlanta, and Lincoln accounted for one-half of college students in HBCUs, and the first three added almost all of the growth. Conversely, the conditions of the other institutions were dire, at least for the "college departments . . . [that] are but adjuncts, and sometimes unimportant adjuncts, to other departments devoted to secondary and primary work."[8]

Du Bois's two surveys also provide unique information on the education of African-Americans at northern universities. By 1910, he had identified 693 such graduates of northern schools, or nearly one-quarter of the number of HBCU graduates. Of that total, in 1900, more than one-third (21 percent in 1910) had graduated from Oberlin, where African-Americans had been admitted since 1837. For 1900–1909, total northern graduates grew to nearly 40 percent of those at HBCUs. The leading universities were tolerant for the most part of a small number of Black students, led by Harvard and later Chicago. Otherwise, such students were admitted to a few liberal arts colleges and some Midwestern state universities. The 1910 Report includes a lengthy description of Black students at the University of Kansas, the second-most prolific producer of Black graduates (a total of sixty by 1909). Most Black students in the preparatory classes never entered the university and of those that did most left by the sophomore year. Still, this was a common pattern for the era and their graduation rate of 28 percent was better than that of White students. This was achieved despite hardships and social segregation. The report notes that almost all Black students came from disadvantaged backgrounds. Ninety percent were self-supporting, working the menial jobs that were available to them. They were compelled to live off campus and rarely participated in athletics or social life. Rather, they formed their own associations and participated in the social and church activities of nearby Black communities. This description would seem to hold wherever a significant number of Black students were present. As for Oberlin, a report from that campus identified the recent appearance of a "color line" that discouraged inter-racial mixing in social gatherings and literary societies. Most discouraging, several of those surveyed were dismayed that "prejudice against the colored man has spread from the South to the farthest point North."[9] This impression is confirmed by Richard Breaux's account in this volume of conditions for African-Americans in Midwestern universities.

At the time of Du Bois's second survey (1910), African-Americans comprised less than one percent of American college students. In the half-century preceding the Civil Rights Era, they labored against heavy odds to achieve progress on two fronts. First, most faced formidable obstacles in preparing for, gaining access to, and studying at institutions of higher education. Second, largely limited to HBCUs, African-Americans would soon struggle to gain control of those institutions so that they might work toward their advancement, rather than perpetuate subordination. This introduction provides only an overview of these historic struggles, but the six studies that follow delve deeply into strategic aspects of these developments.

Expanding Enrollments in Higher Education

The meager enrollments reported by Du Bois improved markedly after 1915. The trigger was the expansion of public secondary education in the South. Although preponderantly favoring White students, Black high school enrollments grew from 15,000 to 100,000 in a decade. Students in HBCUs increased from 2,700 to 12,000 in these years (1915–1925) and the availability of public education allowed these colleges to dispense with some primary and secondary programs. Howard University enrolled one of every six students, while the other HBCUs averaged less than 200 students. One major change was the emergence of college-level programs at the public, land-grant HBCUs, where they had scarcely existed in 1915. In the next ten years college enrollments at HBCUs nearly tripled to 34,000 (1935), with the public share rising from 25 to 37 percent. This progress came with a price. As states grudgingly provided some resources to the 1890 land-grant colleges, they installed Black presidents whose task was to keep students under control and, above all, to avoid politics or protest. These public colleges and normal schools provided African-Americans an opportunity for education but not leadership.[10]

By 1940, the number of undergraduate students at HBCUs increased another 10,000 to roughly 44,000.[11] It was at this juncture that Gunnar Myrdal observed, "increasing education provides theories and tools for the rising Negro protest against the caste status in which Negroes are held."[12] By the early 1950s, that number had risen to nearly 65,000 students. When the Civil Rights Act was signed in 1964, there were over 110,000 students enrolled in HBCUs, 60 percent of them women.[13] The growth of HBCUs was documented through a series of federal surveys. Much less known are the other ways in which African-Americans sought advanced education. Two papers examine these other alternatives, normal schools and study at northern, predominately White colleges and universities.

In "City Normal Schools, Municipal Colleges and Advanced Education for African Americans" Michael Fultz uncovers the stories of little-known institutions in Washington, Baltimore, Saint Louis, Richmond, and Louisville. These segregated institutions provided the opportunity for thousands of local African-Americans to obtain advanced education. By providing a shorter course of study and the advantages of commuting, city normal schools expanded both access and the prospects for completion. The teaching profession was of vital importance to Black communities. It was the chief occupational outlet for educated Blacks as well as the means for educational upgrading of future generations. Fultz explores the philanthropic and social forces that undergirded the expansion of teacher education programs and schools for African-Americans. Of particular interest is Fultz's broad look at the development of Black normal schools and their contributions to surrounding communities.

Figures are incomplete for the number of African-Americans who attended northern colleges and universities between the Du Bois studies and the Civil Rights Era. Black enrollments at the six Midwestern universities examined by Richard Breaux actually declined from 465 in 1930 to 365 in 1936.[14] Nor did conditions of attendance seem to have improved from Du Bois's survey to 1940. By that date, the small number of southern Blacks who came North for graduate or professional education was dwarfed by a much larger number of northern Blacks who traveled to the segregated South to attend HBCUs. The nearly 3,000 such students represented 7.5 percent of HBCU students. The main reason these students migrated South was to enjoy a normal social life on campus and to be able to participate on athletic teams. In contrast, Blacks on northern campuses were effectively ostracized from campus activities and organizations, and were barred from on-campus living facilities. Moreover, they had difficulty finding off-campus housing and were excluded from many all-White facilities. A few Black individuals played on northern university football teams before World War II, but they were all exceptional cases.[15]

Richard M. Breaux's important study contributes to our understanding of this situation. "Nooses, Sheets, and Blackface: White Racial Anxiety and Black Student Presence at Six Midwest Flagship Universities, 1882–1937," depicts racial politics at historically White Midwestern universities. The depressing picture that emerges is one of overt White hostility toward Black students that increased as the twentieth century progressed. Breaux differentiates the various types of White students and their perspectives on African-Americans, race, and racism (including both subtle and blatant examples, such as minstrel shows). His examination of historical documents gives the reader insight into the relationships between Black and White students (or lack thereof) on campus as well as the influence of outside forces, such as the Ku Klux Klan on the universities. The conditions of attendance highlighted by Breaux largely explain why some northern Black students preferred to attend college in the segregated South.[16]

Shifting Ideas about African-American Higher Education

By 1915, the northern philanthropists, including those affiliated with the Rockefeller-sponsored General Education Board, took a new approach toward aiding Black higher education. Over the next few years, the philanthropists shifted the emphasis of their giving from industrial to liberal arts education—albeit for a select group of Black liberal arts colleges. These actions followed a pattern of supporting the strongest institutions that the foundations had established in funding of other colleges and universities.

One of the institutions most affected by this shift in emphasis was Fisk University in Nashville, Tennessee. Fayette A. McKenzie, the White president of the institution, was fixated on pleasing White donors in both the Nashville community and in the Northeast. In his inaugural address in 1915, McKenzie assured White Southerners and northern philanthropists that Fisk would aid in restoring the South to economic prosperity and increased national wealth—precisely the goals of these groups. Under his leadership, the General Education Board agreed, in 1920, to support a $1 million endowment for Fisk. With such large sums pledged to Fisk, the philanthropies were easily able to dominate its board of trustees, displacing the former alliance of Black educators and White missionaries.[17]

In 1923, a memo of the General Education Board called for the collection of more financial support for Fisk and emphasized the urgent need to train "the right type of colored leaders"—leaders who would assist the Negro in becoming a capable worker and respectable citizen. Following this memo, McKenzie curtailed the liberal arts curriculum, suspended the student newspaper, and refused to allow a Fisk chapter of the NAACP. Further, he arranged racist entertainment for Fisk's White benefactors. Clearly, the "right type of colored leader" was one who acquiesced in the segregationist social order in the South. As a result of his suppression of student initiative and narrowing of the curriculum, McKenzie gained both the support of the northern philanthropists and the praise of local Whites.

However, McKenzie's pandering to the southern Whites caused unrest among the students and alienated many of the alumni. Developments on the Fisk campus became known across the country through alumni networks, which were quite strong. Fisk alumnus W. E. B. Du Bois reacted by openly criticizing and challenging the Fisk administration. On February 4, 1925, the Fisk students revolted in a destructive and defiant demonstration. McKenzie belatedly called in the feared Nashville police. The next day, a protest by over 2,500 Black Nashville citizens called for the end of McKenzie's presidency. His position untenable, McKenzie resigned in April of 1925. Fisk's conservative trustees recognized that desire for Black self-determination contributed to McKenzie's downfall, but they nevertheless appointed another White president, Thomas E. Jones (1925–1946). Du Bois praised the student and alumni victory and hailed these groups as the new Black intellectuals who would challenge control of HBCUs by northern philanthropists.[18]

Campus unrest was not unique to Fisk. The mid-1920s were a time of challenge and new ideas—many of them spread by newspapers, radio, and Northern Black students attending southern schools. Lauren Kientz Anderson examines the atmosphere at Fisk as the institution matured in the 1930s under the more conciliatory president Jones, who sought to promote the doctrine of "interracialism." "A Nauseating Sentiment, a Magical Device, or a Real Insight? Interracialism at Fisk University in 1930," explores the challenge to this doctrine raised by Juliette Dericotte and Mabel Byrd—two administrators at Fisk. According to Kientz Anderson, "interracialism" was a half-way house on the road to racial equality in which Blacks and Whites would work together, while conceding White social superiority. By challenging tacit White privilege, these women probably improved race relations at Fisk. In addition to invoking the words of the Fisk rebels, Kientz Anderson also draws on the perspectives of W. E. B. Du Bois, E. Franklin Frazier, and Horace Mann Bond to explicate the impact and implications of "Interracialism."

Howard Intellectuals and the New Negro

Fisk was the leading Black liberal arts college, but Howard was the largest and most prestigious institution—a fully developed university with professional schools that proudly regarded itself as the "capstone of Negro education." Although it was led by White, clerical presidents, academic affairs were largely controlled by Black deans, and Howard students had far more freedom than students at other HBCUs to engage in extracurricular activities. However, the appointment of James Durkee as president (1918–1926) exacerbated the issue of self-determination in a Black university. Durkee sought to centralize administrative authority, even while a new sense of racial pride and self-consciousness was empowering Black intellectuals. In addition, faculty salaries were badly eroded by wartime inflation. Conditions were ripe for the nation's first effort at faculty unionization, analyzed by Timothy Reese Cain in "'Only Organized Effort Will Find the Way Out!': Faculty Unionization at Howard University, 1918–1950."

The Howard faculty organized a chapter of the American Federation of Teachers on two occasions. In 1918, the union had little impact, but it planted the flag of unionization in higher education for the first time. After World War II, a second union chapter was almost unanimously approved by the Howard faculty. In its short history, it worked constructively with president Mordecai Johnson, but was closed in 1950 during the anticommunist hysteria. Black intellectuals at Howard played a conspicuous role in unionizing the campus. Unlike most of the research pertaining to faculty unionization, Cain explores the period prior to the 1960s—a time virtually ignored by many historians. The focus on a prominent Black college is particularly interesting as relationships between the president and faculty are often mixed and volatile. In Howard's case, the faculty members, according to Rayford Logan, were either "fervent admirers or bitter critics."

A desire for self-determination and opposition to "missionarism" among students and alumni forced the resignation of Durkee and the appointment of Mordecai Johnson as Howard's first Black president (1926–1960). Johnson was an authoritarian and controversial leader, but his long tenure brought important advances for the university. He established a rapport with the federal funders that brought substantial increase in resources, defended the academic freedom of Howard faculty, and aggressively recruited Black scholars to create not just a distinguished faculty, but an intellectual center focused on the problems and the progress of the Black community. Howard professors made numerous contributions to this effort. Alain Locke in the philosophy department articulated the cultural assertiveness of a new generation with his anthology, *The New Negro* (1925). In the English department, literary critic and poet Sterling Brown invoked the language and culture of southern rural Blacks. In the law school, William Hastie and Charles Hamilton Houston forged the legal strategy that challenged and ultimately overturned the American apartheid regime of racial segregation. Charles Thompson founded the *Journal of Negro Education*, an important forum, and also led the Department of Education, the College of Liberal Arts, and the Graduate School. In the social sciences, E. Franklin Frazier, Ralph Bunche, and Abram Harris, Jr., fulfilled the roles of scholars and activists.[19]

Louis Ray's, "Competing Visions of Higher Education: The College of Liberal Arts Faculty and the Administration of Howard University, 1939–1960," provides insight into the internal dynamics of Howard during these years by examining the role of the above-mentioned Charles Thompson. As dean of liberal arts, Thompson was a significant voice in administrative policy, but one that often took issue with president Johnson. Thompson favored merit and quality, while the president was more concerned with income and expansion. They first clashed over Johnson's policy of raising tuition during the Depression. Johnson seemingly foreshadowed twenty-first-century high tuition policies by seeking greater income from Howard's traditional constituency among the District's Black middle class. Thompson wanted more affordable costs for Howard's many poor students, as well as financial aid. Johnson naturally prevailed, but Howard's enrollment fell by 21 percent. In the 1940s, Thompson advocated limiting growth and raising academic standards, but Johnson proceeded with his policy of building a larger and more comprehensive university. Given the postwar boom in higher education, Thompson's position appears almost quixotic, but it represented a genuine concern for the intellectual side of the university.

Overcoming Segregation

Howard professors Hastie and Houston worked with the NAACP Legal Defense Fund to crack the legal edifice of southern segregation. In the 1930s, southern states began sending African-Americans to northern universities on scholarships to avoid providing equal facilities in the state. Between 1936 and 1950, the NAACP Legal Defense Fund fought and won several cases that made the out-of-state scholarships unconstitutional as a substitute for equal opportunities at home. The courts ordered states to accept Black students in their state-supported White universities or create separate Black graduate or professional schools. Even under court order, most southern states still found ways to deny African-Americans' admission at the graduate level.

The first higher education lawsuit to reach the United States Supreme Court was *Missouri ex rel. Gaines v. Canada* (1938). The plaintiff, Lloyd Gaines, was a 1935 graduate of Lincoln University in Missouri who sought to attend law school in that state. After receiving a rejection letter from the University of Missouri, Gaines filed a civil action against Missouri. During the trial, the state admitted that Gaines was denied admission based on his race, but the state circuit court sided with the University regardless. Gaines later appealed the case to the Missouri Supreme Court, which supported the state's policy of segregation based on race, and held that Gaines would not be deprived of any constitutional rights as long as the educational opportunities afforded to him by the state were equal to those provided to Whites. The Court also found that because of the out-of-state scholarship fund for Black students, Gaines had the same opportunities as White students at the University of Missouri.

Gaines appealed the decision to the United States Supreme Court, which ruled that the state of Missouri was not providing instruction in law to its Black citizens and deemed the legal education provided by other states to be irrelevant. Because the state had not established a separate law school for Black students, the Supreme Court held that Gaines was entitled to admission to the University of Missouri. Rather than comply with the Supreme Court's decision, the state of Missouri opted to create a new, Black, publicly funded law school. Although the NAACP was ready to argue that the new law school, with only four faculty members, was not equal to that of the University of Missouri, Gaines mysteriously disappeared, most likely murdered. His case nonetheless struck a blow against the duplicitous doctrine of separate but equal.

That doctrine was further undermined a decade later by *Sipuel v. Board of Regents* (1948) and *Sweatt v. Painter* (1950). In the first case, Ada Sipuel applied to the University of Oklahoma law school and was denied admission based on her race. With the help of the NAACP, Sipuel sued the state with the case reaching the Supreme Court. In accordance with the 14th amendment, the Court held that states must provide equal graduate education for Blacks. Unfortunately, the ruling was not specific about how that education was to be provided and, rather than admitting Ada Sipuel to the University of Oklahoma, the state sectioned off an area in the state capitol, designating it the "Negro law school," and hiring three Black faculty members. Eventually, the Supreme Court decided that this practice was unconstitutional and Ada Sipuel was allowed to enroll at the University of Oklahoma.[20]

In *Sweatt v. Painter* (1950), Heman Sweatt had been denied admission to the segregated University of Texas law school. With the help of the NAACP, Sweatt sued the university. Although he lost his case at the state level, the United States Supreme Court forced the University of Texas law school to open its doors to all students regardless of race in 1950.[21] Notably, the court declared in these cases that the states not only had an obligation to provide graduate education for Blacks, but that the education must replicate the intellectual level experienced by Whites.

These legal victories began the process of desegregation in southern higher education. The chief accomplishment was token integration of selective institutions beginning in the border states.[22] At this juncture (c. 1950) discriminatory practices toward Black students in northern universities were beginning to be addressed. For example, Indiana University president Herman Wells, who was unequivocally opposed to racial discrimination, only succeeded in integrating on-campus housing in 1952. The University of Nebraska adopted a nondiscrimination policy in 1949. Hence, there was a great deal of work to accomplish in the North in order to move from mere acceptance of Black students to equitable treatment and, beyond that, to valuing their contributions to the university.

In 1935, Charles Thompson had idealistically signaled the need for some agency that could identify Black students with high academic potential and assist in their education. It would be almost twenty years before historically White institutions began to do this by seriously recruiting and enrolling African-American students. Linda Perkins's "The First Black Talent Identification Program: The National Scholarship and Service Fund for Negro Students" describes efforts to promote racial integration in colleges by placing African-American students in historically White institutions. The NSSFNS identified talented Blacks for colleges and universities before historically White institutions established their own minority recruitment efforts. In 1950, it managed to place almost 200 Black students in northern private colleges. However, its efforts in the South were frustrated for most of that decade. In addition to examining NSSFNS's development and activities, Perkins discusses the changing leadership of the organization as it moved into the 1960s—leadership that changed from White to Black. She also explores the NSSFNS's relationship with the United Negro College Fund, the nation's most influential scholarship fund for African-Americans. The establishment of the NSSFNS has a symbolic significance as well: it represents a turning away from the marginalization of Black students at nonsouthern colleges and universities described above.

Toward the Civil Rights Era

In the South, the legal victories described above launched the process of desegregating higher education—a process with an excruciatingly slow start that proved irresistible in the long run. In 1935, in seventeen border and southern states, no Black and White students were educated in the same classroom or school, from kindergarten to graduate school. Maryland was the first state to "break the color barrier" that year when a legal team led by Thurgood Marshall and Howard's Charles Hamilton Houston forced the University of Maryland Law School to accept a Black applicant. The decisions in favor of Gaines and Sweatt complicated the maintenance of segregated graduate and professional education by requiring states to offer educational facilities for Blacks comparable to those provided for White students. These rulings were implemented at least tentatively in the border states and Virginia, allowing individuals to attend select programs under stringent conditions. But token deseg- regation was nevertheless a symbolic achievement, an opening wedge for further progress. The *Brown* decision in 1954 finally invalidated the doctrine of "separate but equal," once and for all, and the follow-up decision the next year made clear that *Brown* applied to higher educa- tion too. By the fall of 1955, the six border states from Delaware to Oklahoma, plus Arkansas, had begun to admit Black undergraduates. Limited advances were subsequently achieved in the Upper South and the University of Texas. Elsewhere, progress toward desegregation was grudging and the five states of the Deep South were intransigent. It took court orders and violent confrontations to achieve token inte- gration in Alabama, Georgia, and Mississippi in the early 1960s. Only the Civil Rights Act of 1964 signaled the end of legal segregation in higher education.[23]

Still, breaking the color barrier was not the end of the process of integration. The process began with the legally mandated admission of exceptional individuals to select programs. The next step—and a large one—was the admission of Black undergraduates without restric- tion in programs. Allowing Black students to live or dine on campus was yet another barrier to overcome. Participation in academic or social organizations, or on athletic teams, all had to be obtained before the Civil Rights Era could be said to have arrived.

A large scholarly literature now exists on the heroic final phase of the struggle to overcome segregation and discrimination in higher education, culminating in the Civil Rights Act of 1964. The prior drama, covering the first two-thirds of the twentieth century, is much less known or studied. This volume contributes to understanding how African-Americans overcame great odds to obtain advanced education in their own institutions, how they asserted themselves to gain control over those institutions, and how they persisted despite discrimination and intimidation in northern universities. The following papers investigate and analyze strategic aspects of these struggles that transformed the lives and life chances of African-Americans.

Notes

1. Jim Anderson, *The Education of Blacks in the South, 1860–1935* (Chapel Hill, NC: University of North Carolina Press, 1988); David Levering Lewis, *W.E.B. Du Bois: Biography of a Race, 1868–1919* (New York: Henry Holt, 1993).
2. W. E. B. Du Bois, ed., *The College-Bred Negro* (Atlanta, GA: Atlanta University Press, 1900), 107, 111; Lewis, *Du Bois*, 203–10, 261–62.
3. Du Bois, *College-Bred Negro*, 112; William Rainey Harper, *The Prospects of the Small College* (Chicago, IL: University of Chicago Press, 1900), 3.
4. W. E. B. Du Bois and Augustus Granville Dill, eds., *The College-Bred Negro American* (Atlanta, GA: Atlanta University Press, 1910).
5. Du Bois, *College-Bred Negro*, 12–13. Branch Normal College in Pine Bluff, Arkansas, was taken over by Whites after receiving land-grant funds and degraded to a precollegiate level: C. Fred Williams, "The Second Morrill Act and Jim Crow Politics: Land-Grant Education at Arkansas AM&N College, 1890–1927," *History of Higher Education Annual* 18 (1998): 81–92.
6. Du Bois, *College-Bred Negro*, 16–17.
7. Anderson, *Education of Blacks*, 251–56.
8. Du Bois and Dill, *College-Bred Negro American*, 16: enrollment figures in these volumes are incomplete, but indicative of trends.
9. Du Bois and Dill, *College-Bred Negro American*, quote, 96. See also, Cally L. Waite, *Permission to Remain among Us: Education for Blacks in Oberlin, Ohio, 1880–1914* (Westport, CT: Praeger, 2002); Clifford S. Griffin, *University of Kansas: A History* (Lawrence, KS: University of Kansas Press, 1974).
10. David T. Blose, *Statistics of Education of the Negro Race, 1925–1926*, U.S. Bureau of Education, Bulletin No. 19 (1928); Sandra T. Hill, *The Traditionally Black Institutions of Higher Education, 1860–1982* (Washington, DC: National Center for Education Statistics, 1985), 3–11.
11. U.S. Office of Education, *National Survey of the Higher Education of Negroes*, 3 vol. (Washington, DC: GPO, 1942), 3; Bobby L. Lovett, *America's Historically Black Colleges & Universities: A Narrative History, 1837–2009* (Macon, GA: Mercer University Press, 2011).
12. Gunnar Myrdal, *An American Dilemma: The Negro in America* (New York: Harper, 1944), 879.

13. F. Bowles and F. A. DeCosta, *Between Two Worlds: A Profile of Negro Higher Education* (New York: McGraw-Hill, 1971); Valerie Lundy-Wagner and Marybeth Gasman, "When Gender Issues Are Not Just about Women: Reconsidering Male Students at Historically Black Colleges and Universities," *Teachers College Record* (forthcoming 2011; available at http://www.tcrecord.com).

14. Richard Breaux, "Nooses, Sheets, and Blackface: White Racial Anxiety and Black Student Presence at Six Midwestern Flagship Universities, 1882–1937," in this volume: These data were gathered by Du Bois and published in *Crisis*: see note 15.

15. U.S. Office of Education, *National Survey of the Higher Education of Negroes*, 3 vol. (Washington, DC: GPO, 1942), II, 77–91; E.g., Griffin, *University of Kansas*. For football: Lane Demas, *Integrating the Gridiron: Black Civil Rights and American College Football* (New Brunswick, NJ: Rutgers University Press, 2011), 7–11.

16. For the experiences of a select group of Black female students, see Linda M. Perkins, "The African American Female Elite: The Early History of African American Women in the Seven Sister Colleges, 1880–1960," *Harvard Educational Review* 67, no. 4 (Winter 1997): 718–56.

17. Anderson, *Education of Blacks*, 257–70.

18. *New York Times*, January 28, 1925. For a more detailed account of this incident, see Joe Martin Richardson, "The Student Revolt," In *A History of Fisk University, 1865–1946* (Tuscaloosa, AL: The University of Alabama Press), 84–100; Raymond Wolters, *The New Negro on Campus: Black College Rebellions of the 1920s* (Princeton, NJ: Princeton University Press, 1975); Lester Lamon, "The Black Community in Nashville and the Fisk University Student Strike of 1924–1925," *The Journal of Southern History* 40, no. 2 (1975): 225–44.

19. Jonathan Scott Holloway, *Confronting the Veil: Abram Harris, Jr., E. Franklin Frazier, and Ralph Bunch, 1919–1941* (Chapel Hill, NC: University of North Carolina Press, 2002); Wolters, *The New Negro on Campus*, 70–136.

20. Michael Klarman, *From Jim Crow to Civil Rights: The Supreme Court and the Struggle for Racial Equality* (New York: Oxford University Press, 2003); Mark Tushet, *NAACP's Legal Strategy against Segregated Education, 1925–1950* (Chapel Hill, NC: The University of North Carolina Press, 1987).

21. Tushet, *NAACP's Legal Strategy against Segregated Education.*

22. Peter Wallenstein, "Black Southerners and Non-Black Universities: The Process of Desegregating Southern Higher Education, 1935–1965" in *Higher Education and the Civil Rights Movement: White Supremacy, Black Southerners, and College Campuses*, ed. Peter Wallenstein (Gainesville, FL: University of Florida Press, 2008), 17–59.

23. Ibid., 33–36.

City Normal Schools and Municipal Colleges in the Upward Expansion of Higher Education for African Americans

Michael Fultz

This manuscript utilizes case studies of several Black city normal schools and municipal colleges to argue for the need to expand our conceptualizations of "higher education" for African Americans. Through a variety of educational institutions founded in the late-nineteenth and early-twentieth centuries, "advanced education" for African Americans expanded, serving both immediate needs—especially teacher training—while developing an infrastructure for future educational and social advancement.

Historians have had difficulty categorizing normal schools and conceptualizing their role within patterns of American school-going. The general tendency has been to consider these institutions as mere extensions of common schooling—at best, high school "plus," with the "plus" mostly a few lectures in pedagogy and perhaps review sessions in basic academic subjects. But should they be considered by their aspirations, and sometimes by their practice, as fundamentally outside the realm of common schooling, given the "professional" training and "higher" education that characterized the normal school ideal? The seamless transformation of normal schools into teachers colleges, well underway by the 1920s and virtually completed during the 1930s, is an unexplored reminder that the web of higher education in the United States has many historical threads.[1]

These problems of categorization and conceptualization apply with perhaps greater force with regard to normal schools for African

Perspectives on the History of Higher Education 29 (2012): 17-41
© 2012. ISBN: 978-1-4128-4771-1

Americans, concerns spanning the nineteenth and twentieth centuries. The tendency of historical narratives to emphasize Black college-going is understandable, given the denial of educational opportunities during slavery and a national context of persistent denigration of African American intellectual abilities. However, this celebration of undeniable achievements has had hidden and unfortunate effects in terms of crafting a nuanced exploration of the rich and varied institutional infrastructure that characterized African American education from the Civil War through the 1940s. On the one hand, an incomplete understanding of African American higher education has often led to distorted comparisons between Black and White colleges and university at very different stages of their historical evolutions. Black institutions (and Black collegiate populations generally) have commonly been "normed" against White counterparts within single historical periods and in these comparisons Black colleges have often been found "deficient." On the other hand, more to the point of this essay, the role of teacher training and normal schools within the development of African American educational advancement has been fundamentally obscured.

Without question, both directly and indirectly, teacher training drove the development of any sense of "higher education" for African Americans in the aftermath of the Civil War. A narrow focus on the label of "college" or "university" has camouflaged this phenomenon, both in terms of the internal dynamics of particular institutions, in which teacher training almost universally played a central role and with regard to the evolution of Black higher education over time. Fisk University and Atlanta University are widely acknowledged as two of the premier African American institutions of higher education founded in the aftermath of the Civil War. Within the constellation of Black institutional development, however, they were not exceptional insofar as their normal school graduates exceeded the number of collegiate graduates for much of the period prior to the 1900s, reflecting the often considerably larger number of student enrollments in their teacher-training programs. Talladega College, founded in 1867, did not have its first college graduate until 1895; for almost thirty years it functioned as a normal school disguised under a college title.[2]

Similarly, in the first two-to-three decades after the Civil War, the majority of the institutions established by Black or White philanthropy, or by state authorities, to provide some degree of higher education for African Americans were normal schools. According to the US Commissioner of Education report for 1881, there were approximately forty-seven Black normal schools, thirty-four Black high schools, and seventeen Black college and universities; by 1894–95, the number of these institutions had grown to seventy-three normal schools, fifty-seven high schools, and thirty-two colleges. Only two southern states used federal funds from the 1862 Morrill Land Grant Act to aid Black collegiate education (Alcorn University, Mississippi, 1871, and Claflin University, South Carolina, 1872), while two others used this funding to aid Black normal schools (Hampton Normal and Agricultural Institute, Virginia, 1872, and State Normal School for Colored Persons, Kentucky, 1889). In contrast, nine southern states established Black state normal schools before 1890, when the US Congress passed the second Morrill Act, leading to the belated establishment of seventeen Black land-grants. These nine institutions were: State Normal School at Holly Springs, Mississippi, 1870; Lincoln Normal School (later the State Normal School for Colored Students at Montgomery), Alabama, 1871 (one of four Black normal schools to receive state funding that year); Branch Normal College, Arkansas 1873; State Colored Normal School at Fayetteville, North Carolina, 1877; Lincoln Institute, Missouri, 1879; Prairie View Normal School, Texas, 1879; Virginia Normal and Collegiate Institute, Virginia, 1883; State Normal School for Colored Persons, Kentucky, 1886; and State Normal College for Colored Students, Florida, 1887.[3]

Several factors account for these trends. Southern White resistance to establishment of traditional baccalaureate education for African Americans must loom large in any analysis of state funding considerations. Certainly, as well, the overwhelming demand for African American teachers to initiate and to expand Black schooling in the decades after the Civil War pushed demands for "advanced education" of all types, with normal schools readily understood as an essential piece of the emerging pipeline. Moreover, as African American communities and the small but growing number of Black teachers sought to enhance "professionalism," normal schooling was emphasized.

One avenue through which to investigate in more depth the trajectory of higher education for African Americans is via an examination of the city normal schools initiated in the late-nineteenth and early-twentieth centuries. There were five city training schools for African American teachers in 1914, when the first comprehensive nationwide survey of these schools was published by the U.S. Bureau of Education: Miner Normal School, Washington, DC (1879); Sumner Normal School, St. Louis (1890); Colored Normal School, Louisville (1897); Baltimore Colored Training School (1901); and Richmond Colored High and Normal School

(1903). By the mid-1930s three of these institutions—the schools in the District of Columbia, St. Louis, and Baltimore—had become Teachers Colleges, with, in addition, three municipal colleges—Houston Colored Junior College (HCJC) in Houston, Texas (1927); Dunbar Junior College in Little Rock, Arkansas (1929); and Louisville Municipal College (1931)—playing a substantial role in supplying teachers and higher education generally for their respective Black communities.[4]

All of the Black city training schools in 1914 were located in cities with sizable African American populations—the five locales were among those with the nation's twelve largest Black populations—but there was no correlation between having a city normal school and the percentage of the municipal population that was African American. African Americans made up only 6.4 percent of St. Louis's total population around 1914, and only 15.2 percent and 18.1 percent of the population in Baltimore and Louisville, respectively. Yet, these three cities schools had locally sponsored training schools, whereas there were no such schools in Memphis or Atlanta, for example, where African Americans made up 40.0 percent and 33.5 percent of the population, respectively. All five cities that sponsored Black normals in 1914 also hosted White normals, and given local histories and the politics of racial segregation, it is not coincidental that none were located in the Deep South. Three other southern cities, Birmingham (1887), New Orleans (1895), and Charleston (1911), had all established city training schools for Whites, but of the three only New Orleans briefly established a city normal school for African Americans, the Valena C. Jones School in 1923. It must be recognized, too, that the category of city training school itself is somewhat misleading. During the 1920s and 1930s, it was common for penurious southern school boards to exploit the presence of private Black normal schools, colleges, and universities for post-grammar schooling and the provision of teachers for local schools. Institutions such as Avery Normal Institute in Charleston, LeMoyne Normal Institute in Memphis, Chandler Normal School in Lexington, Kentucky, as well countless others, fall within this category. The city of Atlanta, capitalizing on the presence of several prestigious Black colleges, did not fund a public Black high school until 1924; New Orleans school officials fought Southern University's relocation to Baton Rouge in 1913–14 realizing that as a result, they might then be pressured to establish a publicly funded Black secondary school, which they finally did in 1917.[5]

Washington, DC

The best known of the city training schools for African Americans was the Miner Normal School in Washington, DC. Established as the Colored Girls School and intended for free Black women, the institution was founded in 1851 by Myrtilla Miner, a White teacher from upstate New York, whose anger against slavery was exacerbated by her experiences in Mississippi in the late 1840s. Hostility to education for African Americans, however, was not confined to the Deep South, and although the School for Colored Girls attracted a growing clientele, especially among the city's more well-to-do Black families, it also ran into persistent obstacles from White Washingtonians. Miner's ill-health (which lead to her death in 1864), along with financial difficulties, led to the school's closing in 1860.[6]

By the early 1870s, there was a growing need for teacher training to staff the expanding Black and White public school systems of the District and Georgetown. In the fall of 1873, Washington Normal School was opened as a District-sponsored facility for White women. For several years prior to its initiation, young White girls from the grammar schools had been used as substitutes, and sometimes as instructors, in the lower grades. Since there was then no high school for Whites in the District, the normal school was needed for academic purposes as well—"many things must be taught from the beginning," the board of trustees noted in its 1873–74 report.[7]

Just as the Washington Normal School was getting underway, Black students at Preparatory High School, founded in 1870, were being diverted from their schoolwork and hired as classroom instructors. Before they could complete their high school training, academically advanced students in the school's first two entering classes—those of 1870–71 and 1871–72—were assigned to teach in Black primary schools in various parts of the city. This ad hoc resource allocation continued for several years. In the 1875–76 school year, a normal department was organized within Preparatory High, offering a one-year program which paralleled the course of study at Washington Normal. Twelve students were again rerouted from their high school studies, this time to participate in that first teacher-training class. Mary Jane Patterson, the principal at Preparatory High and one of the nation's first Black women college graduates (Oberlin 1862), supervised the normal program.[8]

In 1877, the District entered into an agreement with the trustees of the Colored Girls School—incorporated as the Institution for the

Education of Colored Youth (IECY) in 1863 and better known as the Miner Fund—whereby: (a) two floors of the newly constructed Miner Building were rented to the District to house Preparatory High (where it remained through 1890) and an elementary school; (b) upon recommendation, a selected number of female graduates from the high school would be admitted to the Miner Normal School, which had been established as an independent institution in 1876; and (c) upon graduation from the normal school, these young Black women would have preference for appointment as teachers in Washington and Georgetown schools. (Prior to this agreement, from 1871 through 1875, the Miner Fund trustees had been associated with and financially supported the normal department at Howard University.) In 1879, the arrangement was modified such that Miner Normal became a semipublic institution managed by a joint committee of trustees representing the Miner and District Boards. At the conclusion of the 1886–87 school year, the Miner Board terminated its participation in the 1879 agreement and Miner Normal (officially named Washington Normal No. 2) fell fully under public support and control.[9]

During the period when its reputation for superior training was established, Miner operated under the firm, exacting hand of Lucy Ellen Moten, who was principal for thirty-eight years, from 1883–1920. Moten was the second African American principal at Miner, succeeding Martha Briggs, a former director of Howard University's Normal School, who headed the school after the 1879 agreement was finalized.[10]

Controversies over admissions policies during Moten's tenure at Miner illustrate the fine line several of the Black city normals negotiated, balancing efforts to enhance their standards and serve their constituencies within a context of restricted opportunities and fiscal constraints. Between 1879 and 1890, the number of students admitted annually to Miner was relatively small, mostly in the upper teens and mid-twenties, though in the late 1880s, evidently under community pressure, incoming class size was increased to forty. Yet, because of relatively high salaries and limited employment possibilities for African American professionals outside the educational arena, the Black teaching force was quite stable in District schools, with minimal turnover. Thus, even within a growing system, as early as the mid-1880s or so, all graduates from Miner could not be placed in District schools. In 1890, the school board set a ceiling on admissions at twenty-six. For Moten, this limit was arbitrary and impractical. Motivated by rigorous standards intended to inculcate both "instruction in the art and science of teaching" and "moral character," but constrained by a need for more practice schools and small faculty size—the school had five instructors in 1888, six in 1898—Moten generated considerable local controversy when she sought to raise minimum exam scores for admission from 65 percent to 80 percent on examinations in language, arithmetic, biology, physics, and chemistry. This change in policy, Moten wrote to her Board of Trustees, "will give the Normal School your best material to prepare for teachers and enable us to protect the natural rights of the little ones entrusted to our care."[11]

Although supported by Dr. George Cook, an African American educator who served as the District's Superintendent of Colored Schools from 1868 to 1900 (when the position was eliminated), Moten's proposal was opposed by Calvin Chase, editor of the influential *Washington Bee*, and by substantial portions of Washington's middle and upper-class Black community. The social standing accrued from enrollment at Miner, opposition to the appointment of outsiders to District schools, and limited professional prospects, especially for African American women, produced a pressure-filled mix. Moreover, there was strong sentiment across the District's Black communities that local government should provide more opportunities for African American higher education—aside from Howard University—rather than less. In 1898, a compromise was reached under which the ceiling of twenty-six was removed and all candidates for admission with averages of 80 percent or more would be admitted. Propelled by growing high school matriculation, enrollment at Miner soared. The normal school had 13 enrolled when Moten took over in 1883–84, 30 in 1895–96, 77 in 1905–06, and 174 in 1910–11. (Small numbers of men began to be admitted starting in 1887.) Throughout the remainder of her presidency at Miner, Moten continued to these and other issues she considered essential to high-caliber training. In her last annual report, for the 1919–20 school year, Moten reiterated her proposals that the course of study for elementary school and high school teachers be increased to three years and four years, respectively, that comprehensive model schools replace the hodge-podge of practice schools scattered around the city, and that graduates of Miner be appointed to the schools on the basis of civil service exams to avoid the "unwarranted embarrassment caused by some parents."[12]

Moten's leadership at Miner produced considerable programmatic growth. Prior to mid-1890s, the normal program was an intensive one-year-long course which: reviewed the various branches of study taught in elementary schools; offered professional courses in pedagogy, school management, and psychology; and provided a practicum experience of three weeks of observation and six weeks of practice teaching. One hour per week was also required with alternating lectures on the value and use of educational literature, moral training, and "sensible etiquette," along with practice in vocal culture. Starting with the 1896–97 school year, Miner's program was expanded to a two-year curriculum, a move that had been urged by Moten since the late 1880s. (In 1894, the course of study at M Street High School, the successor to Preparatory High, was expanded from three to four years, which meant that as of 1898, graduates from Miner Normal had completed fourteen years of schooling. Given that in 1871–72, student-teachers had been placed into teaching positions from what would have been their seventh and eighth grades at Preparatory High, this was a marked improvement in educational attainments among Black school staff.)[13]

By 1910–11, Miner Normal had developed seven distinct teacher-training programs for kindergarten, primary, and grammar school teachers, as well as for special teachers of domestic arts, domestic science, manual arts, and drawing. The kindergarten course was a long-term project, initially promoted by Martha Briggs back in the early 1880s, though not adopted until the 1905–06 school year. In 1909, Miner also implemented a one-year training course for college graduates, a program pushed by African American school board member Mary Church Terrell. The twelve students enrolled in this course in 1913 were graduates of such schools as Amherst, Brown, Rutgers, Howard, Cornell, and Oberlin.[14]

In 1927, fulfilling a request made by Moten as early as 1903, but coming seven years after her retirement, Miner was authorized to develop a three-year Normal program. In 1929, a four-year program was authorized. Political posturing played an ironic role in the events that led to upgrading the Black and White normal schools in the District. A US House member from Nebraska publicly criticized the city normals for the virtual monopoly they held over local teaching positions. Supporters of the normal schools countered these accusations, noting that prospective teachers in the District would be at a distinct disadvantage if they were forced to compete against others who had baccalaureate degrees. As a result, Wilson Normal for White teachers and Miner Normal for African Americans were made baccalaureate-granting Teachers Colleges in 1929. Miner's first graduating class to receive the BS degree was in 1933, the same year that the local preference policy for graduates from both schools was discontinued. Admissions restrictions were at first imposed, but later revoked, and by the 1940s enrollment in Miner was more than 700, making it far and away the largest of the Black city-based institutions. From 1930 to 1951, the school's education department was led by Dr. Jane Ellen McAllister, a leading figure in African American teacher education, who in 1929 became the first Black PhD recipient from Teachers College, Columbia University. Miner Teachers College and Wilson Teachers College were merged in 1955 to form the District of Columbia Teachers College, now the University of the District of Columbia.[15]

St. Louis

In 1875, the Missouri General Assembly called upon a reluctant St. Louis school board to "make suitable provision for . . . the purpose of educating the colored children of said city in the advanced studies," and to establish a "department of normal instruction." Later that year, the Washington School, a former White elementary school, was transformed into the "High School for Colored Students." A Black primary school shared the facility. The normal department would have to wait.[16]

Presiding over Sumner High from 1879 until his retirement in 1908 was Oscar Minor Waring, a much respected figure among the city's Black educators. Waring attended Oberlin Academy and Oberlin College on and off in the late 1850s–early 1860s, and from 1867 to 1872 taught in schools for freedpersons in various parts of the South. Prior to moving to St. Louis, he was a mathematics instructor at Alcorn College in Mississippi and also taught in the Louisville schools. His wife Lottie was also a teacher, working at Colored School #1 in the early 1880s.[17]

Under Waring's administration, Sumner High School offered the typical English and classical curriculum of the times, likely not that different from the high school for White students, which had opened in 1853. Enrollment grew slowly in the early years; in 1880, it was the only Black school in the city with a course of study above the sixth grade. Only twenty were enrolled in 1885, the year Sumner had its first graduating class of two. By 1891–92, enrollment was 114; 250 by 1900; and 505 by 1911–12. From the start, the growth and development of the high school were under vigilant oversight by members of the Black community. Ongoing complaints about Sumner's condition and location forced the board to move the school twice: once in the late 1890s; and again in 1910, for the first time into a newly constructed building, on Cottage Avenue in The Ville, one of St. Louis's historic Black neighborhoods then coming into its own as a social and cultural enclave. A map drawn by one of Sumner's faculty members showed that the majority of the aspiring middle-class and working-class student body were already living in this area, their families spreading northwest out of the inner-city.[18]

Unlike the situation in Washington, DC—and more like the situation in many urban school districts south of the Potomac—Black teachers in St. Louis had to fight their way in, riding a wave of community protests. Dating back to the early antebellum period and continuing even after a 1847 state law prohibiting the education of slaves and free Negroes, African Americans in St. Louis had a long tradition of supporting, and teaching in, self-initiated church and private schools. An African American-led Board of Education for Colored Schools sponsored several freedmen's facilities in the 1860s, and was thorough in its selection of Black instructors. Yet the postwar St. Louis School Board hired only White teachers for the city's schools, including the three schools for African American children the city took over in 1866–67. Not until after a round of protests in 1875 did the school board agree that White teachers assigned to colored schools had to receive the same passing score on the teacher's exam as their counterparts in the White schools. Two years later, in 1877–78, the Black community scored an even bigger victory when thirty-four White teachers were transferred and African American teachers were introduced into the Black schools. The impact of the change to Black instructors was immediate: citywide, the number of enrolled African American students more than doubled, jumping from around 1,500 to more than 3,600. A boycott had been lifted.[19]

By the 1890–91 school year, the need for a normal program for prospective Black teachers loomed large. Ongoing community pressure, plus growing African American school enrollments at all levels, pushed the need for more and better trained Black instructors. Thirty years earlier, in 1857–58, a normal program for prospective White teachers in St. Louis had been established. Housed for most of its early history within the local White High, the program provided a tuition-free, preferred (but not exclusive) pipeline for young White women to gain academic and pedagogical training before becoming teachers in the city schools. African Americans sought a similar program for similar reasons. By the time the St. Louis School Board authorized the formation of the normal department at Sumner High at its September 9, 1890 meeting, the issue was one of professionalism and equal treatment rather than academics. The course of study at Sumner was strong enough to allow the young Black women who attended the school to pass the city teacher's exam. Including the twenty-six who graduated from Sumner before the normal department was initiated, all but one of the seventy-two women graduates between 1885 and 1892 became teachers in the St. Louis schools. Fourteen young women made up each of the first two normal school classes; virtually the entire female senior class at Sumner (fourteen of sixteen in the class of 1890 and the class of 1891) continued after graduation for an additional one year of teacher training. By 1900, Principal Waring calculated that 80 percent of Sumner's 224 female graduates had become teachers in St. Louis.[20]

Sumner's normal program matured swiftly. Around 1896, the course of study was increased to two years. In lieu of a true observation and practice teaching facility—which would not be available until 1915 when the Cottage Avenue School, a group of portable structures surrounding Sumner High School, was utilized—an apprentice system was initiated in 1905. As apprentices, young women who had finished their course-work were assigned to an elementary school for half a year, combining observation with supervised teaching of their own. During this semester, students were required to take a course in classroom management. In 1907, Sumner began to offer extension courses for in-service Black teachers, replicating a service offered by the White training program (closed in 1897 and reopened as Harris Teachers College in 1904). By that same year, 1907, Sumner's training program had proved so attractive that the Board of Education imposed short-lived admissions restrictions; the St. Louis superintendent's annual report for 1906–07 reported that some graduates "have had to wait about three years before it was their turn to be called on to serve." When admission to the normal department was cut to six annually—enrollment had averaged in the thirties for eight of the prior ten years—the Black community loudly voiced its disapproval. In 1908, the policy was abandoned, with all young ladies who graduated from Sumner eligible to enter the teacher training program, though with no guarantees for placement. Men were not admitted to the program until 1941.[21]

In June 1921, two years after similar authorization was granted to Harris Teachers College for Whites, the St. Louis Board of Education recommended that the Sumner normal program begin to implement a curriculum leading to an AB degree and to change its name to Sumner Teacher College. Courses for training elementary teachers would take place in the Junior College while the Senior College would provide extension and summer coursework for in-service teachers. Fifteen additional extension classes were soon in place to supplement the regular program. In 1924, a full four-year collegiate curriculum was authorized and the name change to Sumner Teachers College was made official.

The year 1929 proved a banner year for the program. On the one hand, cramped within Sumner, the normal department moved to a newly constructed wing of the Simmons elementary school, also located in The Ville neighborhood. This move severed administrative ties with the high school for the first time in the school's almost forty-year history. With the relocation came another name change, to Harriet Beecher Stowe Teachers College. Highlighting these transformations, thirteen African American women that year received their AB degrees. In 1932, Stowe joined Miner in DC as the only two Black teacher training programs accredited by the American Association of Teachers Colleges.[22]

In January 1930, again pushed by community demands, the St. Louis Board of Education essentially created a liberal arts junior college within Stowe, allowing young men and women who were not preparing to teach to attend the school for two years of coursework. Enrollment soared, reaching a peak of 523 in the 1931–32 school year. The two-year liberal arts program was discontinued by St. Louis authorities for financial reasons in 1932, but the educational void was filled in 1933 when the Board allowed the state's Black land-grant, Lincoln University in Jefferson City, to open a WPA-sponsored junior college division in Stowe's building and under Stowe's administration, though with a separate faculty. In 1938, St. Louis resumed sponsorship of the junior colleges at both of the Teachers Colleges and the temporary Lincoln program was closed.[23]

From 1931 through 1940, both Harris and Stowe were jointly administered by the president of the White institution. In 1940, the year Stowe moved into a newly built facility in The Ville, separate administrators were again reestablished, with Ruth Harris (AB, University of Chicago, 1921; MA, Columbia, 1929), a former student in the normal department and a faculty member at Sumner-Stowe since the early 1920s, assuming leadership. Harris presided over Stowe until the merger of Stowe and Harris Teachers Colleges in 1954. As was the case in Washington, DC, the Black and White Teachers Colleges in St. Louis were among the first educational institutions affected by the *Brown* decision.[24]

Baltimore

Baltimore did not initiate training schools for either Black or White teachers until 1901, when very different motivations propelled the city to move in this direction. There were multiple local sources for White teachers before the turn of the century. In addition to various private colleges and academies, the White-male only Central High School, opened in 1839 and renamed Baltimore City College in 1866, provided small number of teachers from the start. In fact, congruent with the name change in 1866, the city Board of Commissioners extended the course of study to five years "to afford advantages . . . especially to those who may adopt the profession of the teacher as the pursuit of life." The all-girls Eastern and Western high schools, opened in 1844, provided teacher training, as did the Baltimore Female College, opened in 1849 (closed in 1890), with funds from the state for this purpose starting in 1860. The Maryland State Normal School was located in Baltimore from 1866 to 1915 and provided multiple cohorts of White teachers for local schools until cramped conditions forced its transfer to Towson, just outside the city limits. Continued dissatisfaction with these options, however, especially the low standards at the State Normal, led Baltimore to flirt with establishing more systematic training; on and off between 1851 and 1881, city-sponsored normal classes were organized but later discontinued.[25]

In sharp contrast, the need for a normal school for African Americans was mitigated by the fact that African Americans were not hired as teachers in Baltimore city schools until 1889—twenty-two years after the city took over selected freedmen's schools—when Colored Primary School No. 9 opened with twelve Black instructors. "A gradual system of elimination" of White teachers in otherwise segregated Black schools, the formal policy declared by the city council in 1896, was not completed until 1907. Despite the local lockout, several programs for African American teacher training were established in the Charm City dating back to the post–Civil War period. The Centenary Biblical Institute, founded in 1867 and renamed Morgan College in 1890, was one source. The Baltimore Normal School for the Education of Colored Teachers, better known locally as the Howard Normal School, was another. This facility was the outgrowth of teacher training classes established in 1866 by the Quaker-led Baltimore Association for the Moral and Educational Improvement of Colored People. The school's declining fortunes were clearly evident by the turn of the century, and in 1908, its assets were sold to the state, officially becoming State Normal #3. In 1911, it too was relocated outside Baltimore, redesignated as the Maryland Normal and Industrial School at Bowie. Aside from the bureaucratic legerdemain concocted by labeling Morgan College's Princess Anne Academy as the state's Black land-grant institution, Bowie Normal was Maryland's first state-funded Black institution for postsecondary education.[26]

Initiated in January 1901, Baltimore's training class for African American teachers was initially housed in a room on the third floor of the local Black high school, renamed that year Colored High and Training School. (Founded in 1883 as an extension of a Black grammar school, and given the status of a high school in 1889, the year its first class graduated, the school became Frederick Douglass High School in 1925. A year later, its most famous alumnus, Thurgood Marshall, graduated.)[27]

In its first year the curriculum for the Black training class was slim: "most of this time is spent in correcting the papers [in history mathematics and English] of the High School pupils in these subjects," the report for the year ending December 1901 stated. As crafted and developed, however, by Colored High's principals, Hugh M. Browne and J. H. N Waring, both veteran educators in the Washington, DC schools before moving to Baltimore, and their all-Black staff, the curriculum improved dramatically. In 1902, students preparing to teach had their course of study modified in the senior year of high school, followed by an additional year of study and practice teaching. The curriculum for the first "undergraduate" year was now fully articulated, with arithmetic, chemistry, and history, grammar, and literature leading an array of coursework. In the second year of the program, students spent half of every day in their practicum experience and the other half with coursework. One can imagine the student-teachers were fully occupied: the two facilities utilized for observation and practice teaching, Schools No. 107 and 116, were critically understaffed, with the former having two teachers for 688 enrolled students and the other three teachers for 588. In 1905, a full two-year post-high school course of study was introduced; within three years, extension courses were initiated for in-service teachers. In 1909, the Colored Training School was assigned its own principal, although it remained housed within the high school. Enrollment grew over the program's first decade, from nine students in 1901, twenty-four in 1902, seventy-eight in 1905, and eighty-one in 1910.[28]

In 1926, two years after the White training school closed, the name of the Colored Training School was changed to Fannie Jackson Coppin Normal School in honor of the esteemed former principal (1869–1902) of the Institute for Colored Youth in Philadelphia. At the time, the school shared facilities with a junior high school and sported two programs, one for prospective teachers in grades K-2 and the other for the upper elementary grades. In 1931, a three-year curriculum was introduced and in 1938, a full four-year curriculum was initiated. Authorization was also given to grant Bachelor of Science degrees in elementary education.

The next year, marking its new status, the school's name was changed again, to Coppin Teachers College. In 1941–42, with enrollment up to 160, eight men and twenty-seven women received their BS degrees. By the late 1940s, Coppin's situation was becoming increasingly untenable. The need for teacher training for the local Black elementary schools was still pressing, but the school was consistently underfunded and cramped for space. Lack of accreditation by regional agencies (which would not be achieved until 1963) added to the problems. In 1950, the school moved from city to state control, as Coppin State Teachers College.[29]

Richmond and Louisville

In Richmond, Virginia, and in Louisville, Kentucky, the normal schools eventually faded from the educational landscape, although in the latter city, the creation of Louisville Municipal College in 1931 provided a degree of continuity.

In Richmond, the high school in many ways was grafted onto the normal school, at least in terms of initial priorities. Colored Normal School was the brainchild of Ralza Morse Manly, superintendent of schools for the Freedmen's Bureau in Virginia from 1865 to 1870. Fully supported by Richmond's Black community, Manly's intent was to create a teacher training program that would send African American instructors throughout the South and "inspire in the colored people hope and life and self-respect and a generous ambition." Located in the Navy Hill-Jackson Ward section of Richmond, near the only elementary school in the city with an all-African American staff, Colored Normal opened with much fanfare in October 1867 with sixty-five students selected via competitive examinations from various other schools for freedpersons. Observation and practice teaching were in place by 1871 and the first class graduated in 1873. Starting in 1868, Colored Normal received sporadic funding from the Peabody Fund ($100 in 1868, $500 in 1870, and $800 in 1872) in the foundation's attempts to promote model schools and teacher training in southern states.[30]

Progress at Colored Normal stalled between the mid-1870s and the turn of the century. In June 1876, Manly gifted his private school to the city of Richmond. As part of the agreement, its three-year course of study remained intact, but other improvements were notably absent. In fact, by the mid-1880s, around the time of the name change to Richmond Colored High and Normal School in 1886, rank discrimination marked the school's transformation into a public facility: equipment and furniture which once adorned Colored Normal, for example, disappeared one summer only to appear in the White high school in the fall. Moreover, as in Baltimore, Richmond's refusal to hire African American instructors for any of the colored schools except Navy Hill thwarted the development of adequate teacher training. Even the breakthrough in Black teacher hiring policy in 1883–84 did not result in an immediate upgrade to the normal training offerings. It was not until twenty years later, in 1903, that a one-year "postgraduate" course in teacher training was added to the school's curriculum (similar to the arrangement established at John Marshall High School for Whites in 1887–88). In 1912–13, three years after a name change to Armstrong High and Training School, and three years before its shift to African American teachers (the last school in the city to attain an all-Black staff), a second year was added to the normal program. The White training program, now called the Richmond City Normal School and housed in a local elementary school, also became a two-year program in 1912–13. In 1916–17, the Black normal classes were similarly moved to an elementary school, in this case to the Monroe School, housed in the renovated Leigh Street Armory a few blocks away from Armstrong High, a building of great symbolic importance for Richmond's Black community. That same year, the program for African Americans was accredited by the state and a few teachers were trained for sixth and seventh grade assignments. In 1933, due to financial hardships imposed by the Depression, teacher training classes for both Blacks and Whites were discontinued. The normal program had two African American women teachers and an enrollment of 103 (seventy-four young women and twenty-nine young men) when it was closed.[31]

In Louisville, the Black normal program was decidedly a second-class citizen in the city's school system, arguably more so than in any of the other locales through the first decade of the twentieth century. The White normal school was established in 1871; the Black normal in 1897, after the African American community had forwarded numerous petitions. Indeed, the Black normal program was inaugurated only because the Louisville school board was concerned with the costs of having large numbers of African American applicants fail to pass the required teachers exam. The White normal ran for one year until 1895, for a year and a half (three five-month sessions) from 1895 to 1897, and for two years (four five-month sessions) starting in 1898; the Black classes ran for ten months for much of the school's first decade. By 1895, the White normal school had extensive practice classes for the first, third, fourth, fifth, and sixth grades. By way of contrast, in his report for 1911–12, the head of the Black normal school, A. E. Meyzeek, a former principal of

Colored Central High where the program was housed, noted that practice teaching in the now two-year program was just getting underway. Both normal schools were closed at the end of the 1934–35 school year—a statement by the president of the board of education in that year's annual report recounts the history of the "Louisville Normal School," but does not even mention that the Black normal ever existed.[32]

Municipal Colleges

Although none of the three municipal colleges for African Americans in mid-1930s was officially a normal school, the origins and early histories of these institutions, like those of Black city normals, and Black liberal arts colleges generally, were closely linked to community concerns about the provision of teacher training and advanced education.

Louisville Municipal College for Negroes (the formal name until 1942) was opened in 1931 as a unit of the University of Louisville. Its establishment was the result of a decade-long battle between Louisville city officials and the Black community over passage of a school bond that provided additional funds for the University. Spearheaded by the local Urban League, Black voters held firm in their position that unless the city created additional opportunities for advanced education, they would oppose the bond issue. Accredited as a four-year college in 1932, the institution was at the time the only true liberal arts college in Kentucky for African Americans. Teacher training was an important component within the school's core curriculum and in this regard served as a more-than-adequate replacement for the old normal program associated with Central High School; by the early 1940s, more African American teachers in Louisville had attended Municipal College than any other single institution. The school closed abruptly in 1951, a year after the state of Kentucky legislatively eliminated its segregated system of higher education. The way the University of Louisville terminated the contracts of Municipal College's faculty, including those who were tenured, alarmed African American educators nationwide, a stark portent of the wave of teacher "displacement" which would cascade across the South over the next two decades.[33]

Dunbar Junior College in Little Rock, Arkansas, was founded in 1929, coincident with the opening of a new high school facility for African Americans (at first named the Negro Industrial High School, formally dedicated as Dunbar High School in 1930), and was housed in one wing of the high school for several years. The facility that Dunbar High replaced, Gibbs High School, had briefly offered a normal course back in the 1910s, but the program had been abandoned. "Centered around a teacher-training curriculum," according to one authoritative history, Dunbar Junior College also provided courses in the liberal arts and home economics. Within 10 years, by 1939, 77 of the junior colleges's 352 graduates were employed by the Little Rock school system, representing approximately 72 percent of the city's African American teaching staff. In May 1955, to avoid the prospect of integration with all-White Little Rock Junior College (established in 1927), Dunbar Junior College was unceremoniously closed following a secret meeting by its board of trustees.[34]

The continuities and discontinuities between the older normal programs and the new models of municipal colleges were perhaps best exemplified in Houston. HCJC was founded in 1927, the outgrowth of the African American community's ongoing desire to establish a local institution for Black higher education and the administrative program of a new school superintendent who sought to upgrade the city's Black and White teaching force.

For years, the Black community in Houston was miffed by the lack of availability of local opportunities for teacher training and advanced education. In 1924, Wiley College, one of the better four-year Black colleges in Texas, initiated extension classes in education in Dallas, about 150 miles away from its Marshall campus. In 1925, Wiley ventured even further afield, responding to a request from Houston teachers for extension classes in the Bayou City, about 225 miles away. These classes, popular from the start, met in Colored High School with school board's approval. The initiation of the classes coincided with initiatives planned by the city's new school superintendent, E. E. Oberholtzer, hired from a similar position in Tulsa in 1924. Only about 17 of the city's 175 Black teachers had college degrees in 1925 and levels of college education among White teachers were similarly low. Backed by an extensive petition drive in the Black community, Oberholtzer convinced the school board to sponsor local opportunities for higher education, provided financial support would be minimal. In 1927, Houston Junior College for Whites and HCJC began to function under the auspices of the Houston Independent School District, the Black school being the nation's first publicly supported African American junior college. Both schools were self-supporting and dependent on tuition fees, which were initially a somewhat expensive $100 a year.[35]

Enrollment expanded rapidly at HCJC during its first decade, growing from 300 in the summer of 1927, to 700 in 1934, to 1,016 in 1937.

Most of the students during these early years were in-service Houston teachers, who took a variety of evening (from 3 p.m. to 10 p.m.) and summer school courses at Jack Yates Colored High School (opened in 1926), where HCJC was housed until 1946. Through the early 1930s, Prairie View Normal and Industrial College, the state's Black land-grant located about fifty miles away in Waller County, no doubt embarrassed by the fact that Wiley had beaten them to the punch in Houston, offered extension classes at HCJC. Combined with their junior college liberal arts coursework, Black Houstonians could now complete three years of their collegiate experience without leaving the city. In 1934, the same year the White junior college became the University of Houston, a four-year curriculum was initiated at HCJC and its name was changed to Houston College for Negroes. In 1943, the University of Houston began to offer a graduate program in education for in-service African American teachers at Houston College for Negroes, and in 1945 both the University and Houston College were separated from HISD, with the Black school then administered by the University's Board of Regents. Two years later, in 1947, the school was acquired by the state and renamed Texas State University for Negroes, becoming Texas Southern University in 1951. By 1945, at the time of its separation from HISD, 348 of the city's 450 Black teachers (77.3 percent) had received at least some of their training at the school, with 109 or close to one-third, receiving their bachelor's degrees from Houston College for Negroes.[36]

Conclusion

In a recent historiography on gender and Black colleges, Marybeth Gasman titled her thoughtful piece, "Swept under the Rug." This same phrase might be applied to the lack of research examining the role of normal schools in the upward expansion of African American educational attainments in the nineteenth and twentieth centuries. This blind spot, arguably a function of many of the same reasons noted in Gasman's work, has in many ways distorted a comprehensive understanding of the arduous development of educational "ladders" within the African American experience, overlooking key rungs in the process while conflating others.[37]

The problem is longstanding. W. E. B. Du Bois's classic 1900 Atlanta University study, *The College-Bred Negro*, rightly notes that only approximately 9 percent of those attending thirty Black colleges and universities in 1898–99 were enrolled in the collegiate units of those institutions. "In most cases, the college departments of these institutions are but adjuncts, and sometimes unimportant adjuncts, to other departments devoted to secondary and primary work," Du Bois noted when examining his data. Yet he neither discussed nor examined the teacher-training programs these schools sheltered and offered to large numbers of their constituents. Similarly, as editor of the *Crisis*, Du Bois often devoted one issue annually, often in July, to a celebration of Black college-going. In 1915, the special issue contained a section on "The Colored High School." In his commentary, Du Bois lists "Miner Normal, D.C.," "Colored Normal, Louisville," and "Baltimore Normal" as three of the high schools having the largest graduating classes annually. Yet by this date, all three institutions offered two-year *post-high school* teacher education coursework, a distinction Du Bois ignored that is deserving of recognition and its own special category.[38]

In the era of de jure segregation, Black higher education might best be conceptualized as a process over time, with multiple institutions creating of interwoven network. Undoubtedly, for many Black young adults and their families in the late-nineteenth and early-twentieth centuries, college-going and the attainment of a baccalaureate degree was idealized as a long-term goal. This aspiration grew over time. But African American normal schooling of all types, as demonstrated by the city teacher-training programs and other municipal initiatives, played a significant role in the development of traditional higher education, serving as important indicator of advanced education, a marker of professional training, and eventually as a springboard for greater educational attainments.

Notes

1. Benjamin W. Frazier, *Development of State Programs for the Certification of Teachers*, U.S. Bureau of Education, Bulletin, 1938, #12 (Washington, DC: GPO, 1938), 127; Arnold Lee Thomasson, "A Half Century of Teacher Training in State Normal Schools and Teachers Colleges of the United States, 1890–1940," Dissertation, University of Illinois, 1943, 9, 67.
2. Fisk University's first normal class began with twelve students in November 1867; no students were enrolled in college courses until 1871. It was not until the early 1880s that collegiate enrollments began to surpass those in the normal program. See "Fisk University," *American Missionary* 12, no. 5 (May 1868): 102–3; *Catalogue, Fisk University, 1883–84* (Nashville, TN: Marshall & Bruce, 1884), 5, 15. At Atlanta University, the normal program began in 1873; the college department in 1876. Between 1873 and 1907, 370 women and 11 men graduated from the normal department, while 114 men and 28 women graduated from the college department between 1876 and 1907. See Myron W. Adams, *A History of Atlanta University* (Atlanta, GA: Atlanta University Press, 1930), 14–21, 37–38. On Talladega, see D. O. W. Holmes, "The Beginnings of the Negro College," *Journal of Negro Education* 3, no. 2 (April 1934): 185.

3. *Report of the Commissioner of Education for the Year 1881* (Washington, DC: GPO, 1883), lxxxv–lxxvi; *Report of the Commissioner of Education for the Year 1894–95*, vol. 2 (Washington, DC: GPO, 1896), 1334–35; John W. Davis, "The Participation of Negro Land-Grant Colleges in Permanent Federal Education Funds," *Journal of Negro Education* 7, no. 3 (July 1938): 283. On the founding of Black state normal schools, see Edward Mayes, *History of Education in Mississippi*, U.S. Bureau of Education, Circular of Information No. 2 (Washington, DC: GPO, 1899), 266; Horace Mann Bond, *Negro Education in Alabama: A Study of Cotton and Steel* (1939; reprint: New York: Atheneum, 1969), 105–10; Fredrick Chambers, "Historical Study of Arkansas Agricultural, Mechanical and Normal College, 1873–1943," Dissertation, Ball State University, 1970, 9; Eugene Davis Owen, *Early Development of State Normal Schools or Negroes in North Carolina*, MA, University of North Carolina at Greensboro, 1930, 3–4; W. Sherman Savage, *The History of Lincoln University* (Jefferson City, MO: Lincoln University, 1939), 34; George Ruble Woofolk, *Prairie View: A Study in Public Conscience, 1878–1946* (New York: Pageant Press, 1962), 43–46; William Murray Clayborne, "A History of the Teacher Education Programs in Five Negro Colleges of Virginia from 1876 to 1954," Dissertation, George Washington University, 1971, 74; Austin Edwards, "History of the Kentucky State Industrial college for Negroes," Dissertation, Indiana State Teachers College, 1936, 5–6; Thomas Cochran, "History of Public-School Education in Florida," Dissertation, University of Pennsylvania, 1921, 99.

4. Frank A. Manny, *City Training Schools for Teachers*, U.S. Bureau of Education, Bulletin, 1914, No. 47 (Washington, DC: GPO, 1915); William Martin, "A Study in Local Initiative in the Education of Negro Teachers," *Journal of Negro Education* 12, no. 1 (Winter 1943): 24–30.

5. Manny, *City Training Schools*, 104–5; Edgar A. Toppin, "Walter White and the Atlanta NAACP's Fight for Equal Schools, 1916–1917," *History of Education Quarterly* 7, no. 1 (Spring 1967): 3–21; Donald E. Devore and Joseph Longsdon, *Crescent City Schools: Public Education in New Orleans, 1841–1991* (Lafayette, LA: University of Southwestern Louisiana, 1991), 189–91, 207; Myrtle R. Banks, "The Education of the Negro in New Orleans," Master's Thesis, Xavier University, 1935, 189–91.

6. Druscilla J. Null, "Myrtilla Miner's 'School for Colored Girls': A Mirror on Antebellum Washington," *Records of the Columbia Historical Society, Washington, D.C.* 52 (1989): 254–68; Ellen M. O'Connor, *Myrtilla Miner: A Memoir* (New York: Arno Press and the New York Times, 1969), quote on 17; Sadie Daniel, "Myrtilla Miner: Pioneer in Teacher Education for Negro Women," *Journal of Negro History* 34 (January 1949): 30–45.

7. *Twenty-Seventh Report of the Board of Trustees of Public Schools of the City of Washington, 1873–74* (Washington City: M'Gill & Witherow, 1874), 10, 26–27, quote on 26; *Third Report of the Board of Trustees of Public Schools of the District of Columbia, 1876–1877* (Washington City: R. Beresford, 1877), 25–26; *Sixth Report of the Board of Trustees of Public Schools of the District of Columbia, 1879–1880* (Washington: Globe Printing and Publishing House, 1881), 37–41. *The First Report of the Board of Trustees of Public Schools of the District of Columbia, 1874–1875* (Washington City: M'Gill & Witherow, 1876), 120, notes that one portion of the curriculum at Washington Normal included a review of sixth grade arithmetic.

8. *First Report of the Board of Trustees, 1874–1875*, 8, 252; *Third Report of the Board of Trustees, 1876–1877*, 40, 257–259; Lillian G. Dabney, *The History of Schools for Negroes in the District of Columbia, 1807–1947* (Washington, DC: Catholic University of American Press, 1949), 135–38, 163–64.

9. *Third Report of the Board of Trustees, 1876–1877*, 40–41, 259–60; *Sixth Report of the Board of Trustees of Public Schools of the District of Columbia, 1879–1880*, 10, 175–77; Winfield S. Montgomery, "Historical Sketch of Education for the Colored Race in the District of Columbia, 1807–1905," in *Report of the Board of Education to the Commissioners of the District of Columbia, 1904–1905* (Washington, DC: GPO, 1906), 121–31; Bernard H. Nelson, *Miner Teachers College: The First Century, 1851–1951* (Washington, DC: Author, 1973), 17, 31–40; Dabney, *A History of Schools for Negroes in the District of Columbia*, 165–66. The 1879 agreement marks the date considered as the beginning of Miner's status as a city teacher-training facility.

10. *Report of the Board of Education to the Commissioners of the District of Columbia, 1904–5* (Washington, DC: GPO, 1906), 333–34; Thomasine Corrothers, "Lucy Ellen Moten, 1851–1933," *Journal of Negro History* 19 (January 1934): 102–6; Paul Phillips Cooke, *A Collection of Biographical Sketches of the Principals of the Normal Schools, Washington, D.C., 1851–1931* (Washington, DC: University of the District of Columbia, 1983), 32–38.

11. Nelson, *Miner Teachers College*, 46, 51–54, quote on 54; Corrothers, "Lucy Ellen Moten," 106. As was common in the late-nineteenth century, teacher candidates at Miner were required to sign a pledge that upon completion of their studies they would teach in the local public schools for at least two years. This pledge remained in place until 1921. See Dabney, *A History of Schools for Negroes in the District of Columbia*, 66, footnote 248.

12. *Report of the Board of Education to the Commissioners of the District of Columbia, 1904–5* (Washington, DC: GPO, 1906), 334–37; *Report of the Board of Education to the Commissioners of the District of Columbia, 1910–1911* (Washington, DC: GPO, 1913), 257–65; *Annual Report of the Commissioners of the District of Columbia, Vol. IV, Report of the Board of Education, 1919–1920*, 362–65; Nelson, "Miner Teachers College," 51–60, 62, 64, 74.

13. Nelson, "Miner Teachers College," 60–62, 74–80; Dabney, *History of Schools for Negroes in the District of Columbia*, 137, 172; Mary Church Terrell, "History of the High School for Negroes in Washington," *Journal of Negro History* 2, no. 3 (July 1917): 252–66; Montgomery, "Historical Sketch," 129.

14. *Report of the Board of Education, 1910–1911*, 259; Manny, City Training Schools, 106.

15. Nelson, *Miner Teachers College*, 110–12; Winona Williams-Burns and Jane Ellen McAllister, "Pioneer for Excellence in Teacher Education," *Journal of Negro Education* 51 (Summer 1982): 342–57.

16. *Revised Statutes of the State of Missouri, 1879* (Jefferson: Carter & Regan, 1879), 1542–3; Elinor Mondale Gersman, "The Development of Public Education for Blacks in Nineteenth Century St. Louis," *Journal of Negro Education* 41, no. 1 (Winter 1972): 37–40; Julia Davis, "Harris Teachers College and Stowe Teachers College: Growth and Development," Master's Thesis, State University of Iowa, 1941.

17. Julia Davis, *Down Memory Lane: 50th Anniversary Celebration* (St. Louis, MO: St. Louis Public Library, 1976), 5; Ronald Butchart, *Schooling the Freedmen: Teaching, Learning, and the Struggle for Black Freedom, 1861–1876* (Chapel Hill, NC: University of North Carolina Press, 2010), 204; *Twenty-Ninth Annual Report of the Board of Education of the St. Louis Public Schools for the Year Ending August 1, 1883* (St. Louis, MO: Nixon-Jones Printing, 1884), lxxv.

18. *Thirty-Eighth Annual Report of the Board of Education of the St. Louis Public Schools for the Year Ending, June 30, 1892* (St. Louis, MO: The Mekeel Press, 1893), 58–64; *Forty-Sixth Annual Report of the Board of Education of the City*

of St. Louis, MO, for the Year Ending June 30, 1900 (St. Louis, MO: Buxton & Skinner, 1901), 114–20; *Fifty-Third Annual Report of the Board of Education of the City of St. Louis for the Year Ending June 30, 1907* (St. Louis, MO: Shallcross Printing, 1908), 282; Gersman, "Public Education for Blacks in Nineteenth Century St. Louis," 38–44; Davis, "Harris Teachers College and Stowe Teachers College," 37–47. A school board meeting on June 9, 1891, noted a "petition signed by 300 patrons of the Sumner High School asking that a new high school building in an entirely new locality be provided for the use of colored children." See, *St. Louis Public Schools, Printed Record of the Board, Vol. VII, July 1, 1889 to July 1, 1892* (St. Louis, MO: Nixon-Jones, 1892), 593.

19. J. W. Evans, "A Brief Sketch of the Development of Negro Education in St. Louis, Missouri," *Journal of Negro Education* 7, no. 4 (October 1938): 548–52; Selwyn K. Troen, *The Public and the Schools: Shaping the St. Louis System, 1838–1920* (Columbia, MO: University of Missouri Press, 1975), 91–92; Elinor M. Gersman, "The Development of Public Education for Blacks in Nineteenth Century St. Louis, Missouri," *Journal of Negro Education* 41, no. 1 (Winter 1972): 39; Davis, "Harris Teachers College and Stowe Teachers College," 39–40.

20. *Twenty-Sixth Annual Report of the St. Louis Public Schools for the Year Ending August 1, 1880* (St. Louis, MO: Slawson & Co., 1881), 55–77; *Thirty-Eighth Annual Report of the St. Louis Public Schools*, 61–66; Ruth Harris, *Stowe Teachers College and Her Predecessors* (Boston, MA: Christopher Publishing Co., 1967), 13–14; Davis, "Harris Teachers College and Stowe Teachers College," 11–24, 45; *St. Louis Public Schools, Printed Record of the Board, Vol. VII, July 1, 1889 to July 1, 1892* (St. Louis, MO: Nixon-Jones, 1892), 362; *Forty-Sixth Annual Report of the Board of Education of the City of St. Louis, for the Year Ending June 30, 1900* (St. Louis, MO: Buxton & Skinner, 1901), 114–18.

21. Davis, "Harris Teachers College and Stowe Teachers College," 52, 62–69; *Forty-Ninth Annual Report of the Board of Education of the City of St. Louis for the Year Ending June 30, 1903*, 100–101; Manny, *City Training Schools for Teachers*, 107; Robert I. Brigham, "The Education of the Negro in Missouri," Dissertation, University of Missouri, 1946, 243.

22. Harris, *Stowe Teachers College*, 16–29, 62.

23. Harris, *Stowe Teachers College*, 24–47.

24. Brigham, "The Education of the Negro in Missouri," 243–46; Harris, *Stowe Teachers College*, 9, 161. For several years before the merger, the two teachers colleges shared the same catalogue.

25. *Thirty-Eighth Annual Report of the Board of Commissioners of Public Schools* (Baltimore, MD: James Young, 1867), 7; *Fourth Annual Report of the Baltimore Female College* (Annapolis, MD: Richard P. Bayly, 1865), 3–5; Bernard C. Steiner, *History of Education in Maryland*, United States Bureau of Education, Circular of Information, No. 2 (Washington, DC: GPO, 1894), 269; *Report of the Commission Appointed to Study the System of Education in the Public Schools of Baltimore* (Washington, DC: GPO, 1911), 25–27, 55–57; *Thirty-First Annual Report of the Board of Public Schools* (Baltimore, MD: Bull & Tuttle, 1860) 27–30. As the *Report of the Survey of the Public School System of Baltimore, Maryland, Volume 2* (Baltimore, MD: Baltimore School Commissioners, 1921), commented with regard to the State Normal, "Its standards of admission and of training were below those that the city could well afford to require from its own elementary-school teachers," 127.

26. Vernon S. Vavrina, "The History of Pubic Education in the City of Baltimore, 1826–1956," Dissertation, Catholic University of America, 1958, 229–33; Martha S. Putney, "The Baltimore Normal School for the Education of Colored Teachers:

Its Founders and Its Founding," *Maryland Historical Magazine* 72 (Summer 1997): 238–52; *Sixty-Seventh Annual Report of the Board of Commissioners of Public Schools for the Year Ending December 31, 1895* (Baltimore, MD: John B. Kurtz, 1896), xxvi–xxvii, 139–40; Bettye C. Thomas, "Public Education and Black Protest in Baltimore, 1865–1900," *Maryland Historical Magazine* 71 (Fall 1976): 381–91; *Report of the Survey of the Public School System of Baltimore, Maryland, Vol. 2*, 89–92; *The 1941 Survey of the Maryland Public Schools and Teachers Colleges* (Baltimore, MD: Maryland State School Survey Commission, 1941), 364–77.

27. Mason A. Hawkins, *Frederick Douglass High School—A Seventeen Year Period Study*, Dissertation, University of Pennsylvania, 1933, 1–10; Clarence Kenneth Gregory, "The Education of Blacks in Maryland: An Historical Survey," Dissertation, Teachers College, Columbia University, 1976, 419.

28. *Seventy-Third Annual Report of the Board of School Commissioners for the Fiscal Year Ending December 31, 1901* (Baltimore, MD: John Lucas Printing Co., 1902), 4, 59, 108; *Seventy-Fourth Annual Report of the Board of School Commissioners for the Fiscal Year Ending December 31, 1902* (Baltimore, MD: John Lucas Printing Co., 1903), 4, 49, 69; *Seventy-Seventh Annual Report of the Board of School Commissioners for the Fiscal Year Ending December 31, 1905* (Baltimore, MD: WM. J.C. Dulany Co., 1906), 43–44, 97; *Eightieth Annual Report of the Board of School Commissioners for the Fiscal Year Ending December 31, 1908* (Baltimore, MD: WM. J.C. Dulany, 1909), 35, 47, 94; *Eighty-Second Annual Report of the Board of School Commissioners for the Fiscal Year Ending December 31, 1910* (Baltimore, MD: Meyer & Thalheimer, 1911), 81; G. Smith Wormley, "Educators of the First Half Century of Public Schools of the District of Columbia," *Journal of Negro History* 17, no. 2 (April 1932): 134–36.

29. Maryland State School Survey Commission, *The 1941 Survey of the Maryland Public Schools and Teachers Colleges* (Baltimore, MD: Maryland State School Survey Commission, 1941), 376–79; Gregory, *The Education of Blacks in Maryland*, 423–31; Monroe N. Work, ed., *Negro Year Book, 1937–1938* (Tuskegee, AL: Negro Year Book Publishing Co., 1938), 198; G. James Fleming, "The Negro Publicly-Supported Colleges in Delaware and Maryland," *Journal of Negro Education* 31 (Summer 1962): 264–67.

30. Scott Britton Hansen, "Education for All: The Freedmen's Bureau in Richmond and Petersburg, 1865–1870," Master's Thesis, Virginia Commonwealth University, 2008; R. M. Manly, "The Navy Hill Schools, Richmond, Va.," *American Freedman* 3, no. 3 (June 1868): 424–25; Martha W. Owens, "The Development of Public Schools for Negroes in Richmond, Virginia, 1865–1900," Master's Thesis, Virginia State College, 1947, 26–29; *Proceedings of the Trustees of the Peabody Education Fund, Vol. I* (Boston, MA: Press of John Wilson and Son, 1875), "Fifth Meeting of the Trustees, July 16, 1868," 94, "8th Meeting of the Trustees, February 15, 1870," 194–95, "10th Meeting of the Trustees, June 25, 1872," 292.

31. C. A. Lindsay, "A Brief History of the Armstrong High School, Richmond, Virginia," *Virginia Teachers Bulletin* 7 (November 1930): 8–9; *Forty-Fourth Annual Report of the Superintendent of the Public Schools of the City of Richmond, Virginia, for the Scholastic Year Ending June 30, 1913*, 19, 157; Ann Field Alexander, "Black Protest in the New South: John Mitchell, Jr. (1863–1929) and the Richmond Planet," PhD Dissertation, Duke University, 1973), 28–33. *Forty-Eighth Annual Report of the Superintendent of the Public Schools of the City of Richmond, Virginia, for the Scholastic Year Ending June 30, 1917*, 39; Selden Richardson and Maurice Duke, *Built by Blacks: African American Architecture and Neighborhoods in Richmond* (Charleston, SC: The History Press, 2008), 79–80; *Sixty-Fourth Annual Report of*

the Superintendent of the Public Schools of the City of Richmond, Virginia, for the Scholastic Year Ending June 30, 1933, 33, 79, 100, 112.

32. George D. Wilson, *A Century of Negro Education in Louisville, Kentucky* (reprint: Louisville, KY: University Libraries, University of Louisville, 1986), 55–56, 62, 69–70; *Reports of the Louisville School Board for the School Year Ending June 30, 1895*, 124–25; *Report of the Public Schools, Louisville, KY., 1896–97* (Louisville, KY: Geo. G. Fetter Printing Co., 1898), 53–54; *Reports of the Louisville School Board for the School Year Ending June 30, 1898*, 108–10; *First Report of the Board of Education of Louisville, Kentucky, from January 1, 1911 to July 1, 1912* (Louisville, KY: John P. Morton & Co., 1913), 91–92; *Twenty-Fourth Report of the Board of Education of Louisville, Kentucky, from September 1, 1934 to September 1, 1935*, 13–14, 54–55; Brenda Feast Jackson, "The Policies and Purposes of Black Public Schooling in Louisville, Kentucky, 1890–1930," PhD Dissertation, Indiana University, 1976, 200–7. The principal of Central High School when the normal classes were initiated, F. L. Williams, later became principal of Sumner High School in St. Louis, presiding over that city's normal program for twenty-one years.

33. Harvey C. Russell, "Municipal Support of Higher Education for Negroes," in *A Century of Municipal Higher Education* (Chicago. IL: Lincoln Printing Co., 1937), 331–38; Wellyn F. Collins, "Louisville Municipal College," Master's Thesis, University of Louisville, 1976; J. Blaine Hudson, "The Establishment of Louisville Municipal College: A Case Study in Racial Conflict and Compromise," *Journal of Negro Education* 64, no. 2 (Spring 1995): 111–23; *Survey Report of the Louisville Public Schools* (Louisville, KY: City of Louisville, 1943), 168; Oliver C. Cox, "Vested Interests Involved in the Integration of Schools for Negroes," *Journal of Negro Education* 20, no. 1 (Winter 1951): 112–14; Charles H. Thompson, "Negro Teachers and the Elimination of Segregated Schools," *Journal of Negro Education* 20, no. 2 (Spring 1951): 135–39.

34. Faustine C. Jones-Wilson and Erma G. Davis, *Paul Laurence Dunbar High School of Little Rock, Arkansas* (Little Rock, AR: The Donning Company, 2003), 25–34; Faustine Childress Jones, *A Traditional Model of Educational Excellence: Dunbar High School of Little Rock, Arkansas* (Washington, DC: Howard University Press, 1981), 14–17; Martin, "Local Initiative in the Education of Negro Teachers," 25–26.

35. William E. Terry, *Origin and Development of Texas Southern University* (Houston, TX: Author, 1968); Ira B. Bryant, *Texas Southern University* (Houston, TX: Author, 1975); Amilcar Shabazz, "One for the Crows, One for the Crackers: The Strange Career of Public Higher Education in Houston, Texas," *The Houston Review* 18, no. 2 (1998): 124–43; James M. SoRelle, "The Darker Side of 'Heaven': The Black Community of Houston, Texas, 1917–1945" Dissertation, Kent State University, 1980, 87; David A. Lane, "The Junior College Movement among Negroes," *Journal of Negro Education* 2, no. 3 (July 1933): 275, 280–81.

36. Terry, *Origin and Development of Texas Southern University*; Bryant, *Texas Southern University*; Shabazz, "One for the Crows, One for the Crackers," 124–43.

37. Marybeth Gasman, "Swept Under the Rug? A Historiography of Gender and Black College," *American Educational Research Journal* 44, no. 4 (December 2007): 760–805.

38. W. E. B. Du Bois, *The College-Bred Negro* (Atlanta, GA: Atlanta University Press, 1900), 16; "The Colored High School," *Crisis* 10, no. 3 (July 1915): 143.

Nooses, Sheets, and Blackface: White Racial Anxiety and Black Student Presence at Six Midwest Flagship Universities, 1882–1937

Richard M. Breaux

This article links the incidents of campus blackface, hangman's noose, and ghetto party incidents between 2002 and 2009 to similar expressions of racial anxiety among white students who saw the first generation black students desegregate several Midwestern universities between 1882 and 1936. It explores four major expressions of white students' fear, anxiety, and resentment as related to blacks' growing presence and success on campuses in the Midwest: (1) the noted presence and establishment of student honorary Ku Klux Klan and affiliates of the Invisible Empire of the Ku Klux Klan groups; (2) the rise of blackface incidents at white fraternity parties, campus minstrel shows, and in university-sponsored theater events; (3) the placing of racial and ethnic caricatures that ridiculed black students or blacks, in general, in class yearbooks; and (4) the use of these caricatures to specifically ridicule African American Greek-letter organizations.

Few incidents openly demonstrate some white's racial anxieties and resentment toward black success and social mobility into formerly white social, political, and educational spaces than the spate of blackface parties and hanging nooses on American college campuses. Many in the academic community expressed shock and disbelief in 2001 and 2002, when a string of so-called "blackface incidents" came to light after white fraternity parties or variety shows at Auburn and Oklahoma State universities and the universities of Wisconsin-Whitewater, Alabama, and Mississippi.[1] The posting of photographs from these parties on the worldwide web made these events seem more horrendous, yet possible suspensions, condemnation

Perspectives on the History of Higher Education 29 (2012): 43-73
© 2012. ISBN: 978-1-4128-4771-1

by many in the press, and pending lawsuits did not curb such incidents. Between 2002 and 2009 at least fifteen blackface, twenty-six
noose, twenty-four neo-Ku Klux Klan, and over two hundred sixty
racist e-mail, sign-flyer, or graffiti incidents hit the American university with a vengeance.[2] These numbers exclude twenty-six so-
called "ghetto parties" where largely middle-class white college
students engage in what scholars Eric Lott and Michael Rogin call
"racial cross-dressing."[3] Many black and some white and minority
students saw these pictures as hard evidence that even the most overt
forms of racism continue to exist on American college campuses.
"History repeats itself in Blackface,"[4] noted one article, where one
of America's most popular forms of entertainment has resurfaced
with a millennium twist. Others, like the Association for Fraternity
Advisors, saw these incidents as an opportunity to educate white fraternities about the history of blackface. This became a chance to
inform white students about why some students found these party
antics offensive.[5] While a growing body of historical research has
begun to reexamine blackface minstrel traditions with regard to white
working-class culture and identity, few studies have highlighted the
rise of blackface minstrelsy, racial caricature, and white supremacist
groups as a part of white middle-class college culture in the late nineteenth and early twentieth centuries.[6] The difference between these
forms of racialized expression at the turn of the twentieth century
versus similar incidents at the turn of the twenty-first century is that
the earlier responses to increased black student enrollment became
more formalized university traditions, that college administrators
recognized as established and approved custom.

This essay explores the politics of racial stereotypes and racial representation as a customary part of white and black students' experiences
at several Predominantly White Flagship Universities (PWFUs) in the
Midwest. I define PWFUs in the Midwest as the universities of Kansas
(KU), Iowa (UI), Nebraska (NU), Illinois (UIUC), Wisconsin (UW),
and Minnesota (UM). This article also examines how white students
responded to increasing black student enrollment at these six Midwestern universities from 1882 to 1937. In 1937, Charlotte Crump, a black
student at UM, believed that blacks encountered three types of white
students: (1) those who attended multiracial events and went to extreme
lengths to speak to blacks to show their concern for the so-called "Negro
Problem," (2) those who demonstrated little interest in thinking about
racism and discrimination because they felt it was not their problem,

and (3) whites who were overtly "antagonistic" toward all nonwhites.[7] These types transcended place and time and could be found on almost any college campus in the United States during the time. Prior to 1910, the first type of student might come to the defense of black students, particularly athletes at NU, UI, UM, or KU, discriminated against by opposing teams. After 1910, these students joined groups like the YMCA or YWCA, the Cosmopolitan Club, the Negro Forum, or other organizations where white and blacks challenged racism and black exclusion from local eateries or restaurants located near KU, UI, UIUC, and UM.[8] Some of these more racially progressive white students joined the American Student Union in the 1930s and protested local and campus racism among other social and political issues.[9] White students in the latter category drew on popular stereotypes concerning black peoples' cultural and intellectual inferiority to whites to attack black collegians psychologically. These attacks took on various forms, however, I will discuss four major expressions of white students' fear, anxiety, and resentment as related to blacks' growing presence and success on campuses in the Midwest: (1) the noted presence and establishment of student honorary Ku Klux Klan and affiliates of the Invisible Empire of the Ku Klux Klan groups; (2) the rise of blackface incidents at white fraternity parties, campus minstrel shows, and in university-sponsored theater events; (3) the placing of racial and ethnic caricatures that ridiculed black students or blacks in general in class yearbooks; and (4) the use of these caricatures to specifically ridicule African American Greek-letter organizations.

Black students did not suffer this racism in quiet isolation, but their skin color combined with their small numbers exaggerated their absence and presence. While some white students responded to blacks' presence and advancement by placing racist cartoons and caricatures in campus newspapers and yearbooks, black collegians sought to vindicate the race through their academic achievement and social organizations. On all six campuses, white students blacked-up and took to the campus minstrel stage, while black students created social and intellectual empowerment zones or safe spaces among themselves as a shield against campus and community racism. All of these cases reveal the degree to which many white students have a distorted view of America's racial past and viewed racist caricature and Klan symbolism not as serious, but humorous. These cases also capture white students' desires, fears, and anxieties about the real and perceived increased presence/power of blacks on the American college campus and in American society.

Some whites' anxieties concerning upwardly mobile blacks' presence/ power on and off college campuses extended black into the early nineteenth century. In her 1980 essay, Emma Jones Lapsansky examined the influence of black sociopolitical self-determination and advancement on white mob violence against free blacks in Jacksonian Philadelphia. She, like historians Leon Litwack, David Roediger, Eric Lott, Matthew Faye Jacobson, and others, found that physical, verbal, and psychological attacks on African Americans by European Americans were in part the result of economic competition, "spatial turf" controversies, and "concerns over competition for status among upwardly mobile" black and white Americans.[10] More often than not, whites attacked blacks because of black social advancement.[11] As Lapsansky and others note, the illustrations of Edward W. Clay and the emergence of blackface minstrelsy that developed in the nineteenth century and persisted into the twentieth century were the results of white hostility, envy, repulsion, sympathy, and fear.[12]

White college students expressed all these feelings in reaction to the growing presence and advancement of black students at six PWFUs in the Midwest from 1882 to 1937. According to W. E. B. Du Bois', by 1900, sixteen blacks graduated from KU, four earned degrees from UI, UW and UM graduated three each, and two earned degrees from NU. No black earned a degree from UIUC before 1900, in fact an unnamed campus official noted that UIUC had a black senior likely to graduate who was "editor of the student's [news]paper"—he did and that was William Walter Smith.[13] In his 1910 follow-up study, Du Bois noted that black college graduates amounted to sixty from KU, eight from UM, seven from UIUC, and six from NU. The six blacks that had graduated from UW were not noted in *The College-Bred Negro American*.[14] By the 1920s, the largest number of black students enrolled at KU and UIUC, which began to enroll over one hundred black students each academic year by the late 1920s and throughout much of the 1930s. Some of these students were faculty and staff at black colleges who only enrolled during the summer sessions. No more than fifty black students each enrolled at NU, UW, or UM in an academic year between 1915 and 1940. W. E. B. Du Bois recorded the most accurate numbers for these universities in the *Crisis* in the 1920s and 1930s. In 1923, KU, UI, UM, UW, and NU enrolled 83, 55, 18, 3, and 21 black students, respectively. By 1927, all black enrollments increased to 114, 115, 45, 6, and 41. In 1930, KU, UIUC, UI, UM, UW, and NU reported 151, 138, 84, 48, 14, and 30 black students, respectively. In 1933, 149, 141, 58, 34, and

32 blacks enrolled at KU, UIUC, UI, UM, and NU; and in 1936, these universities enrolled 149, 108, 58, 25, and 25.[15] White hostility, envy, repulsion, sympathy, and fear emerged with the earliest black enrollees and became sanctioned part of university customs as black enrollment increased.

The numbers of black students at KU, UIUC, and UI likely resulted from southern universities campaign to maintain racially segregated public colleges and universities and KU, UIUC, and UI's location as northern states that border southern states (all bordered Missouri, and Illinois also borders Kentucky). While significant numbers of KU students were residents of Kansas, UIUC students resided in Illinois, and UI students were residents of Iowa; large numbers of students from Missouri, Texas, Mississippi, Alabama, and Oklahoma also enrolled at these universities. NU managed to attract black students from Missouri as well, but it did not enroll nearly as many black Missourians as KU, UIUC, or UI.

The growing presence of black students and cases of the Invisible Empire of the KKK, honorary-KKK presences, or blackface incidents at PWFUs in the Midwest are more difficult to document in the years before the turn of the twentieth century. Although some form of college yearbook has always existed from scrapbooks to e-books, mass-produced modern yearbook publishing emerged in the United States in the 1880s as advances in photographic technology permitted photographers to be more mobile and the halftone printing and letterpress process made book production less expensive for the producer and more affordable to college students. This is important for at least two reasons: (1) yearbooks are one of a few university publications that affirm and document the presence of black students on college campuses and (2) yearbooks became contested racial terrain over which students affirmed their views about racial hierarchies and racial equality.

The Initial Response to African Americans on Campus

Black students desegregated the Midwestern PWFUs in the 1870s, but only at KU did their numbers begin to grow in any significant manner before 1899. By 1900, KU graduated sixteen blacks, UI graduated four, three blacks each graduated from UM and UW, and one or two earned degrees from NU and UIUC.[16] For many blacks in the late nineteenth and early twentieth centuries, KU symbolized one of the most racially progressive colleges in the United States. It graduated sixteen blacks before 1899 and sixty before 1910. Only one predominantly white postsecondary institution graduated more blacks than KU before 1900 and 1910: Oberlin College. Oberlin represents more of an anomaly than KU, UIUC, UI, NU, UW, and UM which were more representative of the northern public university.

It did not long after blacks first enrolled for white students to show their contempt and envy of black students at UM and KU. The college KKK and blackface incidents made their first noted appearances at these institutions in the 1880s. In 1878, Andrew F. Hilyer entered UM. Hilyer came to Minneapolis from Omaha, Nebraska, in 1872.[17] Hilyer's family had come to Omaha decades before many of the Exodusters came to Nebraska. In fact, the family came to Omaha from Georgia, by way of St. Louis, in 1868. Hilyer worked his way through school by finding employment as a barber.[18] Although information on Hilyer's precollege and college years is sketchy, Hilyer most likely followed a group of relatives who migrated to Minneapolis at an earlier date, and took up residences with this extended family. An article published in the UM *Ariel* described Hilyer as "a mulatto who came to our institution without means or encouragement and paid his way through earnest work outside the university."[19] Not everyone treated of Hilyer so kindly.

The official history of UM notes that, weeks before Hilyer's 1882 graduation, a widely publicized blackface-KKK incident occurred on campus. James Gray, the author of UM's centennial history, notes that a group of poor white students recently disciplined by President William W. Folwell's "blackened their faces, put on Ku Klux Klan costumes, and sought to redress the wrong of having received more demerits than they really cared for."[20] Two professors came to Folwell's defense and the incident drew national attention, not because of the students' actions, but because Massachusetts Institute of Technology alumnus and engineering professor William A. Pike brandished a pistol and shot one of the students in the leg. Gray goes on to write that Pike and President William W. Folwell received letters of support from administrators at other universities, despite criticism from officials in the state government.[21] Gray fails to note, however, why the students had been disciplined before the incident. Had these students harassed Andrew Hilyer? Why did they choose to blacken-up and wear Klan suits weeks before Hilyer became UM's first black graduate? The record remains unclear. Perhaps the students who took part in these events were northern Democrats sympathetic to the southern Democratic Party cause; or perhaps these students were northern democrats upset that yet another Republican governor took office in 1882.[22] Despite potential racial hostilities and a relatively small number of blacks in the Twin Cities, this early blackface-Klan incident occurred at a time when Andrew Hilyer challenged the myth of white intellectual supremacy.

A handful of African American students at KU found acceptance from the white classmates despite an equally obvious climate of white racial hostility. Less than four years after Hilyer graduated from UM, Blanche K. Bruce, nephew of the well-known Mississippi Senator of the same name, became the first African American to graduate from KU. At the time of Bruce's graduation, approximately five or six other black students attended the University. The younger Blanche Bruce came to KU in 1881 after one year of study at all-black Lincoln Institute in Jefferson City, Missouri.[23] He graduated from KU in 1885 with a combined bachelor of arts and bachelor of didactics.[24] Bruce was one of the few black students "identified with the various university literary societies." According to reports in the *University Courier*, the student newspaper from 1882 to 1895, Bruce not only earned a place in the Orophillian Society, but he won several debates between Orophillian and rival campus societies.[25] Orophillian, founded in 1866 as the Acropolis society, developed from a co-ed preparatory department club to an all-male literary society when male students seized control of the group's leadership in 1870. This male-exclusive coup lasted a short time and by 1875, Oread and Orophillian reestablished co-ed membership.[26] Bruce's achievements may have very well been ignored had the Orophillian not established the *University Courier* in 1878–79 to compete with Oread Society's *Kansas Collegiate*.[27]

Many of the first black graduates of PWFUs were praised and damned by their fellow white classmates. Whites admitted a few blacks into some student groups and barred most blacks from others. While some black students sought entrance into mostly white social spaces, others did not. Still others were too busy spending their time between work and school to become involved in campus activities or advantaged themselves of opportunities among Lawrence's local black communities.[28] As the nephew of a United States senator and member of a prominent black family, Blanche Kelso Bruce probably fared a little better than other blacks at KU. As Bruce's membership in Orophillian proves, some degree of racial integration, even if token, existed in KU's student life. Some white students championed a form of racial equality, while others opposed it. Opponents of racial equality segregated, intimidated, and harassed blacks "not because of [blacks'] demonstrated incompetence but because of black success."[29] Some white students hated middle-class black students that made good, even more than poor black students from less prominent families with little or no political and financial resources. These white students resented signs of black achievement and advancement especially when they believed that proposed civil rights legislation pushed the proverbial envelope. In the year after Bruce graduated, at least one white student voiced the following opinion in the *University Courier:*

> When we say there should be equality, we do not mean there should be community. No matter how much we contend with the idea, the fact remains that there is an impassible gulf between the races. Not because one is infinitely higher or better than the other, but because there is a difference in temperament and mental qualities which prevents their having little if anything in common.
>
> For this reason we do not desire to associate with the negroes; neither do the negroes as a class desire to associate with us. It seems as a matter of mutual pleasure that the two societies should be separate and independent . . . . The colored people should be allowed to have their own hotels and theaters, and the same privilege should be granted to the white people. This is what we believe.[30]

The above editorial offers some insight into KU's racial climate in the 1880s. In the same year, KU's *Weekly University Courier* reported on a blackface incident that was supposedly meant to "bridge the chasm which separates the two races."[31] Two white students with "curled hair" and in blackface showed up at a black dance party and flirted with two black women. As these flirtations became more persistent, a young black man in attendance sounded the alarm on the white students when he yelled, "Look heah, you white trash, wat you doin up heah? You ain't no nigger; better black your ears next time." At that moment, a group of older black men surrounded the white students and threatened to beat the intruders black and blue if they did not leave. The white students complied and left the party without further disturbance.

These accounts of the KKK at UM and a blackface incident at KU suggest that even before the black student populations at these institutions ever had the opportunity to increase, white students quickly showed their disapproval of blacks' presence. The KKK episode at UM is particularly interesting because it occurred after the passage of the 1871 Civil Rights Act (also known as the KKK Act) that supposedly led to the demise of the first KKK. It adds weight to some historians' claim that the 1871 Civil Rights Act did not eliminate the KKK but merely forced the KKK underground.[32]

The passage of the Civil Rights Acts in the 1870s did little to change social and political conditions for blacks and the Supreme Court's outlawing of the Civil Rights Law in 1883 laid the foundation for the political disfranchisement of blacks and white violence against blacks for the next several decades. Lynching became one of the most violent extralegal forms of expressions whites used to keep blacks "in their place." Between 1889 and 1932, over 2,785 blacks were lynched by whites in the United States. White vigilantes used lynching to mete out their own type of justice and sent a message to other blacks not to push for social, political, or economic equality with whites. Nooses, in the nonhigher education case of the Jena Six, where in six African American teenagers were charged with the 2006 beating of a white teenager after whites reportedly hung nooses to warn black students not to sit under a tree designated for white students in Louisiana, and on college campuses in the post-Jena Six aftermath are meant to convey the same message. Indeed, historian Jelani Cobb reminds us that, "The noose is an index of insecurity generated by black progress."[33]

At NU and UI, whites were tolerant, almost accepting of the few blacks that enrolled before 1910, but some may attribute this to small number of blacks enrolled at these universities. George Flippin belonged to a campus literary society in the 1890s and S. Joe Brown and Herbert Wright were elected as class officers at UI in 1897 and 1900, respectively. Blacks interested in sports could play on almost any athletic team at UI, KU, NU, UW, UM, and UIUC, before 1912 including baseball at KU and UW, basketball at NU, wrestling at KU, and football and track & field at all six universities. The "kindly" feelings of whites toward blacks at NU and the "little more applause than a white boy" received by black NU graduates noted by an unidentified administrator, probably NU Chancellor Samuel Avery, in Du Bois' *The College-Bred Negro American* may be directly attributed to the fact that nearly half the blacks that enrolled at NU were black men who were athletes, including George Flippin, John Johnson, William Johnson, and Robert Taylor.[34] White and black athletes enjoyed popularity unmatched by all but white fraternity and sorority members. None of these institutions permitted blacks to play intercollegiate basketball after 1912 and KU and NU barred blacks from all intercollegiate sports in 1912 and 1917. Some whites accepted blacks into literary and academic honor societies while other white academic honor societies like Phi Delta Kappa barred all nonwhites through the 1940s. Schools of medicine at NU and UM restricted black enrollment so only two and four black students each graduated before 1940, UI began to restrict black medical student enrollment after 1925, and KU barred blacks from the last two (clinical) years until 1938. By 1940, eighteen blacks had received medical degrees from UI and eleven graduated from UIUC's medical school, none of the other schools had more five black graduates before 1940. Schools of nursing at these institutions were more restrictive than medical schools. As campuses added dormitories to college life, all but UW prohibited blacks from rooming in dorms before 1936. This move toward greater racial exclusion represented an official university policy response to the increased presence/power of African American students; white students responded to this increase in black enrollment by forming neo-Klan groups, performing in blackface, and attacking black students and student organizations.

The Birth of the Ku Klux Klan, a Nation, and the Honorary Klan

As black students entered the Midwestern PWFU in unprecedented numbers, judicially sanctioned Jim Crow and executive branch endorsement of a pro-Klan southern redemption film translated into a Ku Klux Klan resurgence that infiltrated every aspect of life in the United States, including the public college campuses. Between 1915 and 1925, racial violence in the United States increased in unprecedented proportions. James Weldon Johnson infamously referred to the summer of 1919, as the Red Summer, to symbolize the blood that filled the streets of America's cities. During the Red Summer, race riots and lynching occurred in twenty-six US cities including Chicago, Illinois, Omaha, Nebraska, and Duluth, Minnesota. White hate groups proliferated in Champaign-Urbana, Iowa City, Lawrence, the Twin Cities, Madison, and Lincoln.[35] The spirit of white supremacy that arose across the United States during this time, infected KU, UI, UIUC, UM, and NU as well.

The origins of the Ku Klux Klan date back to a group of six Scotch-Irish former Civil War veterans who created the secret order in Pulaski, Tennessee, in 1866. Within a year it expanded to several southern states in response to a radical congress that aggressively championed the rights of southern blacks and federal over states' rights. Historians Michael and Judy Ann Newton argue that after it spread to at least a dozen states, the organization ran into internal problems because members used the Klan to engage in a number of local feuds, gang rapes, and lynchings, while others viewed the Klan as a radical wing of the Democratic Party's political apparatus. Federal legislation forced the KKK to disband in 1871, but the informal locals and vigilante groups continued the KKK's duties of violence against blacks, white, and black Republicans, and so-called "carpetbaggers," northern businessmen with corporate business interest in the South. With the publication of Thomas Dixon's *The Clansman*, in 1905, and the release of D. W. Griffith's 1915 movie *The Birth of a Nation*, the white-supremacy revival that would find its way to a number of college campuses began. The adaptation of Dixon's *The Clansman* into Griffith's *The Birth of a Nation* helped popularize and sanitize the image of the Invisible Empire and make it acceptable to noncollegians and collegians alike. *The Birth of a Nation* was not only the first full-length feature film. With its themes of pure white womanhood, black rapists, chicken and watermelon-eating incompetent southern black elected officials, black Civil War soldiers gone wild, and a Christ-sanctioned chivalrous KKK that restores order and white supremacy, the film's KKK spawned a plethora of imitators. As thousands flocked to see the film, membership in the Invisible Empire became a symbol of whiteness, power, and "100% Americanism."[36]

Before the arrival and after the decline of local affiliates of the Invisible Empire, showings of *The Birth of a Nation* became contested issues between blacks and whites in Lincoln and Minneapolis-St. Paul. Some of the NAACP's most heated campaigns were its local branches' attempts to ban showing the southern redemption classic. A UI alumnus named S. Joe Brown and the NAACP branch in Des Moines, the branch Omaha, and St. Paul's branch led by J. A. Burnquist, had failed to get court injunctions to stop the showing of the film.[37] The ban of the second half of *The Birth of a Nation* at the Rialto Theatre in 1918 became one of the Lincoln branches' major victories. In a public letter printed in the *Omaha Monitor*, local NAACP members thanked both Mayor J. E. Miller and Attorney General Willis E. Reed for "putting '*The Birth of a Nation*' out of commission." Attorney General Reed had taken up the expenses of getting an injunction through his office, thereby saving the Lincoln chapter the court costs.[38]

Although St. Paul branch of the NAACP failed to ban the film in 1915, it got a second and third chance to make good in 1939. In one instance the unidentified theater in St. Paul proposed to show *The Birth of a Nation* and another film titled *Nigger*, a less well-known film about a southern governor forced to resign from office and leave his white love interests because he is discovered to have black ancestry.[39] After several appeals to the St. Paul's mayor, the branch had the so-called "Gus scenes" removed from *The Birth of a Nation*. In the spring of 1940, the third time was a charm. The visual education department at UM planned to schedule a showing of *The Birth of a Nation* to an open audience in Northrop Auditorium. This time the NAACP, the Urban League, and UM's Negro

Student Council joined forces, and despite public protests from several white students in the form of editorials to the *Minnesota Daily*, the UM administrators canceled the film, which by terrible coincidence was reportedly scheduled for a showing in a downtown theater.[40]

Organized groups like the KKK, and popular films like *The Birth of a Nation*, emerged as the ugliest, most harmful, and often most damaging aspects of white supremacy during the Jim Crow era. The presence of student Klan groups and battles over screening of *The Birth of a Nation* on or near college campuses confirm that universities across the country were not immune from such expressions of white supremacy. On January 27, 1915, the honorary KKK became a registered student organization at UIUC. Twelve days later D. W. Griffith's pro-Confederacy, pro-Klan, and antiblack film *The Birth of a Nation* premiered in theaters across the United States. The lynching of Leo Frank in Atlanta in August 1915 and the revival of the Invisible Empire of the KKK at Stone Mountain in October 1915 marked the shift of the KKK from regional influence to national ubiquity.

One of the earliest signs that an honorary Klan had come to the American campus appeared at UIUC in 1916. A group of white male students, who were leaders in various fraternities on campus, established a group called the Ku Klux Klan junior honorary fraternity. The groups' members claimed that the organization had been in existence since 1906, 1908, or 1909, however, the first public record of the groups' presence at the University was in 1916. Although historian Timothy Messer-Kruse maintains that, "there is no evidence that the new organization was in any way tied to the better-known Invisible Empire of the Ku Klux Klan," he points out that both 1906 and 1916 mark the one-year anniversaries of the publication of Dixon's novel and the release of Griffith's film. Moreover, Messer-Kruse points out that William J. Simmons resurrected the Invisible Empire of the Ku Klux Klan with sixteen others in Stone Mountain, Georgia, in 1915—just one year before the first evidence of such a group at UIUC. The honorary Klan at UIUC initiated an average of sixteen juniors per year and grew in popularity and influence until the five chapters of national organization, including UIUC, voted to change its name. Students at UIUC chose the "Tu-mas" because of the misunderstanding and confusion caused by the group's formerly shared name with the Invisible Empire.[41]

By 1919, the honorary Klan emerged at UW as an official student group of the junior class and unregistered neo-Klan groups surfaced at UI, UM, and KU.[42] The group at UW was affiliated with Phi Gamma

Delta fraternity which notoriously dominated homecoming events which included regular blackface performances.[43] The honorary Klan found its greatest support among middle-class elected campus officers and varsity athletes. Although not affiliated with the Invisible Empire, it embraced many of its ideas concerning blacks and European immigrants. By 1923, the Invisible Empire KKK threatened to extend its influence from Madison to UW's students and faculty—it succeeded. Its presence and reputation forced the honorary Klan to change its name.

The honorary Klan at UW changed its name and never enjoyed the same prominence as it had in its early years, but the Invisible Empire established Kappa Beta Lambda among more working-class students as a front for its interests in Madison. Kappa Beta Lambda, a Greek-letter code for the moniker Klansmen Be Loyal, especially attracted students who opted into UW's military cadet corps. Members of this new fraternity failed to wield the power, status, or campus influence of the honorary Klan. However, Kappa Beta Lambda managed to recruit a few students and several UW faculty members. The attitudes of white UW administrators and students permitted the campus presence of Kappa Beta Lambda, but the Board of Regents refused to grant the Invisible Empire use of the UW field house in 1926. One year later, it too changed its name and seems to have eventually broken its bond with the Invisible Empire.[44]

The Invisible Empire of the KKK and neo-Klan group in Iowa City and at UI first appeared in 1917. During the MECCA Engineering celebration and parade for that year, the *Hawkeye* reported, "The parade was headed by a Klu Klux Klan [sic], followed by the University band, which is always essential to this part of the celebration." The captions that accompany the three yearbook pictures of students dressed in Klan robes noted, like the Klan in the 1920s, that blacks were not their major concern. A group of freshman engineers at UI formed the Klan "in order to regain the right of equal suffrage from the women, who have control of our national affairs" and to help students in the College of Liberal Arts "get their rights."[45] According to William E. Taylor, a member of Kappa Alpha Psi enrolled in the UI law school at the time, as early as 1920 African American students at UI appealed to James Weldon Johnson and the NAACP to help end racial discrimination in Iowa City and within the university. William E. Taylor wrote that "the conditions in this city are at present almost unlivable for a colored student. The attitude of hostility is felt most keenly in the matter of housing. No one will rent to colored fraternities and no one will sell in a livable locality."

Taylor reported that a local landlord broke their contract when members of the local Invisible Empire of the Ku Klux Klan chapter organized to outbid the black students. Taylor concluded, "I have been in this city long enough to note the crystallization of sentiment against us. There is an organization of the Ku Klux Klan here, and I have not the least doubt but that they are financing the scheme to affect our ruin." Johnson suggested that the students contact local NAACP chapters but refused to offer any assistance from the national office.[46] One of the difficulties in tracing Ku Klux Klan mentioned by UI William E. Taylor is the paucity of evidence and sources Klan members left behind. Evidence in UI's archives, yearbooks, and newspapers suggests the Klan and the film *The Birth of a Nation* spawned a number of sympathizers who may or may not have been affiliated with an official klavern.

Similar groups that called themselves the KKK either established or attempted to establish a presence at UM and KU. In 1923, the *Minnesota Daily* noted that a number of Big Ten universities had student-run KKK organizations. In the same year, a KKK float appeared in UM's homecoming parade and later that year in the class yearbook—the *Gopher*.[47] By 1924, a group of students at KU calling themselves the "Ku Ku Klan [sic]," dressed in Klan sheets and hoods, marched across campus and performed "stunts" at half-time during football games. Students at KU established this group in 1921 as a male pep club; they also, despite an affinity for Invisible Empire costumes, claimed no affiliation with the Invisible Empire and temporarily changed their name to the "Ku Ku Klub" chapter of Pi Epsilon Pi in 1923. One year later, the state convention for the KKK took place in downtown Lawrence and an advertisement in the *Daily Kansan* announced, "The Kansas University Fiery Cross Club extends a cordial invitation to all Klansmen who are students, faculty, or University employees to become affiliated with" the KKK.[48] These campuses' Klan groups did not take to overtly antagonizing black students, but they had a tradition of appearing at parties, parades, and festivals dressed in white sheets or in blackface.

White campus administrators at NU and white engineering students at UI became wholly intolerant of the Invisible Empire of the Klan and neo-Klan groups on their respective campuses in the 1920s. In 1921, NU Chancellor Samuel Avery threatened to suspend any student who joined the Invisible Empire of the KKK. Days before Avery's announcement, the KKK held an initiation ceremony on the NU campus. To Avery, inequality did not amount to harassment. While black students did not enjoy access to the same campus resources as white students, Avery would not tolerate a secret society with a violent reputation on campus. He argued: "The university should be characterized by a broad liberal spirit of fellowship. Learning knows no distinction on race or color. An organization whose membership is restricted 'to the native born American, white, and protestant' cannot fail to give offense to many students and patrons who in facing the common enemy in the late war showed their 100% Americanism on the battlefields in France." To emphasize his point, Avery explicitly wrote in another letter, "It is therefore ordered that no student of the NU be admitted to membership in the Ku Klux Klan and no unit of the Klan be established within the student body of the University of Nebraska." In 1924, members of the MECCA parade committee at UI made known that "Ku Klux Klan maneuvers will be immediately squelched should it be disclosed that any of their methods are to be enjoyed by the 'paraders.'"[49]

The Invisible Empire was much more of a force in Lincoln, Lawrence, Madison, Champaign-Urbana, and Minneapolis than in Iowa City, yet the KKK was a significant presence in all six states. Invisible Empire rolls in Illinois swelled to over 95,000. Nebraska had some 40,000 Klan members in the 1920s, with over 5,000 members in Lancaster County, which included Lincoln. Historian Michael W. Schuyler notes that Lincoln played host to the 1924 state KKK convention, and one year later 1,500 KKK members marched in a parade through Lincoln's streets. The UIUC armory and the old Illinois Theater played host for the local Zenith Klan No. 56 mass rally in 1923 with guest Imperial Wizard Hiram Evans in attendance. The members of the Klan in Champaign-Urbana had purchased the theater, which had a seating capacity of 1,000, for a klavern. Minneapolis Mayor George Leach forbad members of his police force from joining the KKK and he initiated an investigation of alleged Klan activity at UMN.[50] Nevertheless, some 2,000–2,500 people joined the Minneapolis Klan at an initiation held at Foss Memorial and Olivet Methodist churches in 1921. Historians Kenneth Jackson and Michael and Judy Ann Newton note that the Minnesota Klan reached its height in 1923 when it ran Roy Miner as a candidate for the mayor of Minneapolis against the incumbent mayor. A subsequent libel ruling against the Klan led to its eventual demise in the Twin Cities and its state membership dwindled to less than 500 in 1930, but the Klan maintained a greater presence in St. Paul rather than Minneapolis. Nearly 100,000 Kansas belonged to the KKK by 1924 although the largest chapters functioned in southeast Kansas; as mentioned before, the KKK held its state convention in Lawrence in that year. A combination of legal battles, an anti-Klan governor, and the depression marked a decline in the KKK in the 1930s. Similarly, in Iowa, the KKK rose to prominence on an anti-Catholic and anti-Jewish campaign, but loss momentum during the depression. Approximately, 15,000 Wisconsinites and 7,000 Iowans belonged to the KKK between 1915 and 1944.[51] Only in Indiana, which falls outside the scope of this article, did the Invisible Empire of the KKK become powerful enough to make a bid, although failed, to purchase a private university with the goal of teaching "100% Americanism"—Valpariso University in 1922.[52]

Most whites in Illinois, Iowa, Nebraska, Minnesota, Wisconsin, and Kansas did not join the Invisible Empire of the KKK to intimidate blacks, and not all members were working-class. Klan membership was synonymous with nativism, 100% Americanism, patriotism, Christian values, and whiteness. Historian Robert Neymeyer contends that KKK members were "more mainstream than marginal" and they "were social and economically stable, civic minded, usually from mainstream Protestant churches, and likely to live anywhere, including large cities. They were primarily concerned with local social problems rather than ethnic or racial issues." Other historians of the Invisible Empire of the KKK, such as Kenneth T. Jackson, Lila Jones, and Michael and Judy Ann Newton make similar claims, and add that KKK members across the nation included white doctors, lawyers, politicians, college graduates, and working-class and poor whites. Of course, many of the honorary and neo-Klan members at UI, KU, UW, and UIUC were among the aspiring and future elite.[53]

Minstrel Shows, Frat Parties, and Other Drama

Students from a variety of European ethnic backgrounds participated in their rites of passage to whiteness through dawning blackface or penning caricatures in yearbooks. On all six campuses caricature preceded students dressed in blackface, yet it was the campus minstrel show that proved to be the one of the most popular forms of white entertainment on college campuses. Building on a tradition that harkened back to Jacksonian America and is often attributed to Thomas D. Rice, white students regularly appeared in blackface on campus stages in the 1910s, 1920s, and 1930s. They blacked their faces with burnt cork or some other substance, ridiculed Africans, African Americans, and their cultures and told racist jokes, sang "Negro" songs, and released themselves from the restrictive racial codes of white middle-class and upper middle-class respectability. Moreover, as black students founded black Greek-letter organizations on these campuses and black students individually and collectively challenged white students intellectually and for physical space in student unions, cafeterias, and other pubic campus places, blackface incidents, and campus minstrel shows became all the more common.

Many of the students who first dawned blackface on the campus stage played the dramatic roles of black or Middle Eastern servants, waiters, bootblacks, criminals, happy-go-lucky plantation slaves, postemancipation black buffoons (including the coon, mammy, and sambo), or minstrels in drama and theater departments. As early as 1911, members of the Red-Domino dramatic club at KU included two white students who dressed and played the part of thieves in the production of "The Idle Idol." In the same year, NU students hosted the first "annual University Night" where "minstrel shows, musical numbers, skits, and take-offs dominated the evening's entertainment."[54] Members of the class of 1914 at UM hosted a Vaudeville program that included a skit with white students dressed as banjo playing mammies and dancing, overdressed coons in "Nine Nifty Niggahs." The skit reportedly introduced "the Gold Dust Twins in a new and original dancing scene." The Gold Dust Twins were, of course, the bald, black caricatures that were to Fairbanks Gold Dust Washing Powder what Aunt Jemima and Uncle Ben were to pancake mix and rice. Three years later, white students in UM's College of Forestry performed "Sambo and his Minstrels" at the Forestry Camp in Itasca Park. White students at UW customarily blackened up for events associated with the annual fall homecoming and spring circus parade. The "Engineer's Minstrels" and "Smith Bros. Cough Drop Band" rode or strolled down Madison's streets in the circus and homecoming parades of 1920. Not to be outdone by the neo-Klan in the UI MEECA parade, seven members of the law class appeared in blackface and sang plantation songs in 1925, they followed on the heels of thirty law students who performed in blackface at UI the year before.[55] Not coincidentally, Beulah Wheeler became the first black woman to graduate from UI's law school in 1924, the same year whites appeared in blackface at the UI Law Jubilee. Divorced from their context, these racialized expressions of white anxiety, fear, and jealousy may seem random, but these were no random cases of white student innocence.

Just how often white students hosted such skits, variety shows, or performances remains unclear. Many of college blackface minstrel shows coincided with annual homecoming celebrations in the fall or spring carnivals. At UIUC, students held the Union Minstrel Show every year from the 1920s to 1940, when University president Arthur C. Willard finally helped put an end to this university-supported event.[56] At KU, these shows extended well into the 1940s and included athletic director Forrest "Phog" Allen who not only reveled in barring blacks from KU's intercollegiate sports teams, but performed with four blackface minstrels in a skit which mocked blacks for their failure to assimilate into the dominant culture.[57]

Regardless of if or when these traditions ended, the campus minstrel show first emerged in the 1910s when blacks' numbers at predominantly white Midwestern universities began to exceed a dozen enrollees and blacks began to prove themselves to be whites' intellectual equals. The campus minstrel show served as a means to criticize blacks who successfully entered new fields of study and whose growing physical presence on campus was undeniable and undesirable.

Racial Representation and the College Yearbook

In the late nineteenth and early twentieth centuries, college yearbooks became contested racial territory at UIUC, UI, KU, UM, and NU. Interestingly, blacks who excelled academically and could possibly compete against whites for jobs after graduation received the brunt of a yearbook staffs' criticism and ridicule. Black athletes, particularly those who played for a UIUC, UW, KU, UI, NU, and UM in the late nineteenth and early twentieth centuries, found a bevy of sympathizers among white classmates and yearbook staffs. Perhaps black athletes seemed less intellectually threatening to some white students or perhaps white students could accept blacks in a role that had entertainment value. The staff of the UI *Hawkeye* seemed sympathetic to the outright racism, physical abuse, and violent threats opposing teams meted out to black Hawkeyes. As a track and football star, Frank K. Holbrook was extremely popular among his black and white classmates. In some cases, opposing teams refused to play against UI because Holbrook was black. The November 10, 1896, *Vidette-Reporter* read, ". . . Sinful Treatment of Holbrook by the Missourians."

Unlike some instances when teams forfeited games to protest black players' participation in college athletics or other occasions when black players were forced to sit-out for a game, the crowd in Columbia, Missouri, formed a lynch mob. According to the UI student newspaper, "[t]he Columbians expected trouble was made manifest, not only by the great presence of canes, but clubs, wagon spokes, etc." Fans became more riotous as the game progressed and yelled, "There's the ____ negro," "The Tigers will kill the negro," and "Kill the nigger." According to reports, the other students on UI's team did not abandon Holbrook. Holbrook obviously assessed the situation and determined the odds were not in his or his team's favor, although "[Holbrook] showed no disposition to shield himself in back [of the] others."[58]

Missouri fans also assaulted UI professor Dehn, who officiated the game. According to the report, "when Holbrook tackled a man . . . a Missouri man named Conley, struck the official Prof. Dehn, in the face with his fist." Conley was ejected from the game, but reinstated at the demand of the Missouri coach and for fear of a "riot." At the end of the 1896 season, the *Hawkeye* yearbook staff commemorated the team's 7-1-1 season and the incident at Missouri with a cartoon titled, "Hail the Conquering Heroes Come." This drawing depicted Holbrook and his teammates walking past caricatures of its seven defeated opponents including a Missouri player wielding a stick; the cartoon, unlike many yearbook illustrations of real and fictitious blacks, championed white Hawkeye's stand against overt racism.[59] Missouri refused to play Iowa the next season and the UI won the Western League Championship. Soon after that Holbrook left UI and the state. Despite threats against their own lives, Holbrook's white teammates stood by him in the face of a potential lynch mob.

Black athletes may have been exempt from white ridicule on their own campuses in the late nineteenth century because whites possibly considered this participation acceptable. Certainly, black athletes posed little or no threat to whites who may have wanted to participate in intercollegiate sports. A number of universities, including KU, UIUC, UI, NU, UW, and UM, maintained unwritten policies that limited the number of blacks on any sports team to no more than two. By 1917, KU and NU barred blacks from intercollegiate sports altogether, and UI, UW, UIUC, and UM barred blacks from intercollegiate basketball and wrestling. Blacks could only play on UI's freshmen baseball team after 1921 and at KU Forrest "Phog" Allen made it a personal point to restrict blacks' access to most sports and certain recreational activities in physical education courses.

In the age of mass immigration from Europe and court-sanctioned Jim Crow, the new wave of immigrant students, blacks in student government, and blacks who excelled academically were not as fortunate as black athletes.[60] The 1897 *Hawkeye*, the college yearbook published by the junior class, included an elaborate cartoon and script that mocked UI's black students. The drawings and text combined to make-up a month of the *Hawkeye*'s ethnic calendar section. White students on the yearbook staff assigned blacks, the French, Germans, Russians, and the Irish a month each on their caricature calendar.[61] The staff assigned blacks to June and listed the major campus events day-by-day from the perspective of and in the language of the designated ethnic group. This "June Coon" calendar included drawings of a lazy black farm hand in tethered clothes, an urban black brute strutting down the avenue with an oversized razor, two black men loitering on a street corner smoking drags, a black chicken thief, a confused and puzzled looking black man reading an examination schedule, and two black men happily singing and dancing on a southern plantation. The drawing's themes played on a number of popular and derogatory images of black men circulating through various media outlets (movie shorts, magazines, and newspapers, and popular novels). The bewildered black college student symbolized zip coon, the northern version of the happy, mischievous lazy, black Sambo who fails to successfully integrate and possesses no understanding of the language he uses. Similarly, images like the street loiterer and the man with a razor endorsed the myth that once freed, ex-slaves would either sit around avoiding work at all costs, or quench black men's so-called natural and animalistic thirst for violence, watermelon, and chicken.[62] Members of the *Hawkeye* staff added a fake black dialect to lend "authenticity" to their cartoon. The fact that this illustration appeared in the same year some white students elected S. Joe Brown to Phi Beta Kappa substantiates Leon Litwack's claim about white backlash as a result of black success.[63] Brown, who was also elected junior-class secretary, symbolized upwardly mobile blacks whose credentials brought him into white campus spaces. His achievements brought him a fair amount of attention and press coverage, and this highly visible success likely fanned the flames of white student resentment.

In the years that followed, black students continued to be the focus of white ridicule in the pages of PWFU's yearbooks. White ethnic groups, even during the course of World War I, attracted less attention as they assimilated and made the transformation from white ethnic immigrants to white Americans.

Black Greek-Letter Organizations

Black fraternities and sororities represented that most publicly visible expression of middle-class black culture and upward mobility at Midwestern PWFUs and the high level of visibility afforded African American Greek-letter organizations made their members prime targets of white harassment. Some white students viewed these groups, the houses in which they lived, and their demands to use campus spaces with suspicion, anger, and jealousy. Some whites may have accepted or remained indifferent toward these groups as long as blacks did not try to seek recognition by the Panhellenic Council or the Inter-fraternity Council.

Black Greek-letter organizations could not exist on white campuses unless these institutions had enough black students to maintain such groups. These groups created fear and anxiety among white students concerning blacks' possible invasion of white campus spaces. As individual blacks and black fraternities and sororities began to compete with whites academically, white spaces on campus and in academic programs became more difficult for whites to monopolize. Black Greek-letter organizations first emerged at KU in 1898; however, similar groups with a national affiliation did not appear on PWFU campuses in the Midwest until the 1910s and 1920s.[64,65] With the establishment of local chapters of Black Greek-letter organizations, many whites imagined themselves, their livelihood, and once-white spaces as under siege; they privately and publically ridiculed black students for their accomplishments and their presence on campus.

One of the most obvious and infamous cases where whites at PWFUs in the Midwest ridiculed black fraternities was when Kappa Alpha Nu changed its name to KAPSI in 1915. According to KAPSI's official history, one of the fraternity's founders, Elder W. Diggs, overheard white students commenting on the athleticism and potential fraternity prospects of a black student at Indiana University. When the other white student replied that the student-athlete already belonged to "Kappa Alpha Nig," Diggs corrected him, but grew concerned that his organization had become more commonly known by this derogatory play on Kappa Alpha Nu.[66]

Black Greek-letter organizations proved they were intellectual equals to white Greek-letter organizations and challenged ideas about their own intellectual abilities and those of blacks in general, much to the chagrin of some white students. For example, in its first two years of existence at UI, KAPSI ranked eighth and seventh out of eighteen fraternities.[67] In 1919, members of AKA at UIUC took first place among all sororities on campus. In 1922, Upsilon chapter of APHIA at KU placed second in the standing for highest GPA among national Greek-letter fraternities on campus. A report in the *Daily Kansan* noted that white students fostered an environment that was "intrinsically unjust to" black students.

They paid student fees, but whites excluded them from campus events. Whites viewed black students' presence on campus as a problem rather than an opportunity to dismantle racism. Nonetheless, blacks maintained a "self-sufficient and pleasant social life" as well as a "scholarship record," which some whites could not help but respect and admire.[68] Farther to the east, KAPSI at UIUC ranked sixth in 1924. At NU, Eta chapter of KAPSI rated in the top half of fraternities on campus in 1925. One year later, Psi chapter of KAPSI at UMN accomplished the same feat when it maintained a "B" average.[69] During the 1927–28 academic year, AKA at KU placed sixth out of twenty sororities. In the same year, Eta chapter of AKA at UMN placed first among sororities although the year previously it had placed a dismal and disappointing twenty-first. At UI, also in 1927, KAPSI and APHIA ranked a disappointing twenty-sixth and twenty-ninth, respectively, out of twenty-nine fraternities.[70] Psi chapter of KAPSI at UMN ranked second out of thirty-nine fraternities in 1928.[71] Delta chapter of AKA at KU ranked first among all sororities, black or white, in 1928–29, fell to last place in 1929–30, and "reclaimed [its] throne" in 1930–31.[72] The year that AKA resurfaced as KU's top sorority, DST ranked a dismal last among fifteen and APHIA and KAPSI at KU ranked eighteenth and twenty-third out of twenty-four national fraternities.[73]

Despite comments from whites belittling their accomplishments, black Greek-letter organizations at PWFUs in the Midwest continued to demonstrate that they could successfully compete academically with white Greek-letter societies. In 1930, Eta chapter of AKA at UMN fell to thirteenth out of twenty-seven, but regained the top-ranked slot in the fall of 1931. Ironically, AKA's brother organization at UMN, Mu chapter of APHIA, ranked first among thirty-eight fraternities in the fall of 1931. Much to its collective dismay, Psi chapter KAPSI at UMN ranked last in the same year. Members of APHIA celebrated Mu chapter's accomplishments, however, an anonymous white student wrote to the *Minnesota Daily* in the most condescending tone, that such a feat was not a great challenge for an organization with only three members.[74] Undaunted by this slight, Mu chapter APHIA ranked first again in 1932.

University yearbooks surfaced as a space where white students sought to dictate to black Greek-letter organizations what and who were worthy of equal treatment and significant to student life. In some years, white yearbook staff members placed black students' individual headshots in alphabetical order with the rest of the students; in other years, however, staff members placed all black students' pictures at the end of a section after all the white students. Similarly, when black fraternities and sororities had pictures taken for the yearbook, their group pictures often appeared after all the alphabetically arranged pictures of white fraternities and sororities. This was especially the case in KU's *Jayhawk* where APHIA and AKA almost always appeared on the last pages of the fraternity and sorority sections, respectively.[75] No black fraternity or sorority ever appeared in the NU *Cornhusker*. At UM, UIUC, and UI, black fraternities' group pictures only appeared in their schools' yearbooks two and three times, respectively, in the forty-year period; yet these pictures were a point of pride for black students who consciously made an effort to deconstruct ideals of black people's supposed inferiority and their inability to adapt to desegregation through their manicured appearances.[76]

The images of well-groomed, straight-faced, confident black students dressed in suits or white blouses and dark skirts, challenged the notion that all blacks were poor, frivolous, ignorant, and unlawful. Historian Kevin Gaines reminds us that blacks, in an effort to refute racist caricature, purposely projected "a serious, dignified image" which depicted "representative" blacks as symbols of "uplift and respectability."[77] At first glance, it would be impossible to distinguish white and black fraternities and sororities picture from each other in college yearbooks. Everyone dressed in suits, ties, and freshly ironed white shirts. Similarly, all sororities wore ironed and starched white or light-colored blouses or dresses. At KU fraternities, black and white, customarily included one picture of the outside and one picture of the inside of an organizations' house. Many members of these groups were proudly middle-class, or at least, they aspired to be so. Roy Wilkins, QPSIPHI member and UM alumnus, recalled that he and his fraternity brothers "looked more like a crew of hopeful bankers, than hellraisers" in their yearbook photo.[78] This photo of QPSIPHI appeared in the *Gopher* yearbook the same year as the infamous KKK homecoming float. At no time, did more than one black fraternity and one black sorority picture appear in the same yearbook during the same year although other black Greek-letter organizations existed on these campuses.

The houses black Greek-letter organizations inhabited in Lawrence, Champaign-Urbana, Lincoln, Iowa City, and the Twin Cities became a point of pride for black fraternities and sororities; however, for members of white organizations, these buildings became points of contention. Membership and the purchasing or leasing of a fraternity house provided blacks with a powerful symbol of manhood and womanhood that many college and noncollege blacks did not possess: property ownership.[79] Through collective ownership and leasing, black Greek-letter organizations could spare their members the shame and frustrations of being denied a place to live because they were black. Chapter houses also served as the venue for small parties and informal weekend dances where students could socialize and roughhouse as loudly as they wanted without reprisal from a landlord. Nearly every year that members of APHIA's Upsilon chapter appeared in the University *Jayhawker*, members made sure a picture of the house appeared in the yearbook as well. Members of KAPSI at KU affectionately referred to their house as the Kappa Kastle. It included "a well furnished reception hall, comfortable living room with piano and victrola, a study hall with book cases and long study table for the 'frosh' . . . shower bath, sleeping rooms with double-deckers beds and a secret chapter room" for initiations and chapter meetings. Outside the house members built two tennis courts on the double lot and later installed a basketball court.[80] The chapter house attracted local and national attention for Mu chapter members. Members of the local chapter of Delta Sigma Theta regularly used the Kappa Kastle to host their own parties including the traditional "red hot blowout" before the Christmas holiday. Nonetheless, local whites made attempts to restrict where blacks students could live especially in Lawrence and Iowa City. The case involving KAPSI at UI is noted above; however, in 1930, the Lawrence City Council tried to prevent black students and black Greek-letter organizations from occupying homes near campus, "The negroes are a useful element in the population," wrote the council, "and provision should be made for their welfare, including suitable locations for living." The races should be separated they believed and blacks should not "encroach upon white districts . . . There is no reason why areas adjacent to the University of Kansas should be used for negroes [sic], and such encroachments should stop."[81]

The battle between black fraternities and yearbook staffs, however, did not end here. On at least two occasions, once in the 1917 UI *Hawkeye* and another time in the 1924 KU *Jayhawk*, KAPSI and APHIA became the focus of racist cartoons. The 1917 UI *Hawkeye* noted, "Please note the Kappa feature in this section. They need the advertising." At the bottom of the page a drawing of an overweight black man dressed in a crimson and cream waiter's uniform and wielding a razor blade stood above the caption "Freshie: 'Do the Kappa Alpha Nus go to the Pan Hellenic?' Wise Soph: 'Sure, you always see them serving the punch.'"

The 1924 KU *Jayhawk* included a similar cartoon that read "Alpha Phi Alpha. Motto: 'Damn the Betas.' Color: Same as Thetas, – black and gold. With their rigid qualifications and reputation as an exclusive outfit, it is only fitting that the Alpha Phi Alphas should replace the Beta in the 'Big Five.' Strong on fancy vests, tan shoes, and permanent waves. Honorary Chapter mother, 'Little Eva.' Patron Saint, Abe Lincoln." A drawing of two black men with exaggerated big lips standing next to a bottle of shoe polish and brush accompanied this caption.[82]

Black caricatures have received the attention of a number of scholars. Kenneth Goings argues that such images, like black collectables, "were almost universally derogatory, with exaggerated racial features that helped to 'prove' that, indeed, African Americans were not only differ-ent but inferior as well."[83] More specifically, Goings, Patricia A. Turner, Gerald Butters, and Jan Pieterse provide context for the illustrations mentioned above. The black servant, waiter, and bootblack in clean, starched uniforms were all popularly produced stereotypes of the time. Turner refers to this as the "reasonably neat uncle," and Goings suggests the contemptible black caricatures symbolized the insidiousness of the ex-slave happily serving the old master stereotype.[84] Pieterse illuminates the sociopolitical complexity of racist caricature that represented both real-life racist limitations of labor opportunities for blacks, the accept-ability of "hierarchical integration" among whites, and whites' desire to see nonwhites, and in some cases, non-Anglos, in subservient social positions.[85] Emma Jones Lapsansky argues that white students spe-cifically lampooned middle-class black for their "tendency to adopt the latest forms of dress and furnishings." Whites saw the fancy or upscale dress of middle-class and visibly affluent blacks as a "symbol of black arrogance."[86] Many black students worked in white fraternity houses or for white families, not because they lacked the intelligence or skill to hold other jobs, but because the racialized power dynamics of the time prevented most blacks from finding work outside domestic drudgery. The razor, in the case of the *Hawkeye* cartoon, and the reference to black material excess, Abraham Lincoln, and *Uncle Tom's Cabin's* Little Eva in the *Jayhawk*, play on the popular ideas of the birth of the dangerous emancipated black brute who needed to be re-enslaved to protect him-self and potential white victims.[87] These images and others like them, scholars argue, precipitated the need for a New Negro consciousness; and counter images, like the group pictures of black fraternities and sorori-ties in middle-class business clothes, brought about some vindication for black students.

Conclusion

Despite, or maybe because of their level of educational attainment, working-class, aspiring middle-class, and middle-class members of European American ethnic groups adopted these symbols of terror and used them to solidify their rites of passage into American whiteness. Some whites advocated for racial equality, most were indifferent about the experiences of blacks or any other racial minority on campus. Still some white students negatively responded to black students' academic gains and advances by challenging black students' sense of belonging, their intellectual ability, and their refusal to act or view themselves according to the white supremacist dictates of the time. Such images and symbols of terror became battle scars for black students at UIUC, NU, UI, UM, UW, and KU who bore the brunt of white supremacy but made it a point to de/reconstruct these images of blacks' so-called intellectual and cultural inferiority to empower themselves.

Notes

1.   Thomas Bartlett, "An Ugly Tradition Persists at Southern Fraternity Parties," *Chronicle of Higher Education* (November 30, 2001): 33. Such racist antics are wholly absent from history of white college student culture and the more recent articles on the uses of photographs in the history of education. The classic texts on white student culture remain, Helen Lefkowitz Horowitz, *Campus Life: Undergraduate Culture from the End of the Eighteenth Century to the Present* (Chicago, IL: University of Chicago, 1987) and Paula Fass, *The Damned and the Beautiful: American Youth Culture in the 1920s* (New York: Oxford University Press, 1977). See Kate Rousmaniere, "Questioning the Visual History of Education," *History of Education* 30, no. 2 (2001): 109–16; Ian Grosvenor and Martin Lawn, "Ways of Seeing in Education and Schooling: Emerging Historiography," *History of Education* 30, no. 2 (2001): 105–8; Joan N. Burstyn. "History as Image: Changing the Lens," *History of Education Quarterly* 27, no. 2 (1987): 167–80, on the use of photographs in the history of education.
2.   These numbers were compiled from the "Race Relations on Campus" section of the *Journal of Blacks in Higher Education*, 2002–2009.
3.   Eric Lott, *Love & Theft: Blackface Minstrelsy and the American Working Class* (New York: Oxford University Press, 1995), 6; Michael Rogin, *Blackface, White Noise: Jewish Immigrants in the Hollywood Melting Pot* (Berkeley, CA: University of California Press, 1996), 8.
4.   "History Repeats Itself in Blackface in Whitewater, Wisconsin," *Janesville Gazette* (February 1–3, 1963); "Fraternity Skit Splits UW-Whitewater Campus," *Janesville Gazette* (November 6, 2001).
5.   Dana Williams, "Halloween Warning: Beware of Intolerance," http://www.tolerance. org/news/article_tol.jsp?id=885 (accessed October 22, 2003); Association of Fraternity Advisors, "Blackface on Campus: A Resource for Awareness and Education," October 2003, http://www.64.233.167.104/search?q=cache"XLFZZ145mRMJ: campusumr,edu.studentlife/greek/... (accessed August 1, 2005).

6. These studies are too numerous to list them all. Some of the more pathbreaking work includes: Lott, *Love & Theft*; Susan Gubar, *Racechanges: White Skin, Black Face in American Culture* (New York: Oxford University Press, 1997); Joseph Boskin, *Sambo: The Rise and Demise of an American Jester* (New York: Oxford University Press, 1986); Alexander Saxton, "Blackface Minstrelsy and Jacksonian Ideology," *American Quarterly* 27 (1975): 3–21; Robert Toll, *Blacking Up: The Minstrel Show in Nineteenth Century America* (New York: Oxford University Press, 1974). Sections of David Roediger, *Wages of Whiteness: Race and the Making of the American Working Class* (New York: Verso, 1991), 95–114, 115–31, also analyze the connection between blackface minstrelsy and white working-class identity.

7. Charlotte Crump to Marsh (Marcia Crump), reprinted as "The Free North," *Opportunity* (September 1937), 271, 272, and 285.

8. Herbert C. Jenkins, "The Negro Student at the State University of Iowa: A Sociological Study," M.A. Thesis, State University of Iowa, 1933, 29; Raymond Wolters, *The New Negro on Campus: Black College Rebellions of the 1920s* (Princeton, NJ: Princeton University Press, 1975), 320; Robert Knoll, *Prairie University: A History of the University of Nebraska* (Lincoln, NE: University of Nebraska Press, 1995), 83; David P. Setran, "Student Religious Life in the 'Era of Secularization': The Intercollegiate YMCA, 1877–1940," *History of Higher Education Annual* 21 (2001): 30; Roger Ebert, *An Illini Century: One Hundred Years of Campus Life* (Urbana, IL: University of Illinois Press, 1967), 141.

9. Robert Cohen, *When the Old Left Was Young: Student Radical and America's First Mass Student Movement, 1929–1941* (New York: Oxford University Press, 1993), 212.

10. Emma Jones Lapsansky, "'Since They Got Those Separate Churches': Afro-Americans and Racism in Jacksonian Philadelphia," *American Quarterly* 32, no. 1 (Spring 1980): 55–56.

11. Leon Litwack, *Trouble in Mind: Black Southerners in the Age of Jim Crow* (New York: Vintage Book, 1998), xiii.

12. Lapsansky, "'Since They Got Those Separate Churches'," 54–78.

13. W. E. B. Du Bois, *The College-Bred Negro* (Atlanta, GA: Atlanta University Press, 1900), 36 and 38.

14. W. E. B. Du Bois, *The College-Bred Negro American* (Atlanta, GA: Atlanta University Press, 1910), 27 and 46.

15. "Colored Students and Graduates of 1923," *Crisis* (July 1923): 108, 110, and 112; "The College Negro American, 1927," *Crisis* (August 1927): 185 and 186; "The Year in Negro Education," *Crisis* (1930): 262; "The American Negro in College, 1932–1933," *Crisis* (August 1933): 181; "The American Negro in College, 1935–1936," *Crisis* (August 1936): 252.

16. Du Bois, *The College-Bred Negro*, 28–29.

17. "Andrew F. Hilyer to Booker T. Washington, March 28, 1896," in Louis R. Harlan et al. eds. *The Booker T. Washington Papers, 1895–1898*, vol. 4 (Urbana, IL: University of Illinois Press, 1975), 149–50.

18. Ibid.

19. Quoted in Robert B. Slater, "The First Black Graduates of the Nation's Flagship State Universities," *Journal of Blacks in Higher Education* (Autumn 1996): 80.

20. James Gray, *The University of Minnesota, 1851–1951* (Minneapolis, MN: University of Minnesota Press, 1951), 72.

21. Ibid., 72–73.

22. Minnesota had not elected a Democrat for governor since 1858. Lucius Hubbard took office in January 1882.

23. "Blanche Kelso Bruce," *Who's Who in Colored America* (New York: 1925), 29.

24. Larry Peace, "Colored Students and Graduates of the University of Kansas," in W. E. B. Du Bois, *The College-Bred Negro American* (Atlanta, GA: Atlanta University Press, 1910), 35 and 36.
25. *Weekly University Courier*, October 24, 1884.
26. Clifford S. Griffin, *The University of Kansas: A History* (Lawrence, KS: University Press of Kansas, 1974), 202.
27. Ibid., 204.
28. Du Bois, *The College-Bred Negro American*, 39–40.
29. Litwack, *Trouble in Mind*, xiii.
30. *University Courier*, February 12, 1866; Griffin, *The University of Kansas*, 210.
31. "Incidents and Accidents," *Weekly University Courier*, April 23, 1866.
32. James O. Horton and Lois E. Horton, *Hard Road to Freedom: The Story of African America* (New Brunswick, NJ: Rutgers University Press, 2002), 193; Clayborne Carson, Emma Jones Lapsansky-Werner, and Gary B. Nash, *African American Lives: the Struggle for Freedom*, Combined Volume (New York: Pearson-Longman, 2004), 283.
33. Jelani Cobb, "The Noose," *Ebony* (January 2008): 110.
34. Du Bois, *The College-Bred Negro American*, 26.
35. Michael Fedo, *The Lynchings in Duluth* (1979; St. Paul, MN: Minnesota State Historical Society Press, 2000); Roy Wilkins and Tom Mathews, *Standing Fast: The Autobiography of Roy Wilkins* (New York: The Viking Press, 1982), 41–44; Robert T. Kerlin, *The Voice of the Negro 1919* (New York: E.P. Dutton and Company, 1920), 85–87; Clayton D. Laurie, "The U.S. Army and the Omaha Race Riot of 1919," *Nebraska History* 72, no. 3 (1991): 135–43; William M. Tuttle, Jr., *Race Riot: Chicago in the Red Summer of 1919* (New York: Atheneum, 1974).
36. Michael Newton and Judy Ann Newton, *The Ku Klux Klan: An Encyclopedia* (New York: Garland Publishing, 1991), vii–ix; Kenneth T. Jackson, *The Ku Klux Klan in the City, 1915–1930* (New York: Oxford University Press, 1967), xi–xii.
37. Jack Lufkin, "The Founding and Early Years of the National Association for the Advancement of Colored People in Des Moines," *Annals of Iowa* 45, no. 6 (1980): 450–52.
38. "Word of Appreciation by Colored Citizens of Lincoln," *Omaha Monitor* (July 20, 1918).
39. Based on a play, *The Nigger*, published in 1909 by Edward Sheldon, the National Association for the Advancement of Colored People had the film partially censored had a rape and lynching scenes removed from the film and the title changed to *The New Governor*, see Alan Gevinson, *American Film Institute Catalog: Within Our Gates, Ethnicity in American Feature Films, 1911–1969* (Berkeley, CA: University of California Press, 1997), 713.
40. "Birth of a Nation Showing Banned On 'U' Campus," *Minneapolis Spokesman* (February 23, 1940). See five protests letters from white students who wanted to see the film "Over the Back Fence," *Minnesota Daily* (February 24, 1940); Leonard C. Archer, *Black Images in the American Theatre: NAACP Protest Campaigns—Stage, Screen, Radio, & Television* (Brooklyn, NY: Pageant-Poseidon, 1973), 194.
41. "Ku Klux Klan Announces Twelve Junior Pledges," *Daily Illini* (October 4, 1917): 6; "Twenty-One Sophomores Initiated into Ku Klux," *Daily Illini* (May 11, 1922): 5; "Make Misunderstanding Impossible," *Daily Illini* (January 9, 1923): 4; "Tumas, New Junior Society, Rises from Ashes of Local Klan," *Daily Illini* (April 12, 1923): 1.
42. "Ku Klux Klan," *Illio* (1916): 453; Timothy Messer-Kruse, "The Campus Klan of the University of Wisconsin: Tacit and Active Support for the Ku Klux Klan in a Culture of Intolerance," *Wisconsin History Magazine* (August 1993): 3–5. Also see

Stephanie Lane, "An Analysis of the UIUC Ku Klux Klan and Surrounding Debates," https://www.ideals.uiuc.edu/handle/2142/8735 (accessed January 10, 2011).

43. Messer-Kruse, "The Campus Klan of the University of Wisconsin," 15, 17, 20, and 23.
44. Ibid., 32–38.
45. *Hawkeye* (1917), 162. MECCA was an acronym for Mechanical, Electrical, Chemical, Civil, and Architectural engineering. The parade lasted from 1910 to the 1940s.
46. William Edwin Taylor to James Weldon Johnson, November 2, 1921, series C, part 12, reel 10, frame 0598, NAACP Papers, microfilm, University of Iowa Law Library; James Weldon Johnson to William Edwin Taylor, November 10, 1921, series C, part 12, reel 10, frame 0600, NAACP Papers on microfilm; James Weldon Johnson to L. M. Brown, November 12, 1921, series C, part 12, reel 10, frame 0604, NAACP Papers on microfilm, James Weldon Johnson to Mrs. Thetha E. Graham, November 12, 1921, series C, part 12, reel 10, frame 0606, NAACP Papers on microfilm.
47. Tim Brady, "Almost Perfect Equality," *Minnesota Magazine* (September–October 2002): http://www.alumni.umn.edu/printview/fd18e044-3823-47e6-9100-d8... (accessed July 9, 2005).
48. "Pi Epsilon Pi," *Jayhawker* (1923): 108; "Among Us Ku Kus," *Jayhawker* (1926): 471; "KKK," *University Daily Kansan*, (October 15, 1924); William M. Tuttle, Jr., "Separate but Not Equal: African Americans and the 100-year Struggle for Equality in Lawrence and at the University of Kansas, 1850–1960," in *Embattled Lawrence: Conflict and Community*, ed. Dennis Domer. (Lawrence, KS: University of Kansas, Continuing Education, 2001), 145–46.
49. Samuel Avery to students, September 19, 1921, Samuel Avery to the Committee on the Lincoln Province, September 19, 1921; PRG# 2/2/2 and 05/10/04 Box 2, Samuel Avery Papers, UNLA; Avery quoted in Michael W. Schuyler, "The Ku Klux Klan in Nebraska, 1920–1930," *Nebraska History* 66, no. 3 (1985): 246; "'Radio Nurse' is Parade Feature," *Daily Iowan* (February 24, 1924); Messer-Kruse, "The Campus Klan of the University of Wisconsin," 4, 6, and 15.
50. David M. Chalmers, *Hood Americanism: The History of the Ku Klux Klan*, 3rd edn. (Durham, NC: Duke University Press, 1987), 149, 184–85.
51. Newton, *The Ku Klux Klan: An Encyclopedia*, 291, 308, 395, 422–23; Jackson, *Ku Klux Klan in the City*, 161–62 and 239; Lila Lee Jones, "The Ku Klux Klan in Eastern Kansas During the 1920s," *Emporia State Research Studies* 23, no. 3 (1975): 5 and 39. For more on the KKK in Iowa, see Lenore Goodenow, "My Encounters with the Ku Klux Klan," *Palimpsest* 76, no. 2 (Summer 1995): 52–55; Robert J. Neymeyer, "In the Full Light of Day: The Ku Klux Klan in 1920s Iowa," *Palimpsest* 76, no. 2 (Summer 1995): 56–63.
52. Lance Trusty, "All Talk and No 'Kash': Valpariso University and the Ku Klux Klan," *Indiana Magazine of History* 82, no. 1 (March 1986): 1–36.
53. Neymeyer, "In the Full Light of Day," 59; Newton, *The Ku Klux Klan: An Encyclopedia,* ix–xi; Jackson, *Ku Klux Klan in the City*, 62, 108, 119, and 120; Jones, "The Ku Klux Klan in Eastern Kansas," 37–38; Schuyler, "The Ku Klux Klan in Nebraska," 237–39.
54. "University Night," *Cornhusker* (1919), 84; "Kosmet Klub fall Revue," *Cornhusker* (1939), 153.
55. "The Idle Idol," *Jayhawker* (1911), n.p; "Nine Nifty Niggahs," *Gopher* (1914), 150–51; "Sambo and His Minstrels," *Gopher* (1917), 94–95; "Law Jubilee," *Hawkeye* (1924), n.p; "Law Jubilee," *Hawkeye* (1925), n.p.
56. Ashley Johnson, "Behind the Blackface," *Daily Illini* (February 20, 2004): http://www.illinimedia.com/di/features/712 (accessed July 31, 2005).

57. Tuttle, "Separate but Not Equal," 146.
58. *Vidette-Reporter*, November 10, 1896.
59. "Hail the Conquering Heroes Come," *Hawkeye* (1898), n.p.
60. For more on European immigration to the United States and the stereotypes Americans projected onto them see, Nell Irvin Painter, *Standing at Armageddon: The United States, 1877–1919* (New York: W.W. Norton & Co., 1987), xxiv–xl. On immigration the changing meaning of race and the process of becoming white, see Matthew Frye Jacobson, *Whiteness of a Different Color: European Immigration and the Alchemy of Race* (Cambridge, MA: Harvard University Press, 1998), 39–90. The attempts by these groups to shape schools to their own benefit and the efforts of schools to Americanize European ethnics in school is best covered by David B. Tyack, *The One Best System: A History of American Urban Education* (Cambridge, MA: Harvard University Press, 1974), 104–25 and 217–54.
61. *Hawkeye* (1898), n.p; For an example of newspapers' treatment of blacks, Asian Americans, and ethnic non-Anglo Europeans in the United States, see Matthew Frye Jacobson, *Whiteness of a Different Color*, inserts following page 199.
62. Gerald Butters, *Black Manhood on the Silent Screen* (Lawrence, KS: University Press of Kansas, 2002), 14–40. For a brief description of the major black stereotypes, see Donald Bogle, *Toms, Coons, Mulattoes, Mammies, and Bucks: An Interpretive History of Blacks in American Films* (New York: Continuum, 1989), 4–18.
63. Newspaper Clippings, Schorpp and Hilton, F.K. Holbrook Alumni Vertical folder, UIA. Also see, *Hawkeye* yearbook, 1897, 1898, and 1899. The file is mislabeled Carlton Holbrook.
64. "The Color of a New Fraternity," Kansas *University Weekly* (March 12, 1898). This refutes histories that point to Alpha Kappa Nu at Indiana University in 1903 as the earliest effort to establish a college black Greek-letter organization. See Tamara L. Brown, Gregory S. Parks, and Clarenda M. Phillips, *African American Fraternities and Sororities: The Legacy and Vision* (Lexington, KY: University Press of Kentucky, 2005), 137, 138, and 153; Walter M. Kimbrough, *Black Greek 101: The Culture, Customs, and Challenges of Black Fraternities and Sororities* (Madison, NJ: Fairleigh Dickinson University Press, 2003), 22–23 and 34; and Lawrence Ross, *The Divine Nine: The History of African American Fraternities and Sororities* (New York: Kensington Books, 2000), 30–31.
65. Black students established local chapters of national black fraternities and sororities, such as Alpha Phi Alpha (APHIA), Kappa Alpha Psi (KAPSI), Omega Psi Phi (QPSIPHI), Alpha Kappa Alpha (AKA), and Delta Sigma Theta (DST) at UIUC, KU, UI, NU, and UM in the following years: at UIUC, KAPSI was chartered in 1913, AKA in 1914, APHIA in 1917, QPSIPHI in 1928, and DST in 1932; at KU, blacks chartered AKA in 1916, APHIA in 1917, KAPSI in 1920, and DST in 1924; chapters of KAPSI in 1914, DST in 1919, and APHIA in 1922 materialized on UI's campus; at NU, students established chapters of KAPSI in 1916, DST in 1922, AKA in 1927, and APHIA in 1927; finally, at UM students established APHIA in 1912, QPSIPHI in 1921, AKA in 1922, and KAPSI in 1924: "The Pi Alpha Tau," *St. Paul Appeal*, May 13, 1911; Charles H. Wesley, *The History of Alpha Phi Alpha: A Development in College Life,* Fifteenth Edition (Chicago, IL: Founders Publishers, 1991), 79; Ross, *The Divine Nine*, 30–31.
66. William L. Crump and C. Rodger Wilson, *The Story of Kappa Alpha Psi: A History of the Development of a College Greek Letter Organization, 1911–1971*, 2nd edn. (Philadelphia, PA: Kappa Alpha Psi Fraternity, 1972), 23–24 and 27.
67. Robert E. Rienow, "Scholarship and the University," *Iowa Alumnus* 15, no. 3 (December 1917): 69.

68. "Kansas Commends Colored Students for Grades," *Daily Kansan* (November 24, 1922); Griffin Notes UA/ SH/ 85/ PP/ 14/ Box 22, KUA.
69. Crump and Wilson, *The Story of Kappa Alpha Psi*, 57, 68, and 76–77.
70. "Eta Chapter, University of Minnesota," Ivy *Leaf* 6 (1927–1928): 20–21; "Fraternity Standing," Box 201, folder 28, 1927–28, Jessup papers, University of Iowa Archives.
71. "Signs from Psi," *Kappa Alpha Psi Journal* (October 1928): 13; "Kappa Alpha Psi Makes Record at IU," *Chicago Defender* (November 10, 1928).
72. Amy Delores Estues, "Leaving Their IQ Behind," *The Dove* (November 21, 1929); "Report of Delta Chapter, Lawrence Kans.," *Ivy Leaf* 6 (1927–1928): 16–17; "Delta Doings," *Ivy Leaf* (December 1931): 12–13; "Negro Sorority Awarded First in Scholarship Rankings" *University Daily Kansan* (October 11, 1931).
73. "Negro Sorority Awarded First," *University Daily Kansan* (October 11, 1931).
74. "All-U Grades Hit New Mark Second Time with 1.223; 12 Fraternities Miss 'C' Average," *Minnesota Daily* (September 29, 1931). APHIA and KAPSI ranked thirty-eighth and thirty-seventh out of forty in 1930; "Greeks Set High Scholastic Marks," *Minnesota Daily* (October 1, 1930); Wesley, *The History of Alpha Phi Alpha*, 223.
75. *Jayhawk* (1919), 314; *Jayhawk* (1920), 168; *Jayhawk* (1921), 178–79; *Jayhawk* (1923), 200–01 and 232; *Jayhawk* (1927), 279 and 297.
76. *Gopher* (1922), n.p; *Gopher* (1926), 465; *Hawkeye* (1910), n.p; *Hawkeye* (1921), 43.
77. Kevin Gaines, *Uplifting the Race: Black Leadership, Politics, and Culture in the Twentieth Century* (Chapel Hill, NC: University of North Carolina Press, 1996), 68–69. For essays on the use of photographs and African American educational philanthropy see Michael Bieze, "Booker T. Washington: Philanthropy and Aesthetics," and Marybeth Gasman and Edward M. Epstein, "Creating an Image for Black College Fundraising: An Illustrated Examination of the United Negro College Fund's Publicity, 1944–1960," in *Uplifting a People: African American Philanthropy and Education*, ed. Marybeth Gasman and Katherine V. Sedgwick (New York: Peter Lang, 2005), 39–63 and 65–88.
78. Wilkins, *Standing Fast*, 46.
79. Martin Summers, *Manliness and Its Discontents: The Black Middle Class and Transformation of Masculinity, 1900–1930* (Chapel Hill, NC: University of North Carolina Press, 2004), 27.
80. "Mu Radio Musings," *Kappa Alpha Psi Journal* (November 1924), 8; "Kansas City Notes," *Kappa Alpha Psi Journal* (October 1924), 13.
81. Report of the City Planning Commission, "A City Plan for Lawrence, Kansas," 1930, Kansas Collection, Lawrence Public Library.
82. *Hawkeye* (1917), 461; *Jayhawk* (1924), 439.
83. Kenneth Goings, *Mammy and Uncle Mose: Black Collectibles and American Stereotyping* (Bloomington, IN: Indiana University Press, 1994), xiii.
84. Patricia A. Turner, *Ceramic Uncles and Celluloid Mammies: Black Images and Their Influence on Culture* (New York: Anchor, 1994), 20; Goings, *Mammy and Uncle Mose*, 34.
85. Jan Pieterse, *White on Black: Images of Africa and Blacks in Western Popular Culture* (New Haven, CT: Yale University Press, 1992), 124 and 129–31.
86. Lapsansky, "Since They Got Those Separate Churches," 63 and 65.
87. Butters, *Black Manhood on the Silent Screen*, 31, 32, 36, and 52–57. For more on images that evoke Harriett Beecher Stowe's *Uncle Tom's Cabin*, see Pieterse, *White on Black*, 62, 133, and 170; Turner, *Ceramic Uncles & Celluloid Mammies*, 45–49 and 70–88.

A Nauseating Sentiment, a Magical Device, or a Real Insight? Interracialism at Fisk University in 1930

Lauren Kientz Anderson

On October 7, 1930, satisfied that he was making the world safe for African Americans, President Thomas Elsa Jones welcomed his faculty to the fall meeting. The white president of historically black Fisk University felt confidence seep into him from the beautiful new library walls around him—walls erected through his fund-raising efforts. Partially finished Aaron Douglas murals carved black history into the walls and complemented the shelves of leather bound books. Jones also emanated confidence because of a recent achievement in racial harmony. As a forward-thinking liberal, committed to racial justice, he refused to acquiesce when a New Jersey hotel insulted the Fisk Dean of Women, Juliette Derricotte. After his pressure, the hotel agreed that the black woman could enter the hotel for the conference as long as she stayed out of the public areas. This compromise pleased Jones. It represented the epitome of racial justice, which he sought throughout his presidency—polite conversation that led to a gradual change and emphasized interracial cooperation.

At the October 1930 meeting, members of the faculty rejected this form of racial justice as inadequate and criticized Jones' administration as discriminatory. The meeting began when Jones introduced a group of new advisors. Different expressions passed across black and white faces—ranging from indifference to hostility to welcome. Mabel Byrd,

Perspectives on the History of Higher Education 29 (2012): 75-111
© 2012. ISBN: 978-1-4128-4771-1

a young black research assistant, sprang to her feet, frustration creasing her brow. Staring straight into the president's eyes, she requested that he explain his recent choices. Why were all the freshman advisors white? In particular, why was a woman from Georgia, that "most prejudiced of environments," more "qualified to advise our freshmen than Negro women, who at least knows the Negro youth, his difficulties, his environment, her needs?"[1] She brought up more problems, including the new houses Jones had built for white faculty while asking black professors to live in dormitories with students.

Before Jones gathered his thoughts to respond, A. A. Taylor, black historian and Dean of Academics, protested that he and Jones had not considered race in the choice of the advisors and that, indeed, he did not see color when he looked in the mirror. E. Franklin Frazier and Horace Mann Bond, not yet the nationally known scholars they would become, stood in support of Byrd with Ann Boie, a white woman. The three agreed

Figure 1. Mabel Byrd for Her 1931 Rosenwald Application (Reproduced with Permission from Fisk University Franklin Library's Special Collections)

that they too had noticed a consistent pattern of discrimination in Jones' administration.[2] Jones, however, was flummoxed. He believed he was doing a great service to the black race by building up a university that rigorously defended black Americans' right to achieve the highest level of education any human could attain. He had learned from the many misguided and blatantly discriminatory actions of his predecessor, Fayette McKenzie, who had been asked to resign by the board after calling in riot police on students exercising free speech. In response to Byrd's accusations, Jones began to explain each of the decisions called into question. Most of the faculty, black and white, remained silent, so he gathered courage and believed the room supported him. They seemed to agree that it had just been a "misunderstanding"—that Byrd, Frazier, and Bond simply did not know Jones' reasons, which had nothing to do with race.[3]

At the end of the faculty meeting, Jones asked Byrd and Frazier to stay behind. He called their protest an instance of unacceptable disloyalty to Fisk, said that they did not have to remain in their positions, and accused them of starting a "race riot" by "misinterpreting" his actions.[4] These were no petty threats; he suggested that they were undermining the university and potentially starting something akin to the bloody race riots of 1919 or those "riots" that started a month-long student strike in 1925. Byrd's honest opinions, supposedly a hallmark of profitable interracial dialogue, had earned her a serious condemnation and a threat to her job.

Introduction

In this paper, I use the communication between Juliette Derricotte, Mabel Byrd, and Thomas Jones at Fisk University and their wider contexts to examine interracialism, a philosophy which compelled many of the subtle changes in race relations in the interwar period. Distinct from the more commonly studied concept of "integration," interracialism inspired good will and motivated action among liberals, while also drawing hatred and enmity from some blacks and whites.[5] It had all the flaws of a moderately liberal concept—promising limited change only after compromise with the opposition. Some, like Derricotte and Jones, believed interracial dialogue and communion would lead to lasting change; others, like W. E. B. Du Bois and Byrd, believed that "a facet of all interracialism connotes and denotes subserviency to white supremacy veiled or blatantly open."[6]

The philosophy of interracialism, which motivated Jones to assume the presidency of Fisk and helped him build Fisk into a successful institution, did not just describe the process of whites and blacks interacting. In some gatherings, people used it to express their fear of sex between black men and white women.[7] For liberals, though, it connoted a particular type of struggle for racial justice—one marked by dialogue, education, and patience rather than protests, boycotts, and legal changes. Most of the whites interested in improving life for African Americans, such as Quakers, NAACP members, or liberal Protestants, were interracialists.

The structure of the paper follows the three categories that Marion Cuthbert, friend of Derricotte and Talladega College's Dean of Women, used to explain the different reactions to interracialism—a "magical device," a nauseating sentiment, and a "real insight." Her speech, "Honesty in Race Relations" argued that honesty was the lifeblood of interracialism and yet honesty was constantly being feared, avoided, and punished. Some people regarded interracialism as a "magical device" that would solve all racial problems. Many whites had indeed felt a transformation so intense that it could be magical when they had first encountered an educated, well-spoken black person. Everything about American society taught them that they should expect blacks to be un-intelligent and subservient. Once they met individuals like Derricotte, Byrd, and Du Bois, they wanted to share the transformatory experience with others. Being on the other side of that transformation—having people exclaim over and over again at their speaking abilities—tried the patience of many blacks. After too many of these experiences, many began to view interracialism as a nauseating sentiment which distracted people from concrete solutions.[8] For example, one of Byrd's criticisms of Jones was that he was a member of the "spine-less inter-racial group in the South." Still others thought it just might be a real insight with practical use, as long as interracialists thoroughly examined the strengths and weaknesses of the strategy.[9] Glenda Gilmore tracks the successes of interracialists: "Interracial cooperation commissions opened channels of communication, built mutual respect among in-dividuals, and succeeded in condemning lynching and reducing its frequency."[10]

This paper will examine these three different reactions to interracial-ism through the lens of Fisk University in the early years of the Jones administration. This era witnessed growth pains as Fisk transitioned from a white funded and administered school to one driven by the needs and desires of black people. In the midst of that transition, Jones and his interracial faculty had to find a way to work together to build the university. Criticizers and builders were both needed in this development. Builders were more likely to be interracial in this period because they recognized the necessity of working pragmatically with whites. Criticizers, on the other hand, saw the world the way it should be and attempted to transform the present to look like that future image.

One of the reasons that Jones reacted so differently to Mabel Byrd and Juliette Derricotte was because of the way that they communicated with him. Byrd, a criticizer, had just returned from two years in Geneva, Switzerland, where she became convinced that pacifists and interracialists, who preferred compromise above all else, neglected justice and failed to challenge white supremacy. Derricotte, a builder, had made interracialism her life's mission along with improving education for black women. She had been inspired by the fruitful interactions between the whites and blacks she witnessed during her tenure with the headquarters of the Young Women's Christian Association (YWCA). Byrd and Frazier believed they embodied the values of the New Negro in presenting their disagreements directly to Jones, but he responded in the old way of refusing to listen to anything other than conciliatory speech. They were "angry black men and women," not productive members of the faculty, in his opinion. Jones could listen to and aid Derricotte because she spoke with a mixture of reconciliation, gentleness, and candor that charmed everyone she met.

Sometimes whites argue that blacks see discrimination where it is not intended, as indeed Jones did in the wake of Byrd's criticism, but that is often because whites are unable to acknowledge their own prejudices or consider the idea that though well meaning, they might harbor unrecognized racism. It was easier for Jones to make a small effort, like securing a private accommodation for Derricotte at her national conference, than it was to admit that discrimination might have been at the heart of his administration. Jones thought his administration was "color-blind," but when whites are color-blind, they still tend to act according to the dictates of white privilege. At the same time, interracialism was more powerful than a simple "Uncle Tomism," or acceptance of white supremacy by whites and blacks, would suggest. Small changes could accrue to make meaningful changes; in other words, the interwar period's small changes prepared US liberals and government officials to support the civil rights movement after World War II rather than violently suppressing it (as happened in South Africa when the same tactics were tried). The conflagrations at Fisk illustrate that both protest and dialogue—criticizers and builders—were needed, depending upon the circumstances and the people involved.

Fisk Student Uprising

Throughout their discussions in 1930, everyone at Fisk heard the echoes of the 1924–25 student uprising. In the year of the uprising, the students protested President Fayette McKenzie's administration because of its severe limitations on student life, its endangerment of female students, and its refusal to listen to the ideas and plans of black students, faculty, and alumni. In 1930, Jones tried desperately to avoid the mistakes of his predecessor, Byrd tested the newly won authority of blacks at Fisk, and Derricotte expanded students' freedoms. These echoes necessitate a brief analysis of the 1924–25 transformation in Fisk leadership.

One of the sparks of the strike was W. E. B. Du Bois' 1924 commencement address, which laid out the full complaints of students and faculty. He had gathered these items directly from the students through his daughter, Yolande, a graduating Fisk student, and through his role as Fisk's most famous alumnus. McKenzie had abolished the student council and most of the athletic associations. He refused to allow the new black sororities and fraternities on campus. He even went so far as to punish students who volunteered to clean up the university grounds. Du Bois' criticism led to McKenzie's retrenchment and a campaign by both leaders to woo influential people connected to Fisk to their side.[11] Initially, black newspapers and the white trustees remained on McKenzie's side because he had successfully raised the endowment to a million dollars.[12] Students spent the whole school year of 1924–1925 trying to convince the Board of Trustees of the rightness of their stance. The winds changed after a spring demonstration by the students, who picketed, stated their demands, broke some windows, and then went to bed. McKenzie called in the riot police. Officers who had only recently looked the other way during a lynching of a local black businessman invaded the dormitories and hauled black students out of their beds. Several were arrested that night and the following day, even some McKenzie had had his eye on who were not actually on campus that night. This seemed to make clear that the raid was a set-up.[13]

Almost all the students boycotted the campus after that incident, except those financially obligated to stay because of scholarships. They went home or were put up by local members of the black Nashville community. The Board of Trustees finally listened and McKenzie resigned. An interim president reinstated the student council, athletics, and opened the campus to Greek life. The trustees finally settled on Thomas

Elsa Jones to be the new president, and he brought his enthusiasm for interracialism to campus.[14]

Interracialism—An Introduction

Before enumerating the different kinds of support for and criticism of interracialism at Fisk, let us examine what was meant by the term in 1930. Among liberal whites and blacks, discussions about race relations in the 1920s tended to focus on improving interracial cooperation (as opposed to changing laws, ending Jim Crow, or establishing social equality). This was in distinct contrast to the majority of moderate and conservative whites, who automatically equated any talk of interracial collaboration with black men having sex with white women and so advocated stringent segregation. It was also in contrast to the many blacks who focused on creating safe separate spaces in the 1920s, like those who followed Marcus Garvey.

The primary components of interracialism's effort to improve cooperation between the races were: education to expand individuals' tolerance of difference; gatherings of educated, genteel members of both races together for discussion; religiously motivated change; and emphasis on personal transformation leading to social transformation. This was an heir of the Progressive Era's concept of "uplift," because the people who built up black spaces using that concept at the turn of the nineteenth century had begun to be accepted into white spaces; for example, federations of white club women invited black club women to their national conferences, the YWCA hired young educated black women, and the number of black students at primarily white institutions grew exponentially. Interracialism was markedly different from the activism/collaboration dichotomy sometimes attributed to W. E. B. Du Bois and Booker T. Washington in that era, described by Kevin Gaines as "the clash between blacks' communal quest for social justice and individualistic imperatives of survival."[15] The Niagara Movement represented Du Bois' actualization of the quest for social justice, while Washington's empire was built upon solutions that accepted segregation and racism. In contrast, interracialism emphasized social justice, while bringing blacks and whites together to talk in some semblance of equality. It also emphasized individual transformation for both blacks and whites, but often not systemic change. It tended to be very modest and pragmatic in its goals and stressed patience in waiting for change to come.

"Interracialism" as a distinct philosophy has been lost to history, subsumed as it was into the idea of "integration." Interracialism was less than full integration. People could support genteel gatherings, without supporting interracial marriage, housing equality, nondiscrimination in employment, etc. Whites could also support interracialism in the form of whites working for the improvement in the lives of blacks without working side by side with blacks. For example, Will Alexander of the Commission on Interracial Equality always started his speeches promoting interracial cooperation by condemning interracial marriage. The fear of intermarriage, or "social equality" haunted a lot of interracial dialogue and stopped progress.

Interracialism—Magical Device

During the interwar era, many white organizations began to recognize that the treatment of African Americans within the United States was a major moral question for all Americans to face. Three groups are particularly important for this paper. First, the YWCA slowly moved toward integrated national conferences, with segregated local branches, and was one of the largest employers of educated black women outside of the schoolroom, including both Derricotte and Byrd in their twenties. Second, the Quakers developed the Race Relations Institute and influenced Jones' thinking. Third, the Commission on Interracial Cooperation (CIC) was the largest Southern-based interracial organization and one with many connections to Fisk faculty and administration (including Charles Johnson and Juliette Derricotte).[16] The last two, in particular, responded to the violence of the "Red Summer" race riots of 1919 and tried to find a peaceful means for whites to coexist with African Americans. Many members of these organizations, particularly whites, seemed to believe that just getting black and white individuals into the same room to talk would accomplish amazing things, because it had within their own lives. Speaking to educated blacks had transformed their understanding of race and they believed this transformation could be replicated and would have a sustaining power to overcome widespread American racism. These were the type of groups that Cuthbert identified as believing that interracialism could be a "magical device."

Young Women's Christian Association

Interracialism became a major focus of the YWCA after black members grew in number after World War I. Local branches were segregated and white leadership usually held financial control over the black branches, causing much frustration among black secretaries.[17] However, the national YWCA did begin to recognize its black members and started developing a policy on race relations that emphasized interracial harmony and "Christian sisterhood." For instance, the YWCA published a pamphlet to help educate Americans about race relations. Its readers were told that "[a]mong the many evils with which our American life is confronted, none seems so acute or aggravated as the relationship between the races" and "[u]ntil Christian white women stand by negro [sic] women, giving them that human protection and respect which is the right of womanhood the world over, there will be little progress in racial solutions. Womanhood and motherhood are among the few things deeper than race."[18] Nancy Robertson points out that "[w]hite women in the YWCA, especially class-privileged women, spoke of womanhood as universal; they argued that [. . .] there was a 'bond of common womanhood deeper than all racial separateness.' In so doing, they suggested that *all* women had traits that bound them with other women."[19] The black and white YWCA leadership believed that "women had a special mission to promote harmony in a divided world by bringing the familial values of the private realm into the public. Then, people working together—black and white, worker and industrialist, woman and man—would build the 'Kingdom of God on Earth.'"[20] The ideals of universal harmony and sisterhood could be a powerful motivator or a simplistic sentiment.

Black YWCA workers believed this rhetoric to different extents—some, like Derricotte believed that it held the promise of the future, while others believed hypocrisies among white YWCA members annulled its promises of unity.[21] White women in the YWCA pushed black women to consider their gender above their race, but separating the two was impossible. Individuals could only choose which to emphasize. The YWCA nurtured both Derricotte and Byrd in their young adulthood. Derricotte embraced the spirit of interracialism because she met a wide range of white and black women in the United States and abroad who fulfilled its promise with grace and hope. At the same time, she had patience with mistakes. Her lifelong motto was "there is more to know than I am knowing; there is more to love than I am loving."[22] This mantra gave her the personal peace to return to women who had insulted her, usually without meaning to, and try again to influence them away from racism. She had a remarkable success record in transforming individuals' perception of race—black women toward greater pride in themselves and white women toward greater awareness of the particular struggles of the blacks they encountered but did not know.[23]

In contrast, Byrd's experience with the YWCA made her want to know more about structural and economic solutions. She saw enough hypocrisy within the whites she encountered that she did not believe in the ability of individuals to transform their own personal racism, let alone society. It was frustrating that the YWCA segregated local branches, which often meant fewer resources went toward the black branches and blacks were excluded from well-appointed YWCAs downtown. Byrd recognized the necessity of hard facts in proving discrimination and so began to pursue economic training, first in New York City and then in Europe, before joining Charles Johnson as a research assistant at Fisk. After her appointment there, she pursued a master's in economics at the University of Chicago. These two complicated reactions to the interracialism of the YWCA indicate how much promise and peril there was within the philosophy. It was not easily rejected as ineffective with Derricotte's witness, but neither was it easily accepted, with the evidence of hypocrisy that followed so many white interracialists.

The Quakers' and Jones' Interracialism

As the YWCA influenced the philosophies of Byrd and Derricotte, so the Quakers influenced Jones. Quakers were among many pacifist groups that rose in power following WWI, though they, of course, had a long tradition of influence in the United States. They recognized the violence that arose out of racism (particularly symbolized by the race riots following WWI) and often included platforms on improving race relations in their yearly mandates. The Quakers founded groups to speak and educate about race relations and, because of their peace-based religion, they chiefly emphasized the use of cooperation and compromise over protest.[24] The Philadelphia Arch and Race Street Meetings were particularly influential and the ones Jones, a lifelong Quaker, visited whenever he could. The Arch and Race Street members stressed the importance of bringing together the best of both races to talk together and educate each other.

Like the YWCA, these groups of Friends maintained a level of segregation in their meetings. For example, Dr. Virginia Alexander, a very engaged member, was officially a co-opted member during her years of active participation. She was not a full member because she was black.[25] Her official status represented a compromise between those who wanted her to be a full member and those that were worried that her presence would change the nature and honesty of the conversation.[26]

It was this group that supported the idea of Crystal Bird Fauset (a black woman) to create the Swarthmore Institute on Race Relations in 1933, which emphasized the tenets of interracial education while moving the conversation more toward social science and less toward individual religious transformation. This institute continued at Swarthmore under the leadership of Fisk professor Charles Johnson, until he moved it to Fisk in the 1940s.[27] As with so many of the strange compromises the Quakers made with their black collaborators, the Race Relations Institute had a dark underbelly of discrimination that Quakers tried to paste over with pleasantries. African Americans attended, co-led, and spoke at the Race Relations Institutes in the 1930s on the Swarthmore campus, but they could not have returned in the fall as students because the private Quaker school did not accept black students.[28]

Inspired by the Quakers' talk of interracialism, Jones eagerly accepted the job at Fisk. Both a scholar and an activist, he wanted to make a positive intervention in American race relations. Like most college presidents in the nineteenth century, he had a background in theology (B.D. Hartford Theological Seminary, 1915), but like those in the twentieth he also had a Ph.D. (Columbia University, 1926, sociology). He became aware of American racial ideology while spending 1917–1924 in Japan as a YMCA missionary. In Japan, he witnessed American actions that could only have resulted from racism.[29] He thought that these actions were based in "a philosophy of race difference erroneously assumed to exist between white and coloured people." Determined to help America "right the wrong done the great and sensitive nation of Japan, I went to see what I could do at Fisk University."[30] Jones' strange leap in topic from America's role in Japan to African Americans' difficulties in the home of their birth could be interpreted a few ways. He was not exactly equating Japanese with African Americans, but he was suggesting that a similar kind of racial discrimination affected them both and that aiding blacks in the United States could somehow redeem a situation in Japan. This could be seen as a corollary to Du Bois' idea of the "color-line" running through the twentieth century, or as the privilege of the white man to consider everyone else "other." Either way, it indicated his ignorance of American race relations, which he freely admitted.

Jones tried to explain the connection between the Japanese and Fisk by showing how his openness to one situation made him suitable for the other. His admiration for the Japanese made Jones appropriate for the position of Fisk president, he argued, not because it gave him specific skills or experiences, but because it reflected his openness, willingness to question, and enthusiasm. "I wished to know the facts about race. I was sure that the so-called facts which had appeared in books about the Negro were as distorted as those which had appeared in other books about Japan," he wrote. "I wished to know for myself and at first hand."[31] This attitude was attested to by black diplomat, author, and scholar James Weldon Johnson; he remembered that "no one can hear President Jones talk about Fisk without feeling the galvanic force of his tremendous energy and enthusiasm."[32] This did not mean that Jones was immune to many of those "so-called" facts about race in the United States and, indeed, he brought many stereotypes about blacks to Fisk. In many ways, Jones approached Fisk as a foreign mission field in the way he had entered Japan. He took with him to Nashville his steadfastness, his good humor, and his faith, as well as his awkwardness, self-consciousness, and paternalism.

The summer before arriving at Fisk, Jones had his own moment of "magical" transformation. He was living at the International House on Columbia University's campus. One day while shaving, a black person greeted him. At first, Jones was affronted by the familiarity of this person, probably a servant. Then he realized that the man was an African student and had earned his place by his merits, just as Jones had. He gave himself a lecture—"'Here am I, a teacher, resident in International House which is 'open to students irrespective of race, creed, or color' and yet I am allowing the prejudices of my youth to come forth.'"[33] He lectured himself not because he owed the black student pleasantries because he was a fellow human, but because the black man was a fellow student, with equal merit to Jones. This emphasis on educated people of each race meeting was a hallmark of interracial thought. The one episode did not rid Jones of all the "prejudices of my youth."

The newly minted Ph.D. arrived at Fisk in 1926 to a student body and campus still recovering from the strike the year before. Students had been reprimanded by President McKenzie for pulling weeds, so one of the first impressions Jones had of his new home was that it was "grown up in weeds and very tall grass. . . . It looks like an abandoned home of some sort," he wrote a friend. "It gets my goat to look at it."[34] In among his educational goals, he set about improving the physical and aesthetic landscape of the campus. The beautified physical plant improved morale and increased the feeling that students were engaged in a serious academic endeavor.

Jones' two primary goals at Fisk were securing its financial future (which included paying off a large debt that was due) and hiring the "best faculty and build[ing] the best equipment possible to give the Negro race a college second to none in the United States."[35] In addition to the new Cravath library, Jones also built new chemistry and biology labs. He took on McKenzie's goal for a million-dollar endowment, but instead of only focusing on white philanthropists, he also raised significant contributions among Fisk alumni. To accomplish these two goals, Jones had to convince white and black citizens of his good intentions. After one representative of the General Education Board met with Jones, he wrote tellingly "If I don't miss my guess, he will be more popular among the white people of Nashville even than Dr. McKenzie, and, from what he tells me, he has already taken the steps necessary to cut off criticism among the colored radical group from the source from which it might probably come."[36] To "cut off criticism," Jones vacillated between taking the criticism seriously and attempting to silence the criticizers. He consistently overestimated his popularity among African Americans and his ability to soothe their concerns.

One area in which Jones did earn appreciation from African Americans was his openness with regard to social activities. While Fayette McKenzie mistrusted the students in every way (requiring, for instance, that every extracurricular activity have a faculty member present), Jones immediately expanded the number and range of acceptable clubs and activities.[37] Sororities and fraternities joined the campus for the first time and athletics received an infusion of cash. He also encouraged all disciplinary issues to be handled through the Student Council in conjunction with the Dean of Men or Dean of Women. Jones wanted students to act appropriately because of peer pressure and positive relationships with faculty. So instead of dictating "a course of action or arbitrarily impose a penalty for the infringement of a rule, the Dean of Men and the Dean of Women try to build a public opinion that will maintain order through the Student Council." Faculty would influence student government "by gaining the students' confidence, bringing them into faculty homes, and aiding any group to discipline one of its recalcitrant members."[38] This was a significant change from the McKenzie era because it showed that Jones had enough confidence in black students' and faculty's moral character to leave discipline up to them. When Juliette Derricotte was Dean of Women, some female students celebrated Halloween with such passion that a girl's arm was broken, another suffered a hot water burn, and pieces of furniture were ruined. Jones gave Derricotte his "complete confidence and support" to take care of it and let her proceed with a discipline plan that gave students a great deal of autonomy. Jones did not let the event change his idea of African Americans; he just chalked it up to student behavior.[39] Rather than characterizing all African Americans as the same, Jones was able to see nuance and difference—an important first step to eradicating one's own racism. However, he did not remain open to the ways that his subconscious could influence his decisions, resulting in a preference toward white faculty. This was one of the primary concerns raised by Mabel Byrd in 1930.

Southern Liberals—Commission on Interracial Cooperation

In addition to national and northern groups writing about and working for improved race relations, like the YWCA and the Quakers, most of the Southern whites willing to talk about improving life for African Americans were interracialists. "The oldest and best known of all of the interracial committees working in the field of race relations," according to Rufus Clement in a 1944 *Journal of Negro Education* article, was the CIC. A group of churchmen established the CIC immediately after the race riots of 1919 in Atlanta, GA. While primarily a white-led organization (Will W. Alexander was the major force behind it), the leaders included prominent black men like Robert R. Moton, the president who succeeded Booker T. Washington at Tuskegee, Dr. John Hope, president of Atlanta University, and Charles Johnson of Fisk. They produced "hundreds of thousands of different pieces of literature" and spawned 800 state and local committees, through which "many of the best people of the South have come to know one another and to know further that most of the racial stereotypes which had developed in the minds of whites concerning Negroes, and Negroes concerning whites, are false and can not be substantiated by fact."[40] The CIC tended to be one of the NAACP's primary competitors for supporters and resources in the South. Both organizations were interracial, but whereas the NAACP fought segregation in all its forms, the CIC opposed injustice without challenging segregation. It focused on fighting the most egregious forms of racism, like lynching and race riots, as well as putting the "best" of blacks and whites (i.e., upper class, cultured, and professional) in conversation with each other.[41] In 1926, Du Bois praised Will W. Alexander's leadership of the CIC, while acknowledging the "magical" nature of many such committees; "For a long time inter-racial committees fiddled away and made believe they were discussing co-operation between the races. But now and then a few of them, and a few individuals, have taken the matter seriously and have gone in for discussion. And one of these is Will W. Alexander of

Atlanta." His praise for Alexander arose when the white man garnered criticism for refusing to defend the Jim Crow car on railroads because "it works an injustice." For this statement, Alexander "was ordered out of town [. . .]; he was traduced in the newspapers; and the white preachers declared in a formal resolution that he was not a suitable man 'to take the lead in the discussion and direction of race relations'!"[42]

Interracialists emphasized dialogue largely because honest conversation about race was so difficult to achieve. The southern whites' idea of race was "too sacred to talk about, too absolutely right to criticize, too portentous to be challenged."[43] The CIC's greatest success was to challenge that aura of sacredness around race. However, the CIC did not live up to Du Bois' hopes for it. Frazier, Byrd, and Du Bois found unacceptable the CIC's acceptance of the basic legal structure of the South as well as the linguistic hurdles it went through to attract white southern support.

Interracialism—Nauseating Sentiment

The interracial sentiment that most frustrated many African Americans was the persistent paternalism that emanated from white adherents and its acceptance of segregation.[44] An Atlanta University colleague of Du Bois' remembered how this paternalism played out in criticism of Du Bois during the founding of the NAACP; "The high presumption was then [1910] and still is [1968] that colored people would always be amenable to 'cooing' while the whites would do the 'operating'!"[45] Many blacks felt like interracialist whites required "subserviency to white supremacy."[46] Interracialism was both an heir to Du Bois' pressure for integration and activism articulated in the Niagara Movement's creed and an heir to Booker T. Washington's need to project an air of subservience in order to accomplish his goals, even while being distinct in its emphasis on blacks and whites working together. This complicated amalgam is represented in Du Bois' response to interracialism, which as a philosophy he often challenged, but when it worked in reality, he praised.

W. E. B. Du Bois' Response to Interracialism

When Du Bois visited Fisk early in Jones' tenure, he spotted great progress as well as all the places of potential conflict; several of his observations pointed at the tensions that interracial interaction suffered. Du Bois thought that Fisk was the most modern of the universities he visited, particularly in the freedoms allowed to students. They could eat breakfast when they liked, they could smoke, and men and women could mix. Yet, while Jones was surprised to meet so many cultured and well-mannered black people, Du Bois worried that the new black faculty did not have the proper manners to hold the position they did. He suggested that the development of their knowledge had gone before the development of their "culture." They had not yet learned "enough not to proceed the hostess out of the dining room."[47] In this notation, Du Bois recognized that good manners helped professional blacks to be taken seriously. At the same time, it reflected Du Bois' very formal personality.

While Du Bois worried about blacks being cultured enough, he also worried that the Fisk administration was still too easily swayed by the opinions (and pocketbooks) of whites in Nashville and beyond. He warned Jones from the pages of the *Crisis* about these whites—that "unconsciously they will seek to dominate and advise," and that Jones might find it easier "to defer to this public opinion, rather than to the more reticent and poorly expressed public opinion of the black world." Fisk could not give in. It "went on the rocks in a former administration because the Chamber of Commerce of Nashville tried to set standards for it. The standards of Fisk University are being set today by its own Alumni and the colored world. It must continue in this line despite Vanderbilt, Peabody and all white Nashville."[48] An interracialist would try to blend the desires of each group together. Du Bois maintained that African Americans must have control over Fisk, despite the external political and financial pressures of the white world.

As long as Fisk was shaped by African Americans, Du Bois delighted in witnessing interracial communication. During a reception after a lecture on the Russian Revolution (something else that excited Du Bois), teachers and students mingled, including white professors, black students, black professors, a few white students from Vanderbilt, "and fifteen or sixteen representatives of foreign peoples: Chinese, Italians, South Americans, Russians, Dutch, Swiss, and others." Du Bois rejoiced in it; "It was an unusual and inspiring scene."[49] There was something in Du Bois that hoped peaceful interracial and international mingling could lead to real change, though he did not have hope that that social-izing would be some kind of magical device that would change people by its sheer existence. It was not easy for educated African Americans who worked alongside whites to whole-heartedly dismiss all the tenets of interracialism. The delicate balance they had to maintain between their self-pride and their cooperation with others is indicated in Du Bois' visit to Fisk.

Mabel Byrd's Response to Interracialism

Mabel Byrd took much of the inspiration for her challenge of President Jones in 1930 from Du Bois. She had become a family friend of his during her years in New York City in the early 1920s. They frequently corresponded while she was abroad and when she returned to the United States and saw the situation at Fisk, he was the one she turned to.[50] Byrd argued that when interracial and pacifist groups focused on peaceful cooperation and criticized those who would protest the regime rather than try to educate it to be better, they built up white supremacy instead of tearing it down. Byrd thought interracialism was just people talking about getting along, without making real change. And the talk diverted attention from what really needed to be done. That was why interracialism was nauseating (in Marion Cuthbert's formulation). Byrd articulated this at the 1929 Women's International League for Peace and Freedom (WILPF) annual meeting held in Prague. She had just finished her two years working for the Bureau of International Labor (linked to the League of Nations) in the forced labor division.

In her speech to the WILPF gathering, Byrd synthesized what she had learned from two years in Europe, as well as her prior years as a secretary in the Portland, Oregon, Harlem, and Brooklyn YWCAs. The peace and reconciliation preached by the YWCA and WILPF only went so far. Byrd believed it was not worth forfeiting one's dignity and rights for the sake of maintaining peace. Acknowledging a previous speaker who said, "cooperation instead of conflict is the outstanding fact of evolution," she argued that "it is difficult to understand how cooperation can be substituted for conflict until those whose rule is dominant are led to change their attitude toward the minority or dominated group."[51] It was the burden of the dominant group to realize first "that their conviction of superiority is false, that because they find themselves in a dominating position, is no true sign of their inherent superiority; secondly that there is no divine right for one race to rule another; and thirdly, that the disturbances made by the minority groups are the constant attempts toward a real cooperation in the body politic."[52] She directly challenged those in the audience who would condemn African Americans for protesting because they stirred conflict rather than working toward cooperation. The representatives of dominant groups in the audience needed to recognize that cooperation, under the standing social system, tended to always favor the dominant group. To Byrd this meant that pacifists' encouragement of respectful race relations would not contradict their "investment in whiteness," because in actuality interracialists propped up white rule by urging patience and conversation over protest and action.[53]

When she arrived at Fisk from Geneva in 1929, Byrd was determined to face discrimination head on if she encountered it, but during her first year, she was handicapped in this determination by working on a Rosenwald research project that required a large amount of discretion in its execution. She traveled all over the South interviewing white employers about their attitude toward and treatment of black employees; she could not speak her mind without jeopardizing her fact gathering mission. In Birmingham, for instance, she interviewed the white president of a black industrial high school who had been threatened by the KKK for trying to improve the physical plant of his campus.[54] She reported this as just one of many facts about the schools she encountered. Returning to Fisk full-time in 1930, perhaps she felt emboldened to protest the discrimination she witnessed on campus, because she had been so limited in her protest avenues the year before. She thought the university would encourage protest, as it had in the wake of the student strike in the mid-1920s, yet Jones met her protests with the claim that she was trying to start a race riot. There are parallels in Du Bois' experiences with the NAACP, which an Atlanta University colleague remembered; "Some of the founders like Villard were simply unable to accept Dr. Du Bois' insistence upon *absolute candor and forthrightness* of equality of white and colored" [emphasis in original].[55] Interracialism was built on the idea of "Honesty in Race Relations" (the title of Marion Cuthbert's speech that gives this article its arrangement), and yet too much honesty seemed to topple the structure.

E. Franklin Frazier's and Horace Mann Bond's Response to Interracialism

Byrd had the advantage of a short-term position. She could act like an external observer and intellectual, while the colleagues that supported her challenge of Jones, sociologist E. Franklin Frazier and historian Horace Mann Bond, had to worry about their lasting careers at the institution. They wanted to be the forthright speakers of truth canonized in New Negro ideology, but they had to temper that with caution to protect their positions. One of the greatest difficulties for African Americans who disagreed with prevailing white attitudes was the need to get along with their supervisors in order to keep their professional positions. Even when they lived in all-black spaces, eventually there was a layer of power controlled by whites. When Frazier and Bond spoke with Jones, he had the power of an administrator, so they had to be careful how they spoke. But in private settings and letters, they tended to be more critical of the status quo than Jones was and derided the care they had to take when speaking to him.

Frazier had arrived at Fisk in the same year as Byrd (1929) trailing "the shadows [of] being a radical Negro, believing in racial equality."[56] He and his wife Marie had fled Atlanta the year before under threat of violence following his article "The Psychological Factors in Negro Health," which suggested that racism was a form of mental illness in the minds of European Americans.[57] Frazier documented his commitment to resisting tyranny and injustice in his first *Crisis* article, "The Negro and Non-Resistance." In it, he castigated interracialists who believed love and Christian morality would change white attitudes. He argued, "The Negro does not want love. He wants justice. [. . .] The Negro is asking that those who administer justice shall administer it in accordance with the principles of democratic justice which are embodied in the organic law of the United States." Justice should not depend upon love or kindness (words frequently used by interracialists) because it "is impersonal." Frazier argued that the main difficulty in the South was that white people had not attained a conception of impersonal justice. Frazier urged his readers to let go of nonresistance as a false component of Christian humility, and instead fight all instances of racism. "Perhaps, in the distant future, men may love each other so that they will not need to define their rights and duties in society; but in the present stage of social evolution, we prefer to fight for the observance of the established principles of democratic political society."[58] Frazier never stopped his searing published critiques, but life circumstances did force him to learn an element of caution.

Given Frazier's public support for resistance and his criticism of Christian values, it is a surprise that Jones agreed to hire Frazier at all. After the Fraziers spent a year in Chicago for Franklin to begin his Ph.D. studies at the University of Chicago, Charles Johnson invited him come to Fisk to work on Frazier's vast study of African American families. President Jones only agreed to hire him if the still controversial professor would provide his own salary out of his SSRC grant. Jones privileged faculty who were not only qualified in teaching and scholarship, but also showed "balance of personality, enthusiasm for their work, and regard for the deeper values in life."[59] Christian faith meant a great deal to Jones, as did quiet, peaceable personalities. On some level, Frazier recognized this and therefore moderated his criticisms. He and Horace Mann Bond each chose not to engage in some conflicts in order to maintain their positions.

Bond remembered one conflict when he and Frazier divided on whether or not to protest. Bond supported a student who desired to picket a segregated restaurant in Nashville. The administration banned the boycott, which led students to protest on the Fisk campus itself. In response, the administration sought to expel the student leader. They asked a faculty committee to make the final decision. Bond remembered being the only professor out of six to support the student. When he asked Frazier why he had voted against the student, Frazier suggested that the only reason Bond defended the student was that he "had never been fired from a job," whereas Frazier knew that sting and had to be careful.[60] Perhaps it was Frazier's support for Byrd's criticism of Jones at the 1930 faculty meeting, and Jones' subsequent threat to remove Frazier from Fisk, that first brought it home to Frazier how careful he would have to be at Fisk.

Early in his Fisk career, historian Horace Mann Bond complained to Jones that students were manufacturing complaints about racism—precisely what Jones felt Byrd was doing at the 1930 faculty meeting. After studying HBCUs other than Fisk, he wrote, "in the first place, one is more and more impressed with the ease by which [. . .] an entirely worthless student can bring serious trouble and array behind him the public opinion of Negroes through an utterly worthless appeal to race pride. This in the last analysis gets down to present one's case to the prints first and most thoroughly."[61] This would have confirmed Jones' opinion that many of the times African Americans raised the issue of discrimination, they were simply being oversensitive and misinformed. Jones repeated this often in the 1930 conflict with Byrd and Frazier. For instance, when Jones reflected upon the first trustee meeting following Byrd's protest, he believed he had found a measure of interracial peace. He wrote, "I think white people saw that my loyalties are firmly tied up with the group which I represent as President of Fisk University, and I think the colored people saw that it was time to shut up a lot of these vague and groundless rumors of discrimination."[62] Bond recognized what he was doing when confirming for Jones that some students did indeed play "the race card." He had earlier described navigating a professional life between the demands of one's conscience and those of a white employer's as one of the "frightful muddles of my generation." He could "never quite decide just how far to carry protest, or accommodation. I am opinionated enough to believe that by a determined effort, by assiduous practice of the art of fooling the white folks, I can become a great Race Man or a big Niggra as they would have it. However, I cannot bring myself to smile the little smiles and say the little things that pave the way for grandeur."[63] Even though he could not make those accommodations, he was also not ready to exchange his academic career for militant activism.

Whether to protest or accommodate were daily choices for blacks in the interwar era. Unlike during the civil rights movement, when protests were publicized, most protests were done alone and left unremarked upon. Instead, it was the people who accommodated who seemed to get the furthest and who could perhaps make the biggest difference by the choices they made once they had acquired power. One of the things that makes the interwar era unique was the power of white leadership, the gradual opening toward black leadership, and the incremental daily choices about whether to protest or accommodate that all black leaders engaged in.

Interracialism—Real Insight

The outline of this analysis of interracialism is based upon Marion Cuthbert's diagram of responses to interracialism—those that thought it was a magical device, a nauseating sentiment, or a real insight. She and Juliette Derricotte, friends, devoted their lives to the final category.

Cuthbert, who had been called the "Du Bois of womanhood" for her intelligence and leadership, was not unaware of the problems that challenged interracialism's promises.[64] She criticized black and white assumptions that simply educating people would make them somehow more tolerant and empathetic or that simply using social science to describe a problem would end it. "I know of nothing more fallacious than the idea that if the problem is pointed out, described, that problem will disappear."[65] She believed that "once two groups of people considered the problem the problem would remain the same as before and the division would be greater" through the increased knowledge.[66] Perhaps she had learned a hard lesson from her years representing the YWCA, which prided itself for encouraging positive interracial relations through education. Cuthbert explained that education was at most a starting point, because "there is in human nature courage enough to do something about a problem that is understood and those of us of the minority group who can to ourselves and to other people tell what is wrong find that we are stimulated and encouraged to do something about it more than when we are working in some fake situation that is a troublous dream."[67] Furthermore, white people who "actually understand" then become inflamed with "a passion for justice" and "will gird themselves up to do something about it." Simply slapping an "interracial" label on a group or discussion would not achieve this passion or these actions.[68] Nor would the other extreme of dismissing interested whites or anything labeled interracial.

After criticizing interracial groups' sole dependence upon education, Cuthbert then challenged the idea that social science and generalized theorems were the best way to solve race discrimination. Rather than turning people into statistics, she argued that "[t]here is no way for us to deal adequately with our race problem unless we sense it is composed of individuals, every one of them worthwhile, every one of them to be counted upon and in some way developed in this whole schema; no masses of any group with one remedy for all but the accepting of the mass as a mass composed of individuals."[69] Echoes of Derricotte can be heard in this line, since both she and Derricotte strove to see and to encourage others to see the full humanity of everyone around them. Cuthbert explained that individual human worth was first made clear by Christian teaching and then by modern clarification.

Cuthbert directed her attack not only on social sciences at the level of individual or statistic; she also directed it at the unemotional logic that was meant to be applied to problems.

> This is, again, for both sides of the issue, both for whites and black people, an emotional problem which must be accounted for in our personal lives. Many Negroes find it hard to trust individual white people, to feel that they are worth while; many whites find it just as difficult. Now, until we have such concepts of an actual, worthwhile-ness of all people, not as a problem, not as an issue, not as a battle ground, but as human kind and human folk, we are going to make no progress whatsoever with our problem.[70]

Cuthbert offered no suggestions for how to bring these concepts into reality, other than to acknowledge once again that the work she (and Derricotte) had labored in was at the individual level—each student they spoke to, each YWCA secretary they mentored, each international person they introduced to black culture, each white woman they befriended—it was those women and men who would push race relations forward. Cuthbert did not actually reject social sciences or education; she provided a corrective to the overemphasis upon social sciences' powers which she witnessed among those who viewed interracialism as nothing more than an ineffective sentiment. She was even then pursuing her doctorate at Columbia University. Her thesis studied, with a mixture of modern social scientific methods, the way that black women reintegrated into their communities after earning a higher degree.[71] Cuthbert combined intellectual, logical study with an emphasis upon the illogical and emotional aspects of racism.

Cuthbert arrived at her conclusions of interracialism's effectiveness through her experiences within the YWCA. During the same summer as she gave the speech that anchors this essay, she participated in the inaugural Swarthmore Race Relations Institute sponsored by the Quakers. According to news coverage of the event, Cuthbert praised the YWCA for continuing to open up to the advancement of black secretaries in its ranks. For example, she noted:

> Recently Florence Wilson was selected to represent the industrial group of the YWCA at a national conference. Thus, for the first time, a member of the Negro race has deserved and been awarded an important position of national scope in the Y [that was not directly related to African American concerns]. As they become fitted for the work, Negro workers will be given these important positions and it is only a question of time until there is a Negro on the national board of the YWCA.[72]

With such a statement, she seemed to be advocating patience and waiting for things to change, even while working for the change. She also focused narrowly upon limited integration of one organization, not the transformation of society. As she had explained in her NAACP speech earlier in the summer, she was more willing to talk about the positive changes she witnessed rather than further rail against what was missing. This speech frustrated Du Bois for its acceptance of gradual change—he called her a "trimmer"—and he rejected any comparison that might be made between them.[73] The difference between Du Bois and the two Deans of Women Cuthbert and Derricotte was that Du Bois' primary responsibility and passion was to write and critique. The women's purpose and passion was to build and create education and social facilities for women. Interracialism appealed more to the pragmatic side of the women because it offered concrete solutions whose small gestures they could see manifested in front of them. Du Bois' vision of an equal, just future remained far away. Derricotte and Cuthbert saw what worked while Du Bois saw what could be. Both types of people were necessary.

Juliette Derricotte's Response to Interracialism

Juliette Derricotte devoted her life to encouraging dialogue across the races, motivated by a sense of Christian love that arose out of duty and real emotion. Though she faced severe challenges, she also developed meaningful friendships that transformed the understanding of race within the individuals she met. She had to fight to keep love at the forefront of her reactions, because she was not immune to discrimination and racism. After traveling abroad, for example, she wrote to a friend, "When I share the fellowship of many races without regard to color or creed I find an unconquerable peace of soul and I am very sure that it is the peace which will solve our problem, and yet the first act of discrimination produces a destructive hatred inside of me."[74] She did not expect that interracialism would automatically bring her love in return. Rather, she knew she would have to "love and not be loved." Sometimes she could do that, could "give everything and care naught about the return" and in response she found "the inconquerable peace of the soul," but at other times she wanted "to be loved." That desire brought a "great torment of soul," because it seemed to always be accompanied by conflict.[75] It took great courage and perseverance for Derricotte to remain committed to interracialism, which she did until her tragic death at the young age of thirty-four.

Figure 2. Juliette Derricotte (Reproduced with Permission from Fisk University Franklin Library's Special Collections)

Derricotte understood the complexity of interracial relationships from an early age because her mother, Laura Derricotte, was white. Descended from parents who had moved South following the Civil War, Laura nevertheless lived as a black woman in order to be with her husband and mother her six biracial children.[76] The first time Juliette Derricotte remembered recognizing race was when her mother took her to a dry goods shop and the shopkeeper treated her with respect till he spotted the little brown-skinned girl, no more than five. Suddenly, he refused to serve the mother or treat her as a customer. In her adolescence, Derricotte realized the sacrifices her mother had made, not just in the realm of race, but also by choosing motherhood over the life of the mind. She decided to redeem her mother's life through her own choices, starting with college. Mrs. Derricotte urged her daughter to go to a school with an all-white faculty so that she would have a positive experience with whites. Her mother probably hoped that white missionary stock, like her own parents, would treat her daughter better than the white Georgians she had grown up around. Derricotte did indeed have a successful experience at Talladega College in Alabama and came to love and admire her professors. At college, she joined the YWCA among many other organizations. Upon graduation, the national YWCA recruited her to join them in New York City.

Derricotte was surprised in her new position by two divergent things. One was how much work there still was to be done in building up YWCA resources for black members. Two was the way that her white supervisor treated her. Her boss expected her to have insight into many different arenas of YWCA work, not just work devoted to African Americans. That surprised and encouraged her.

Working for the YWCA, Derricotte also witnessed interracialism cause real changes in the people she met. The national conferences became steadily more integrated. Indeed a group of white and black students together nominated her at a national conference to represent the YWCA at the World's Student Christian Federation in 1924 in England.[77] She toured the United States speaking to black and white college students, encouraging both groups to see the other as fully human and with similar struggles. One time she overheard two white male students discussing her visit and deciding to call off the KKK protest scheduled because of how much they admired her speech and decorum.[78] Another time, she and a white coworker arrived at an integrated college in the Midwest. The black students on campus would only talk to Derricotte and the white students would only talk to her coworker. They left the students with concrete instructions on how to encourage interracial dialogue on campus. When they arrived a year later, the students had been working together fruitfully for a year, particularly doing a volunteer project together. Derricotte was glad to see the latter because it meant they were working together for a cause outside of themselves instead of just sitting around talking about race.

After her death, white women remembered how much Derricotte had transformed their understanding. One wrote "What she has done for individual women's lives is probably not to be estimated; and what she has done for the interracial understanding which she so longed to promote is infinitely more than can be counted." Many women have said to me, who have heard her talk, "From this time on my whole mind is changed on this matter. I never have met a woman like that before, and what she has said, and her own fine personality, have utterly changed my ideas."[79] Another expressed even more specifically how much she had been transformed: "that Jule made a different woman of me. I was a bigoted young Kentuckian when we first knew each other, but I couldn't with any self-respect remain that kind of a person working by the side of her."[80] Derricotte's bearing, kindness, and intelligence is mentioned in almost all of these letters. It was essential in overturning white stereotypes of African Americans. Two decades later, the leaders of the civil rights movement knew the importance of the character of their symbols when they chose to promote Rosa Parks' arrest over that of the unwed mother Claudett Colvin for the same actions.

Derricotte experienced an even greater level of interracialism abroad during her many visits to foreign countries as a YWCA emissary. On each trip, she was greeted with enthusiasm and care by members of different races. At the same time, she learned of racial and ethnic conflict around the world that put African American and white conflict into a global perspective. She witnessed people of historically antagonistic groups start to heal these old wounds by meeting under the banner of Christianity and peace. The start was nonetheless slow. She wrote to her family after many white YWCAs in Asia hosted her, "Everyone has been unbelievably nice & hospitable but there often occurs a certain awkwardness or uncertainty or even the evidence of a great effort being put forth. We are ever so young as American whites and Negroes in this matter of social mingling."[81] Only continuation of the mingling would bring maturity to Americans. Out of her experiences abroad, Mabel Carney of the Columbia University Teachers College asked Derricotte to help her set up an annual series of interracial lectures. Derricotte was one of the first speakers.[82]

Derricotte worried that some of the changes that had come to black campuses in the wake of student and alumni calls for greater autonomy would destroy one of the interracial spaces that she had worked so hard to build. She bemoaned the loss of the "fine old white personalities" that had long taught at the schools in favor of young black teachers, just out of graduate school. When Derricotte went to Talladega as an undergraduate, the whole faculty was white and yet she loved her time there.[83] The younger black professors did not know how to live in the South; they were "very impatient with certain things which they have to go up against in the South. There is missing much of the old 'personal relations' of the older days."[84] The white professors at Fisk recognized Derricotte's sympathy. One remembered that she helped "in blending the new [professors] with the old."[85] Derricotte described Mabel Byrd as an old friend to Jones, but she probably found her sorority sister's confrontation with Jones an illustration of this impatience. Derricotte worried that these changes in faculty meant the passing of these campuses as "the one place where we can prove that an interracial community can exist."[86]

Derricotte's push for interracialism, marked particularly by significant interracial fellowship, friendship, and common work, was different from the kind of integration many black Americans strove for—an integration that allowed blacks equal opportunity for success without requiring significant interaction with whites.[87] These ideals were based first in her daily, weekly interactions on black colleges and with black and white students. She had seen, experienced, and, most importantly, enjoyed interracial fellowship and she had witnessed the personal growth of blacks and whites through that fellowship.

Derricotte's tragic death brought about a dramatic showdown between supporters of interracialism and supporters of protest. In the fall of 1931, Derricotte and three students were driving to Georgia to visit her mother. Just outside of Dalton, Georgia, their car collided with another and Derricotte and one of the students were thrown from the car. The brand new hospital was closed to African Americans, so Derricotte and the student were taken to the house of a black woman that served as an examination room for most local blacks. White doctors examined them there and did what they could. As soon as Derricotte's friends and colleagues at Fisk heard about the accident, they came down and decided the two women should be moved to a black hospital in Chattanooga, Tennessee. Both passed away soon after the long and bumpy car ride.

Many different groups and organizations called for an investigation into the circumstances surrounding Derricotte's care. One of Derricotte's white friends went back to Dalton and interviewed witnesses to the accident. When she inquired of one white man why no one thought to take the two injured women to the hospital, he replied "we don't take 'em there." The NAACP demanded to know what happened. The Quakers sent urgent inquiries to President Jones. All the different groups Derricotte had touched during her short life of thirty-four years wrote their condolences and their urge for something to be done. The CIC took charge of the investigation. Several different details emerged. Some recorded the black woman's house that served as an exam room to be filthy and unfit, while others thought she was quite capable. Du Bois assembled all these divergent details for a long *Crisis* article showcasing the differences between the CIC's report and the witnesses he found.

The CIC said that all that could be done had been done. Jones reported this to his Quaker friends with a sigh of resignation and sadness and they accepted it in the same vein. Many of Derricotte's friends, white and black, pointed out that what the CIC meant was that all that could be done *for a black person* had been done, and that was unacceptable. The CIC meant to record that no personal racism had occurred. The white doctors did all that they could to help Derricotte, but she was simply too far gone from her injuries to be helped. Du Bois and others insisted that people recognize the structural racism that had occurred. Despite his own tendency to accept the CIC's report, Jones had also come to understand how racism transcended individual feelings. He wrote a fellow Quaker that "the remedy lies in attempting to break down the whole segregation system which ostracizes the Negro and then fails to provide him with as good educational, health, and legal protection as that accorded to whites."[88] The solution he articulated, though, was still along the same interracial lines—cooperation among the elite—"the best white and Negro citizens of America should put forth increased effort to see that this sort of thing cannot continue to happen."[89] One of Juliette's friends from the YWCA recognized the potential power of her death: "For it may reach the hearts of white people as no inter-racial addresses have yet done," yet hers was the only letter among hundreds sent to the Derricotte family which mentioned the injustice of the death.[90] Most others ascribed it to God's will and/or expressed profound shock and grief.[91] Derricotte had spent her life transforming individuals' understanding of racism, but it did not help in her last minutes because she had run into strangers who did not know the quality of her character, but only the color of her skin.

Conclusion

In 1930, President Thomas Elsa Jones of Fisk University faced a conundrum common to white liberals in the interwar era. They were used to being in charge and yet were beginning to realize the validity and necessity of black leadership. How could they honor the talents of newly educated blacks while not facing their own privilege? Jones decided to favor black faculty and students who concentrated on the positive aspects of the campus and did not challenge his authority. Within those constraints, Derricotte, Charles Johnson, and others flourished with an unusual amount of personal authority. However, his difficulty with African Americans who contradicted and challenged his admin-istration led to his eventual retirement after World War II, replaced by Johnson.

Du Bois also faced a conundrum in the early 1930s in relationship to his alma mater. He had been instrumental in the overthrow of Fayette McKenzie, and many expected him to continue to be a watchdog of the campus. That was why Byrd solicited his opinion and help when she encountered Jones' policies of faculty appointments, housing, and salaries. Du Bois, however, recognized that he had achieved the primary goal he had sought in 1924–25—Byrd, Derricotte, Frazier, Bond and others were in the room with Jones, able to critique his work. There were African Americans on the trustee board. Black students, faculty, and alumni had a certain amount of power at Fisk, and it was now their turn to use it to build the institution. He recognized that his role as outside intellectual had led to the best outcome and it was time for the administrators and educators to build the campus. In the summer of 1933, he recounted to his friend Lillian Alexander his "pleasant time at Fisk" and how some at Fisk had been terrified of his visit, while others were gleefully awaiting his attacks on Jones, and everyone was "on tip-toe." But it was not his "business continually to try to straighten out Fisk. [. . .] So I wrote to Jones beforehand and explained that the rumors that I was coming to criticize him were all wrong. I was com-ing to talk on Negro education and that is what I did."[92] Fisk was ready to fly on its own, after the careful pushing out of its nest by its most famous alumni.

This essay's brief analysis of Fisk University in the 1930s indicates how challenging it was to foster profitable interracial dialogue. Both sides needed to be humble and invested in real change. The whites involved needed to be ready to cede their historical place of privilege and leadership. African Americans filled three necessary roles—critical outsider intellectual, like Du Bois and Byrd; positive developer of education and mentor to students, like Derricotte; or social scientist gatherer of facts and developer of theorems, like Byrd and Frazier. The latter category represents the transition in race relations dialogue from the Christian interracialism of the 1920s to the social science-dominated interracialism of the 1930s.

Honesty bedeviled interracialism. It was central to fruitful dialogue and yet race seems to squelch honest opinions, then as now. Calling someone a racist is an effective end to a conversation. Byrd attempted to honestly critique her superior's understanding of race, but he could not bear to hear that he might be discriminatory. At the same time, Byrd found it difficult to conclude that Jones' actions might have any reason other than race at their basis. Instead of attempting to work through the problem, Jones threatened Byrd's position and called her disloyal to the university. When she named her essay "Honesty in Race Relations," Marion Cuthbert saw what was needed and what was most difficult to achieve—positive race relations that could actually transform the United States' racial regime. As the 1930s wore on, even those who had espoused interracial cooperation began to focus more on transforming the structure of society instead of persuading individuals out of their racism.

Notes

1. Mabel Byrd to W. E. B. Du Bois, October 9, 1930, Reel 30, Du Bois Papers microfilm.
2. Mabel Byrd, October 9, 1930, Reel 30, Du Bois Papers microfilm; TM Brumfield, "Minutes for Faculty Meeting," minutes (Fisk University, October 7, 1930), Box 31 Folder 13, Thomas Elsa Jones Papers (1-71) Fisk.
3. Byrd, October 9, 1930; Brumfield, "Minutes for Faculty Meeting."
4. Ibid.
5. Not many scholars have studied interracialism as a distinct philosophy. Glenda Gilmore is one exception; Glenda Elizabeth Gilmore, *Defying Dixie: The Radical Roots of Civil Rights, 1919–1950* (New York: W. W. Norton & Company, 2008), 235. The interracialism I am discussing is not to be confused with that which Werner Sollors maps in Werner Sollors, *Interracialism: Black-white Intermarriage in American History, Literature, and Law* (New York: Oxford University Press, 2000). It is about love and sex across the color lines, not about the meeting of educated African and European Americans to discuss the future of race relations.
6. William M. Brewer, "Some Memories of Dr. W. E. B. DuBois," *The Journal of Negro History* 53, no. 4 (October 1, 1968): 346.
7. For example, see Sollors, *Interracialism*.

8. Cuthbert explained, "For some people the inter-racial experience has been one so inept, so futile and so sentimental that they have become nauseated and have refused to consider any such part of our American problem." Marion Cuthbert, "Honesty in Race Relations," Speech (Chicago, IL, July 1, 1933), Reel 9, NAACP 1 papers microfilm.

9. Ibid.

10. Gilmore, *Defying Dixie: The Radical Roots of Civil Rights, 1919–1950*, 235.

11. "Fisk Alumni Hears Du Bois on M'Kenzie," *Chicago Defender*, January 24, 1925.

12. For example, see "Fisk University Mass Meeting a Grand Occasion," *Philadelphia Tribune*, April 23, 1921; "Rosenwald and Party Visit Fisk University," *Chicago Defender*, April 23, 1921; "Dr. Du Bois Creates a Stir," *Norfolk New Journal and Guide*, July 21, 1923; W. E. B. Du Bois, "Black Colleges," *Crisis*, January 1924, sec. Opinion; "Fisk Graduates Work to Meet Offer of Rosenwald," *Chicago Defender*, March 29, 1924; "Fisk Graduate Elected to National YWCA Board," *Chicago Defender*, May 17, 1924; "Endowment of a Million for Fisk University," *Norfolk New Journal and Guide*, July 19, 1924; "Fisk's Million Dollar Endowment Fund," *Opportunity*, August 1924; W. E. B. Du Bois, "Opinion: Fisk," *Crisis*, October 1924; "Fisk University Opens New Term," *Norfolk New Journal and Guide*, October 18, 1924; "Hold Founder's Day Program at Fisk 'U'," *Chicago Defender*, November 29, 1924.

13. This included George Streator, who kept Du Bois informed and later worked as an interim editor of the *Crisis* during the 1934 conflict over Du Bois' role in the NAACP. Martin Anthony Summers, *Manliness and Its Discontents: The Black Middle Class and the Transformation of Masculinity, 1900–1930* (Chapel Hill, NC: University of North Carolina Press, 2004), 265.

14. Howard University was the first to follow Fisk's example. Unlike Fisk, though, the Howard board appointed the first black president of the school, Mordecai Johnson. He was also a scholar and a minister.

15. Kevin Kelly Gaines, *Uplifting the Race: Black Leadership, Politics, and Culture in the Twentieth Century* (Chapel Hill, NC: University of North Carolina Press, 1996), 4.

16. B. B. Eleazer to I. T. and Laura Derricotte, November 10, 1931, Box 2 Folder 44, Ken Oilschlager - Juliette Derricotte Collection, 1924–1950, Archives and Special Collections, J. D. Williams Library, The University of Mississippi. This collection will be called the Derricotte Papers from here on.

17. Anna Arnold Hedgeman, *The Trumpet Sounds: A Memoir of Negro Leadership* (New York: Holt, 1964).

18. YWCA National Board, "Interracial Cooperation: Helpful Suggestions Concerning Relations of White and Colored Citizens," Reel 107, YWCA Papers microfilm, 12, 35.

19. Nancy Marie Robertson, *Christian Sisterhood, Race Relations, and the YWCA, 1906–1946* (Urbana, IL: University of Illinois Press, 2007), 2.

20. Ibid.

21. Robertson, *Christian Sisterhood*, 2.

22. Winifred Wygal, "Juliette Derricotte: Her Character and Her Martyrdom," *Crisis*, March 1932.

23. Marion Cuthbert, *Juliette Derricotte* (New York: Womans Press, 1934).

24. Arch Street Committee on Race Relations, "Annual Report," 1930, Box 2 Race Relations Institute Collection, Swarthmore College Friends Historical Library; Arch Street Committee on Race Relations, "Minutes," January 19, 1932, Box 2 Race Relations Institute Collection, Swarthmore College Friends Historical Library;

Arch Street Committee on Race Relations, "Minutes," October 5, 1932, Box 2 Race Relations Institute Collection, Swarthmore College Friends Historical Library; Arch Street Committee on Race Relations, "Minutes," December 27, 1932, Box 2 Race Relations Institute Collection, Swarthmore College Friends Historical Library.

25. Alexander was an important public health doctor in Philadelphia, ran a woman's health clinic out of her home. She was the sister of Raymond Pace Alexander, prominent lawyer, and the paramour of W. E. B. Du Bois during the late 1920s and early 1930s. David L. Lewis, *W.E.B. Du Bois: The Fight for Equality and the American Century, 1919–1963* (New York: Henry Holt, 2000).

26. Arch Street Committee on Race Relations, "Minutes", May 31, 1929, Box 2 Race Relations Institute Collection, Swarthmore College Friends Historical Library; "Committee On Race Relations," Minutes, November 19, 1929, Box 9, Swarthmore College Friends Historical Library; Arch Street Committee on Race Relations, "Annual Report"; Arch Street Committee on Race Relations, "Conference on Race Relations," Minutes, May 3, 1930, Box 2 Race Relations Institute Collection, Swarthmore College Friends Historical Library.

27. Katrina M. Sanders, *"Intelligent and Effective Direction": The Fisk University Race Relations Institute and the Struggle for Civil Rights, 1944–1969* (New York: Peter Lang, 2005); Patrick J. Gilpin, "Charles S. Johnson and the Race Relations Institutes at Fisk University," *Phylon 1960* 41, no. 3 (Qtr 1980): 300–11; "Race Relations Institute," 2007, http://www.fisk.edu/rri/index.htm (accessed March 7, 2010).

28. "Barred," *Norfolk New Journal and Guide*, September 23, 1933.

29. He was confused to watch the United States provide generous assistance following an earthquake one day, but then within a few weeks ban Japanese immigrants to America because they were deemed unfit residents.

30. Thomas Elsa Jones, "Japanese Banzais for Americans," in *Quaker Adventures: Experiences of Twenty Three Adventurers in International Understanding*, by Edward Thomas (New York: Fleming H. Revell Company, 1928), 139–45.

31. Ibid., 142.

32. James Weldon Johnson, *Along This Way: The Autobiography of James Weldon Johnson*, 1st edn. (New York: Da Capo Press, 2000), 407.

33. Harry Edmonds, "The House with the World Within," *The Rotarian*, October 1938.

34. Thomas Elsa Jones to Vincent Nicholson, September 14, 1926, Box 1 Folder 6, Jones (1-71) Fisk University.

35. Thomas Elsa Jones to Hilda Howard, September 8, 1926, Box 1 Folder 6, Jones (1-71) Fisk University.

36. Leo M. Favrot to Mrs. Trawick, September 11, 1926, Box 1 Folder 6, Jones (1-71) Fisk University.

37. Summers, *Manliness and Its Discontents*, 275.

38. Thomas Elsa Jones, *Progress at Fisk University* (Nashville, TN: Fisk University, 1930), 42.

39. Juliette Derricotte, report, November 2, 1929, Box 31 Folder 4, Jones (original) Fisk University; Thomas Elsa Jones to Juliette Derricotte, telegram, November 6, 1929, Box 31 Folder 4, Fisk University Special Collections; Juliette Derricotte to parents, November 7, 1929, Box 31 Folder 4, Thomas Elsa Jones Papers (1-71) Fisk; Thomas Elsa Jones to Juliette Derricotte, November 13, 1929, Box 31 Folder 4, Fisk University Special Collections.

40. Rufus Clement, "Educational Programs for the Improvement of Race Relations: Interracial Committees," *Journal of Negro Education* 13, no. 3 (Summer 1944): 320.

41. Ibid., 318.
42. W. E. B. Du Bois, "Opinion: Will W. Alexander and the South," *Crisis*, August 1926.
43. Ibid.
44. Harold Cruse and Jerry Gafio Watts, *Harold Cruse's The Crisis of the Negro Intellectual Reconsidered* (New York: Psychology Press, 2004), 53.
45. Brewer, "Some Memories of Dr. W. E. B. DuBois," 345.
46. Ibid.
47. W. E. B. Du Bois, "A Pilgrimage to the Negro Schools," *Crisis*, February 1929, 67–68.
48. Ibid.
49. Ibid.
50. Mabel Byrd to W. E. B. Du Bois, March 5, 1923, Du Bois Papers, http://oubliette. library.umass.edu/view/pageturn/mums312-b020-i333/#page/1/mode/1up (accessed March 7, 2010); Mabel Byrd to W. E. B. Du Bois, March 23, 1923, Du Bois Papers, http://oubliette.library.umass.edu/view/full/mums312-b020-i334 (accessed March 7, 2010); W. E. B. Du Bois to Mabel Byrd, June 6, 1923, Du Bois Papers, http://oubliette.library.umass.edu/view/pageturn/mums312-b020-i336/#page/1/ mode/1up (accessed March 7, 2010); Mabel Byrd to W. E. B. Du Bois, May 31, 1927, Reel 21, Du Bois Papers microfilm; Mabel Byrd to W. E. B. Du Bois, July 8, 1928, Reel 21, Du Bois Papers microfilm; Mabel Byrd to W. E. B. Du Bois, August 22, 1928, Reel 21, Du Bois Papers microfilm; W. E. B. Du Bois to Mabel Byrd, November 1, 1928, Reel 21, Du Bois Papers microfilm; W. E. B. Du Bois to Mabel Byrd, to Byrd while in Geneva, December 7, 1928; Mabel Byrd to W. E. B. Du Bois, December 23, 1928, Reel 21, Du Bois Papers microfilm.
51. Mabel Byrd, "Racial Conflict within Countries," in *Report of the Sixth Congress of the Women's International League for Peace and Freedom*, English (Geneva: International Headquarters, 1929).
52. Ibid.
53. Ibid.
54. Mabel Byrd and Franklin J. Keller, "Reports on the Industrial Status of Negroes" Published by the Julius Rosenwald Fund, 1930, Fisk University Special Collections; "Makes Industrial Survey," *The Pittsburgh Courier* February 1, 1930, 5.
55. Brewer, "Some Memories of Dr. W. E. B. DuBois," 345–46.
56. Frazier as quoted in Adelaide Cromwell, "Frazier's Background and an Overview," in *E. Franklin Frazier and Black Bourgeoisie*, ed. James E. Teele. (Columbia, MO: University of Missouri Press, 2002).
57. E. Franklin Frazier, "Psychological Factors in Negro Health," *Journal of Social Forces* 3, no. 3 (March 1925): 488–90.
58. E. Franklin Frazier, "The Negro and Non-Resistance," *Crisis*, March 1924, 213–14.
59. Jones, *Progress at Fisk University*, 21.
60. Wayne J. Urban, *Black Scholar: Horace Mann Bond, 1904–1972* (Athens, GA: University of Georgia Press, 1992), 56.
61. Horace Mann Bond to Thomas Elsa Jones, November 21, 1932, Box 26 Folder 19, Jones (original) Fisk University.
62. Thomas Elsa Jones to L. Hollingsworth Wood, November 28, 1930, Box 14 Folder 23, Jones (original) Fisk University.
63. Urban, *Black Scholar*, 57.
64. Lillian Alexander to W. E. B. Du Bois, November 1, 1933, Reel 39, Du Bois Papers microfilm.
65. Cuthbert, "Honesty in Race Relations."

66. Ibid.
67. Ibid.
68. Ibid.
69. Ibid.
70. Ibid.
71. Marion V Cuthbert, *Education and Marginality: A Study of the Negro Woman College Graduate*, Educated women (New York: Garland, 1987).
72. "Institute at Swarthmore College Comes to Close," *Chicago Defender*, September 9, 1933.
73. Alexander to Du Bois, November 1, 1933.
74. Juliette Derricotte to Jane [Juanita Saddler], [1924], Box 3 Folder 50, Derricotte Papers.
75. Ibid.
76. The census takers recorded her race as black, but Derricotte told Frazier that her mother was white on one of his family surveys. Juliette Derricotte and E. Franklin Frazier, "A Study of the Negro Family Form No. 616", n.d., Box 131-97 Folder 1, E. Franklin Frazier Papers MSRC; "Athens Ward 4, Clarke, Georgia, Roll: T623 187, Page: 3B," Twelfth Census of the United States (Washington, DC: National Archives and Records Administration, 1900), Ancestry.com, Provo, UT: The Generations Network, Inc.
77. "Selected as One of 5 Women to Go Abroad Soon," *Pittsburgh Courier*, June 14, 1924.
78. Cuthbert, *Juliette Derricotte*.
79. Lucetta Daniel to Mrs. Derricotte, November 15, 1931, Box 3 Folder 1, Derricotte Papers.
80. Gladys Bryson to Mrs. Derricotte, November 15, 1931, Box 3 Folder 4, Derricotte Papers.
81. Juliette Derricotte to family, March 11, 1929, Box 1 Folder 21, Derricotte Papers.
82. Mabel Carney to Mrs. Laura Carney, November 16, 1931, Box 3 Folder 9, Derricotte Papers.
83. Mary Jenness, *Twelve Negro Americans* (Freeport, NY: Books for Libraries Press, 1936), 168. Derricotte and Frazier, "A Study of the Negro Family Form No. 616."
84. Juliette Derricotte to Max Yergan, July 24, 1929, RG 58, Box 13, Folder 191, Yale Divinity Library Special Collections.
85. Dora Scribner to I. T. and Laura Derricotte, November 11, 1931, Box 2 Folder 58, Derricotte Papers.
86. Ibid.
87. See for example Anderson, *The Education of Blacks in the South, 1860–1935*; Banks, *Black Intellectuals*.
88. Thomas Elsa Jones, November 30, 1931, Box 31 Folder 5, Jones (original) Fisk University.
89. Ibid.
90. Belle C. Morrill to Mrs. Derricotte, January 16, 1932, Box 3 Folder 33, Derricotte Papers.
91. It is strange that none of the people so outraged by Derricotte's death, like W. E. B. Du Bois, Walter White, or Langston Hughes, sent condolence letters to her parents like her acquaintances and friends from HBCUs and the YWCA did. It makes me wonder if the letters from famous people were separated and lost. It was a lucky break that these letters were found in a thrift store and donated to the University of Mississippi. See Boxes 1–3 of the Ken Oilschlager—Juliette

Derricotte Collection, 1924–1950, Archives and Special Collections, J. D. Williams Library, The University of Mississippi.
92. W. E. B. Du Bois to Lillian Alexander, June 23, 1933, Reel 39, Du Bois Papers microfilm.

Bibliography

Archive Collections

1910 Census. Canonsburg Borough, Washington County, Pennsylvania, April 29, 1910. http://www.ancestry.org (accessed February 7, 2010).
Du Bois, W. E. B. Papers. University of Massachusetts Amherst, microfilm, accessed at Michigan State University.
Johnson, Charles. 1-21. Fisk University Special Collections.
Jones, Thomas Elsa. Original and 1-71. Fisk University Special Collections.
Ken Oilschlager—Juliette Derricotte Collection, 1924–1950, Archives and Special Collections, J. D. Williams Library, The University of Mississippi. Race Relations Institute Collection. Swarthmore College Friends Historical Library.
Kotschnig, Walter. Papers, SUNY Albany Special Collections.
National Association for the Advancement of Colored People Papers 1, microfilm.
Spingarn, Joel Elias. Papers. Moorland Spingarn Research Center, Howard University.
Young Women's Christian Association Papers, Sophia Smith College, Smith College, microfilm.

Newspapers and Magazines

Chicago Defender
Crisis
New York Times
Norfolk New Journal and Guide
Opportunity
Philadelphia Tribune
Pittsburgh Courier

Primary Sources

Brewer, William M. "Some Memories of Dr. W. E. B. DuBois." *The Journal of Negro History* 53, no. 4 (October 1, 1968): 345–48.
Byrd, Mabel. "Racial Conflict within Countries." In *Report of the Sixth Congress of the Women's International League for Peace and Freedom*. English. Geneva: International Headquarters, 1929.
Cuthbert, Marion. *Juliette Derricotte*. New York: Womans Press, 1934.
———. *We Sing America*. New York: Friendship Press, 1936.
———. *Education and Marginality: A Study of the Negro Woman College Graduate*. New York: Garland, 1987.
———. "'The Negro Today' Church and Society (January 1932): 1-2." In *Harlem's Glory: Black Women Writing 1900–1950*, edited by Lorraine Elena Roses and Ruth Elizabeth Randolph. Cambridge, MA: Harvard University Press, 1996.

Franklin, John Hope. *Mirror to America: The Autobiography of John Hope Franklin*. 1st edn. New York: Farrar, Straus and Giroux, 2005.
Hedgeman, Anna Arnold. *The Trumpet Sounds: A Memoir of Negro Leadership*. New York: Holt, 1964.
Jones, Thomas Elsa. "Japanese Banzais for Americans." In *Quaker Adventures: Experiences of Twenty Three Adventurers in International Understanding*, edited by Edward Thomas, 139–45. New York: Fleming H. Revell Company, 1928.
———. *Progress at Fisk University*. Nashville, TN: Fisk University, 1930.

Secondary Sources

Banks, William M. *Black Intellectuals: Race and Responsibility in American Life*. New York: W. W. Norton, 1996.
Clement, Rufus. "Educational Programs for the Improvement of Race Relations: Interracial Committees." *Journal of Negro Education* 13, no. 3 (Summer 1944): 316–28.
Cromwell, Adelaide. "Frazier's Background and an Overview." In *E. Franklin Frazier and Black Bourgeoisie*, edited by James E. Teele. Columbia, MO: University of Missouri Press, 2002.
Cruse, Harold, and Jerry Gafio Watts. *Harold Cruse's The Crisis of the Negro Intellectual Reconsidered*. New York: Psychology Press, 2004.
Gaines, Kevin Kelly. *Uplifting the Race: Black Leadership, Politics, and Culture in the Twentieth Century*. Chapel Hill, NC: University of North Carolina Press, 1996.
Gilmore, Glenda Elizabeth. *Defying Dixie: The Radical Roots of Civil Rights, 1919–1950*. New York: W. W. Norton & Co, 2008.
Gilpin, Patrick J. "Charles S. Johnson and the Race Relations Institutes at Fisk University." *Phylon 1960* 41, no. 3 (Qtr 3, 1980): 300–11.
Gilpin, Patrick J., and Marybeth Gasman. *Charles S. Johnson: Leadership beyond the Veil in the Age of Jim Crow*. Albany, NY: State University of New York Press, 2003.
Kientz, Lauren. "Untrammeled Thinking: The Promise and Peril of the Second Amenia Conference, 1920–1940." PhD, East Lansing, MI: Michigan State University, 2010.
Lamon, Lester C. "The Black Community in Nashville and the Fisk University Student Strike of 1924–1925." *The Journal of Southern History* 40, no. 2 (May 1974): 225–44.
Lewis, David L. *W.E.B. Du Bois: The Fight for Equality and the American Century, 1919–1963*. New York: Henry Holt, 2000.
Lipsitz, George. *The Possessive Investment in Whiteness: How White People Profit from Identity Politics*. Philadelphia, PA: Temple University Press, 1998.
Reed, Touré F. *Not Alms but Opportunity: The Urban League & the Politics of Racial Uplift, 1910–1950*. Chapel Hill, NC: University of North Carolina Press, 2008.
Robbins, Richard. *Sidelines Activist: Charles S. Johnson and the Struggle for Civil Rights*. Oxford, MS: University of Mississippi Press, 1996.
Robertson, Nancy Marie. *Christian Sisterhood, Race Relations, and the YWCA, 1906–1946*. Urbana, IL: University of Illinois Press, 2007.
Sanders, Katrina M. *"Intelligent and Effective Direction": The Fisk University Race Relations Institute and the Struggle for Civil Rights, 1944–1969*. New York: Peter Lang, 2005.
Sollors, Werner. *Interracialism: Black-White Intermarriage in American History, Literature, and Law*. New York: Oxford University Press, 2000.

Summers, Martin Anthony. *Manliness and Its Discontents: The Black Middle Class and the Transformation of Masculinity, 1900–1930.* Chapel Hill, NC: University of North Carolina Press, 2004.

Urban, Wayne J. *Black Scholar: Horace Mann Bond, 1904–1972.* Athens, GA: University of Georgia Press, 1992.

"Only Organized Effort Will Find the Way Out!": Faculty Unionization at Howard University, 1918–1950

Timothy Reese Cain

This article explores the long history of unionization at Howard University, demonstrating the important roles that the institution and its faculty played in efforts to organize educational workers. Faculty at Howard were the first to form an American Federation of Teachers local on a college campus and, years later, the first to bargain for a faculty contract. In between a separate local galvanized faculty around campus, metropolitan, and national issues. The unions' initial successes and longer-term struggles reflect both local situations and larger battles over organized labor.

College faculty unionization began in November 1918 when twenty-nine members of Howard University formed the Howard University Teachers Union and affiliated with the American Federation of Teachers (AFT) as Local 33. Nearly three decades later, in February 1947, Howard faculty voted 130–1 in favor of being represented by a very different union, the Howard Branch of the United Public Workers of America, Congress of Industrial Organizations (UPW-CIO). Three months later, the union successfully bargained the first contract between a faculty and a college or university in the nation. In between, a third union local, the Howard Teachers Union (HTU—AFT Local 440) counted Doxey A. Wilkerson, Ralph Bunche, E. Franklin Frazier, and W. Alpheus Hunton among its members and was central to social activism in Washington, DC, debates over academic freedom at Howard, and the clashes over communism that split the AFT. This essay examines the largely

Perspectives on the History of Higher Education 29 (2012): 113-150
© 2012. ISBN: 978-1-4128-4771-1

ignored unionization of college faculty before the 1960s by focusing on organizing at a single institution at the nexus of racial, professional, and political debates. In doing so, it offers historical background to modern considerations and responds to calls for more scholarship on white collar and public unionization.[1] Further, while understanding early faculty attempts and experiences with unionization is in itself important, this essay contributes through its exploration of the efforts of leading Black intellectuals at Howard University, "the leading site, despite internal and external pressures to the contrary, of black intellectual radicalism in academe during the interwar era."[2] It addresses shortcomings in our understanding of the interplay of politics and faculty activism while meeting Ellen Swartz's recent challenge to "'re-member' American educational history" by correcting the exclusion and misrepresentation of African Americans' roles in standard historical interpretations.[3]

This essay is informed by and responds to gaps in several different strands of literature on higher education, unionization, and African American intellectual history. Despite the importance of unionization in modern higher education, few scholars have considered the beginnings of the movement and fewer have studied, or even acknowledged, the Howard unions. Histories of the CIO ignore college faculty. Those of the AFT offer slight treatment of early faculty organization, even though professors played increasingly important roles that far outweighed their numbers. William Edward Eaton noted that the Great Depression facilitated some faculty organizing and, along with Marjorie Murphy, mentioned Howard faculty as participants in the battles over communism or as part of legislative efforts.[4] Until recently, only Jeannette A. Lester's dissertation addressed faculty unionization in depth, providing an overview of the activities of AFT college locals over a fifty-year period. This essay expands and complicates her interpretations of Locals 33 and 440, pointing to more varied reasons for their founding and broader ranges of activities and accomplishments, while also extending the analysis beyond the AFT to include the crucial role of the CIO.[5] The larger disregard of early faculty unionization implicates the relative neglect of professional workers in treatments of labor history and the emphasis on K-12 educators in discussions of teachers unions. With few exceptions, those who have considered the history of faculty unions have either implicitly or explicitly indicated that they were insignificant prior to the beginning of collective bargaining in the 1960s.[6] This perspective is problematic, including because these unions offered important outlets for faculty activity, provided opportunities for united action, and revealed key aspects of the conditions of faculty employment. Moreover, faculty successfully bargained almost two decades earlier than is generally acknowledged.

Jonathon Scott Holloway's *Confronting the Veil: Abram Harris Jr., E. Franklin Frazier, and Ralph Bunche, 1919–1941*, an intellectual history of three faculty members involved in Local 440, examined the social, political, and intellectual ideas swirling around the campus and community, including a page on Frazier's union activities. Holloway's contributions are significant as they locate these Howard University social scientists within their intellectual and cultural contexts. Holloway argued that the HTU became a primary outlet for social activism among faculty, although he did not engage with the topic after a brief listing of some of the protests with which the local was involved.[7] The vast literatures on race and labor also offer important insight into social, political, and economic activities, although without explicit attention to unionization at Howard University. Labor historians cite Frazier's and Harris' scholarship on African American workers, but the field's larger focus on the organization of manual laborers largely precludes consideration of the union activities of Frazier, Harris, and their colleagues.[8] Through its consideration of AFT, UFWA, and UPW-CIO locals at Howard University, this essay begins to address these omissions.

Faculty Unionization Begins at Howard

The years around the turn of the twentieth century saw great change in American higher education. Some colleges reoriented themselves toward research, some eliminated preparatory departments, many shifted their curricular offerings and administrative operations, and many expanded greatly in size. These changes occurred across institutional types, as small colleges became research universities, normal schools became teachers colleges, junior colleges separated from high schools, and other institutions reconsidered their roles in a widening educational landscape. Along with these changes came concern and criticism, including among faculty who sought professionalization and freedom from overreaching presidents and governing boards. With these criticisms and celebrated violations of academic freedom, elite faculty formed the American Association of University Professors (AAUP) in 1915 as a way to legitimize faculty input into governance and protect faculty interests. The AAUP rejected unionization for more than a half century, arguing that it would bias the professoriate on labor issues, divide faculty rather than unite them, and diminish the professional nature of the occupation.[9] Still, other educators saw benefits in unionization, and in April 1916, four unions from Chicago and one from Gary, IN, formally affiliated as the AFT and received a charter from the American Federation of Labor (AFL). They were soon joined by teachers in New York, Washington, DC, and other municipalities in creating a national union seeking improvement in teachers' working conditions, job security, and remuneration.[10] The early union celebrated Columbia University professor John Dewey's support but was an organization of and for K-12 teachers. At its July 1918 convention, though, the AFT loosened its membership criteria and allowed for union locals on college campuses. Beginning with the founding of the Howard University Teachers Union, college and normal school faculty formed twenty AFT locals over the next two years.[11]

Howard University has played an important and unique role in the history of American higher education. Chartered by the United States Congress in 1867 and initially funded by the Freedman's Bureau, the institution had a special commitment to educating members of underserved populations, including but not limited to African Americans. Although technically a private institution, its location in the nation's capital and mission linked it to the federal government, a tie that was strengthened by congressional appropriations beginning in 1879. These funds, though needed, were not unencumbered and were especially vulnerable as annual gifts to the institution without authorizing legislation until 1928.[12] The first two decades of the twentieth century saw significant change at Howard related to larger shifts in American education, as well as changing ideas about the purposes of higher education for African Americans and roles for African American intellectuals. Internal factors, including unstable leadership, institutional expansion, and curricular restructuring, combined with external events such as World War I to make the period especially tumultuous. In July 1918, the institution named James Stanley Durkee as its eleventh president. Rather than stabilizing Howard, Durkee's appointment contributed to continuing discord, including due to his elimination of the institution's preparatory department, his administrative centralization, and concerns over racial bias and cultural misunderstanding.[13]

Concomitant with these shifts were changes in the experiences of faculty members at the institution, with Walter Dyson terming the period from 1890 to 1920 as one of "rapid degradation of the professor in University affairs."[14] Dyson, a professor and institutional historian, pointed to this decline in faculty power and status as central to faculty looking outside the institution for support. He noted that teachers who had been emboldened by the war were drawn to the AFT as a fighting organization.[15] On November 18, 1918, one week after the end of the war and four months after both Durkee was appointed president and the AFT loosened membership criteria, Dyson and a group of colleagues applied for an AFT charter. This initial group of twenty-four men and five women, many of whom were instructors in the institution's undergraduate division, included faculty who were simultaneously serving in administrative roles such as dean of men and librarian, as well as activist, lecturer, and former member of the Washington, DC, Board of Education member Mary Church Terrell, who lacked a formal position at Howard.[16]

From its founding, Local 33 was interested in changing Howard's governance and providing faculty with greater input into institutional affairs. Its constitution noted a desire to unite faculty from across the institution to affect change in educational standards and working conditions, and correspondence with the AFT national office further indicates a focus on democratizing the institution.[17] In 1919, when the institution's faculty appointed a committee to address "Rules for Cooperation between Faculty, Officers of Administration and Trustees," they included three Local 33 officers and at least one other union member among the five committee members.[18] The local supported the efforts but lacked formal standing to participate in an official capacity. Even more troubling for the local, the resulting report, which called for an elected Committee on Administration made up of faculty members with direct access to the Board of Trustees, went unheeded. Indeed, although labor writer V. B. Turner noted that the union had a "membership of 38 cooperating with the university organization in bringing about desirable change" in August 1919 and Callis later claimed the union "flourished," Dyson termed its experiences as "struggling desperately" after "rendering itself impotent" by a constitutional provision against striking.[19] Indeed, there is no clear evidence that Local 33 affected academic administration or control at the institution.

The local's second concern was the larger solvency of the institution and its implications for both faculty conditions and educational quality. At its fourth national convention in December 1919–January 1920, the AFT supported Local 33 by passing a resolution in favor of the Howard Board of Trustees' recent request for a substantial increase in federal appropriations. In doing so, the AFT called on all members to communicate their backing to their congressmen.[20] Demonstrating at least conditional institutional acceptance, Emmet J. Scott, the newly hired secretary of Howard University, requested that the AFT forward the resolutions to the chairs of the appropriations committees of the House of Representatives and the Senate. AFT Secretary-Treasurer Freeland G. Stecker complied, but there is no evidence that the resolution had any affect.[21] More importantly, this reliance on federal funding complicated the local's existence, and Scott's approval of the union activity was not uniformly shared among institutional leaders—as became apparent in the ensuing months.

These years just after World War I were particularly contentious as anti-German sentiment turned into a fear of anything deemed un-American, returning veterans had difficulty finding work in grim economic times, workers clashed with employers in episodes such as the Boston Police Strike and the Seattle General Strike, and racial tensions exacerbated difficult conditions. Washington, DC, was among the urban centers affected by these events, including the bombing at Attorney General Alexander Palmer's residence in June 1919 and the race riots in July 1919 that left multiple people dead or wounded. Both the Red Scare and the Red Summer influenced the course of unionization at Howard and highlighted the continuous political and racial divides as the institution fought for support and approval from Congress. In January 1920, congressional pressure on the institution increased when Senator Reed Smoot (R-Utah) endangered Howard's financial standing by threatening to block any further appropriations to the institution unless Albert Rhys Williams' *Seventy-Six Questions and Answers on Bolsheviks and Soviets* was removed from the library. The tract, which had been donated to the library by a student, justified the Soviet government and exaggerated its successes. Durkee immediately removed the offending material, apologized for it ever appearing in the library, and wrote to Smoot that he believed that the government should suppress such publications. In ensuing years, Durkee remained leery of crossing Congress and sought to defuse potential political controversies on campus.[22] It was in this context that Howard University Teachers Union struggled to survive and, on April 3, 1920, the local voted itself out of existence.[23] Local member McLeod Harvey explained to the AFT that the administration could not afford to "antagonize in the slightest the feelings of even unreasonable government officials."[24] Combined with the administration's concerns regarding the AFT's connections to the AFL, the union voted itself out of existence over the objection of a few of its members. The nation's first faculty union succumbed to internal and external pressure, as did all but one of the AFT locals in the era.[25]

New Institutional Leadership and New Pressures

The mid-1920s was a tumultuous period at Howard University, with Durkee often at the center of the troubles. In 1925, simmering controversies over authoritarian management came to a head with student strikes involving the nature and content of the compulsory chapel services, dismissals of long-standing faculty and administrators, alumni protests, and accusations that the president accosted faculty with whom he disagreed. The controversies had racial overtones since Durkee, who was White, simultaneously presided over a Whites-only institution in Boston. When Durkee was alleged to have called a professor a "contemptible cur," some interpreted it as demeaning to all African Americans. These events and accusations were covered in publications including *The Crisis* and *The Afro-American*, with the latter running a series of anonymous columns calling for Durkee's dismissal and referring to the institution as the "Durkee plantation."[26] Shortly after W. E. B. DuBois' scathing critique in *The Nation* in March 1926, Durkee succumbed to the accumulated pressure and submitted his resignation. He was replaced by Mordecai Johnson, the man who would lead Howard until 1960.[27]

Johnson, a Baptist minister and the first African American president of the institution, was a strong and, at times, controversial leader. With the assistance of Julius Rosenwald, the General Education Board, and continuing (rather than annual) congressional appropriations, Johnson quickly provided a more stable foundation for Howard and improved its faculty, infrastructure, and curricular offerings.[28] Through his strong administration, his dynamism, his ability to overpower those with whom he disagreed, and his overriding belief in his own ideas and abilities, he also generated continuous controversy, including among faculty who often resented their lack of voice in the institution's governance. As Logan noted, "Very few of those who have known President Johnson hold neutral views about him; the vast majority are fervent admirers or bitter critics . . .. There is, however, one view about him on which friends, adversaries, and neutrals tend to agree—that he possessed a 'Messianic Complex.'"[29] Some outside of the institution were simultaneously concerned about Johnson's leadership, resulting in an investigation into the use of federal funds and harsh alumni challenges over Johnson's treatment of Dean Lucy Diggs Slowe and other matters. Several times during the era, members of the House of Representatives questioned Johnson's politics and accused him of espousing communist principles and enabling the radicals on his faculty to do so. These accusations often included calls for increased governmental oversight of the institution, threats to it appropriations, and challenges to Johnson's continued leadership.[30]

These charges involving communism at Howard were both indicative of larger trends in American education and in response to local events. The 1930s saw both greater freedom for college faculty to pursue leftist political and social ideas and a backlash against those pursuits.[31] At Howard, Johnson's outspokenness combined with larger societal shifts, including those caused by dissatisfaction with the collapsed economy, to allow for the faculty to engage in numerous scholarly and activist endeavors that were previously prohibited. Further, at several points during his presidency, Johnson defended academic freedom and the rights of his faculty to pursue controversial political questions. In 1933, he told Congress that while he was not a communist, he disagreed with those who believed that communists should be persecuted or believed that the "Russian experiment" was without any value. Two years later, he responded to congressional concern by claiming that the institution would be better off without federal support than without academic freedom, a position supported by Secretary of the Interior Harold Ickes, who headed the government's oversight of the institution.[32] Although the stresses on leftist faculty increased across the nation as the decade progressed, Johnson was largely, if not entirely, able to protect his politically active faculty during this era. For, as he noted in 1953 amidst House Un-American Activities Committee investigations into Communist Party infiltration into American institutions, "It would be better that our American institutions lose the last dollar than that we should turn our faculties into a group of frightened sheep, afraid to think independently, and afraid to go out to dinner for fear that they may accidently sit down by somebody who is a member of the Communist Party."[33] Still, the freedom was not universal, and some of the limits eventually implicated unionization and led to the departure of faculty members such as Doxey Wilkerson.

It was in this atmosphere of restricted involvement in institutional administration but freedom to lead political lives that Howard University was able to secure numerous leading intellectuals for its faculty, including Frazier, Harris, Bunche, Hunton, Alain Locke, Sterling Brown, William Hastie, Charles Thompson, and Charles H. Wesley.[34] Also significant, increasing social protests and political activism around racial segregation and class divisions engaged many at Howard. In 1933, Howard faculty members Harris, Bunche, Brown, Charles Houston, and Emmet Dorsey, as well as Frazier, who moved from Fisk University to Howard shortly thereafter, attended the Second Amenia Conference at Joel Spingarn's estate in New York. The conference brought together more than two dozen young African American activists and intellectuals to examine the National Association for the Advancement of Colored People and the relationship between economic change and civil rights.[35] Closer to home, Howard faculty engaged in, led, or challenged the political, social, and intellectual movements swirling around Washington, DC. With its educated African American population but strict segregation, the city became a locus of activism. The New Negro Alliance was founded in 1933 to protest discriminatory hiring practices at stores serving African American patrons. The organization attracted both support and criticism at Howard, with Hastie serving as the organization's legal counsel but Bunche and Harris bemoaning its emphasis on racial solidarity over economic change. Two years later, Howard hosted a conference on "The Position of the Negro in Our National Economic Crisis," which led to the formation of the National Negro Congress (NNC), one of the most significant progressive organizations of the period. Students were similarly involved in social and political activism, including campus protests of the Scottsboro Boy's treatment in 1931. Following Bunche's success in being served at the White-only congressional cafeteria in 1933, undergraduate Kenneth Clark, who later played a celebrated role in *Brown v. Board*, led a group of thirty students in an attempt to gain similar access. The students were arrested and threatened with expulsion by Johnson but were saved by Bunche's intervention. The following year, 150 students participated in protests of lynching and the student newspaper, *The Hilltop*, was a frequent outlet for political and social commentary. By the mid-1930s when students took part in the national student strike against war, then, Howard University was awash in activism.[36]

The AFT Returns to Howard

Concurrent with these events at Howard, the national AFT recovered from the difficulties of the period just after World War I and made inroads into colleges and universities. With a changed political and economic climate, the union expanded, quadrupling its membership by the late 1930s. Beginning with the 1928 founding of Local 204 at Yale University, college faculty demonstrated more interest in unionization and the AFT increasingly attempted to recruit them, including through the creation of a Committee for Organizing the Colleges and Universities. By the end of the decade, almost 2,000 college faculty had joined locals on their campuses. These locals were formed to help foster social change, to support K-12 teachers in their own efforts to unionize, and to fight for academic freedom. College faculty also increasingly assumed leadership positions in the AFT, including Yale educator Jerome Davis and Teachers College professor George S. Counts, both of whom served as president. Of course, as the decade progressed, the AFT faced internal struggles over communism. These appeared in 1933 and 1935 with charges of Communist Party domination of the Teachers Union of the City of New York and the resulting mass exodus of liberal anticommunists from the local. Struggles became more pressing in the later years, eventually resulting in the 1941 revocation of charters of three locals, two of which had significant college faculty membership.[37]

The exact chain of events that led to faculty unionization returning to Howard University remains somewhat obscured, although the faculty at the institution did receive material from the AFT encouraging organization just before the founding of HTU (Local 440). Hylan Lewis, a founding member, later recalled both institutional and societal catalysts:

> The organization, changing leadership, and programs of this pioneering faculty union at Howard reflected a conjunction of forces. Initially, the precipitant for a resort to unionism was an acute conflict between a senior faculty member and the president of the university. This happened against a backdrop of long-term dissatisfaction, frustration, and even anger among some senior faculty—much of this directed at the president—and the changing climate of the times, which featured generally aggressive trade union expansion—eventually, if not initially, in part fueled by Marxian and "old left" ideology and politics.[38]

In early January 1936, twenty faculty members applied for a charter from the national union and, led by Eugene C. Holmes and Bunche, organized their first meeting for later in the month.[39] On January 18, the group officially accepted its charter in the presence of AFT National Vice President Mary T. Grossman, was addressed by President of the National Recovery Administration John Donovan, elected temporary officers, and appointed committees to begin its program. It was at this point that, in the words of temporary president Henry A. Callis, "Local 440 began its life."[40]

The local's by-laws were completed in March and noted the importance of the labor movement and its role as a progressive force for change. It described unionization as a means to unite educators with other laborers and to "co-operate in this field in the advancement of education and resistance to all reaction." The local claimed that it would not interfere with appropriate administrative authority but that "where issues arise which are clearly those of academic freedom or discrimination against individuals on grounds of race, or of social, religious, economic, political opinions or activities, the Teachers' Union will be prepared to have a fair investigation made and appropriate proposals brought forward."[41] Finally, it argued that the current economic distress was threatening retrenchment in educational offerings and that the union would do all that it could to prevent retrenchment, expand opportunities, and improve teaching. Less than a month later, in his annual report, Callis elaborated on these ideas, linked Local 440's goals to those of the larger AFT, and pointed to the specific needs of African American students and educators in a segregated society. At the same time, he emphasized the class issues involved. He argued:

> Education nationally is affected by the enactment of laws requiring teachers' oaths in twenty-one states. Negro education remains throttled. Economic forces have circumscribed the Negro intellectual and the Negro laborer alike. We are just beginning to see the identity of our interests. We have yet to understand that this is the identity of all workers, and not solely of race . . . .[42]

Callis pointed to the segregation that prevented Howard students and faculty from partaking in the cultural opportunities that Washington, DC, offered and that closed careers and positions to African Americans. The economic strife of the 1930s had extended and exacerbated the problems.

> [T]he depression has brought the professional, the artisan and the day worker together. The way to a satisfactory solution lies in the organization of all workers. Every effort to strengthen the protection of human welfare meets with resistance. By joining ourselves through the American Federation of Teachers, with the American Federation of Labor, we place ourselves in position to increase our knowledge of and experience with the labor movement. We should certainly offer intelligent leadership to Negro labor and hasten the democratization of all labor. For seventy years the Negro has been a suppliant for civil rights and social justice. If we can enlist organized workers in support of this cause, the objective will be won. For seventy years other methods have failed.[43]

Local 440 was then, from its beginning, interested in social, racial, and economic issues at the local and national levels.

Local 440's Social and Political Activity

Local 440's founding offered Howard faculty a new avenue through which to channel their social activism. With an organizational ethos that allowed for considerable work outside the institution, HTU addressed racial and economic issues within Washington, DC, while also working to strengthen ties to other labor federations. Indeed, as Wilkerson later noted, the members of the union "were also—some of us most fundamentally—concerned with labor as a force for social progress, and the activities of the Howard Teachers Union extended far beyond campus, in support of working men's struggles in many places."[44] The local supported student political activity and considered founding a Workers Educational School. In the late 1930s, HTU passed a resolution against neutrality in the Spanish Civil War, called on Congress to support the loyalists in their battle against fascism, and supported the American League for Peace and Democracy's "Lift the Embargo Campaign."[45] In 1939, the local was among the organizations supporting the Citizen's Committee for Fair Taxation, which appeared before Congress in opposition to a proposed sales tax in the District of Columbia and in an effort to change the tax code to benefit individuals instead of businesses.[46] The union was also involved in broader labor issues, keeping its members informed on the battles over minimum wages, supporting other unions in the city, and advocating for WPA workers and programs.[47]

Although other issues were considered, most of this work with other labor and social groups involved protesting the segregation that blighted Washington, DC, and much of the nation. Only weeks after its founding, HTU launched a campaign against discrimination at the National Theatre's production of *Porgy and Bess*, which included Howard faculty member Todd Duncan performing as Porgy. The theater had never before allowed African American attendees and posted guards at the doors to try to prevent African Americans from passing as White to gain admittance. Led by Bunche, HTU rallied support from other labor groups in the city, met with the theater's management, and threatened to picket the theater with the support of other local unions.[48] The National Theatre agreed to suspend its policies for the performance, although it reverted to them immediately after *Porgy and Bess* concluded. In ensuing years, HTU pushed for additional exceptions to the policy and further worked to end segregation at other venues, including following the Daughters of the American Revolution's refusal to allow Marian Anderson to perform at its Constitution Hall in 1939.[49] HTU similarly protested exclusionary practices in the federal government, in organizations such as the American Library Association, and within other unions, while also working with organizations including the NNC for larger social change.[50]

Institutional Interests and Academic Freedom

Johnson's autocratic administration provided a backdrop of discontent that fostered the union, but there is no record of a particular grievance or institutional event having precipitated HTU other than Lewis' aforementioned recollection. The local's constitution pledged to protect academic freedom, but it appears to have been more of a larger principle and national consideration rather than related to a recent local event. No mention was made of specific institutional concerns at the founding, and existing correspondence from the opening months similarly neglects institutional issues.[51] During the 1937–1938 academic year, though, the local began focusing more explicitly on the situation at Howard, first by supporting a petition for increases in instructors' salaries and then by forming a committee on tenure and salary to make recommendations to institutional authorities.[52] These efforts took on new urgency a month later with the announcement of the impending dismissal of Callis, effective after a one-year leave of absence. At the time, Callis was an associate professor of medicine with nine years of service and a past president of Local 440. Particularly galling for Callis and the members of Local 440 was the institution's refusal to provide a reason for the dismissal or to provide a fair and adequate hearing.

Based on Callis' case, the local appealed to the Faculty of the College of Liberal Arts to immediately formulate recommendations for new tenure and dismissal policies. The faculty unanimously concurred and authorized its Committee on Tenure and Retirement to propose changes to institutional policy. This committee, which included several HTU members, endorsed a policy substantively the same as the one proposed by the union. It included reviews of proposed dismissals by an elected faculty committee, faculty members' rights to hearings before said committee prior to dismissals, and formal charges being presented in detail.[53] The Board of Trustees approved the plan and, in the summer and fall of 1939, it received its first test. Indicative of larger difficulties within the School of Medicine, Dean Numa P. G. Adams informed another HTU member, Assistant Professor Moses Wharton Young, that he was being released for insubordination. HTU protested, and the elected faculty committee reviewed the case. The committee found that the dismissal was unwarranted and recommended to the board that Young be retained—a recommendation that the board upheld.[54] Although things remained somewhat troubled in the school, tenure was more secure than had previously been the case, in large part through HTU's work.[55]

These HTU efforts for change in the tenure system aided Young, but they were too late to assist Callis. For two years, the members petitioned the board for reconsideration, called on outside agencies to protest the dismissal, and urged the institution to reinstate their former colleague. Local 440 appealed to the AFT national, which had recently become much more active in the area of academic freedom, to provide support and funding for their efforts, including through the recently created National Defense Fund. The local generated publicity about the case and alleged an antiunion bias in the College of Medicine, claiming that the trustees allowed the bias to continue by not reinstating Callis.[56] In response, the trustees invited the Adjustment Committee of HTU to present its case to a committee of the board and indicated a willingness to hold a hearing. This hearing, though, was refused as inadequate when it was learned that it would merely be an opportunity for Callis to make a statement before the committee but without the involvement of administrative officers to protect them from the embarrassment of defending their actions.[57] Finally, in March 1940, an investigatory committee of the AFT National Academic Freedom Committee visited Howard University at HTU's request. Led by New York University Dean of General Education Ned H. Dearborn, the committee interviewed the parties to the situation, reviewed documentary evidence, and determined that the institution had not violated any of the formal policies or procedures in effect at the time of Callis' dismissal. Still, it found that the institution had abridged the policy that it had since approved; had violated what the union considered standard practice; and had acted unethically by not stating charges, providing a true hearing, or continuing a faculty member with the presumption of tenure.[58] Although willing to address the larger issues, the trustees refused to reconsider Callis' termination.

This interest in faculty rights also led Local 440 to express an interest in collective bargaining, something that was still new to education. In November 1939, Hunton, who had been elected HTU president earlier that year, requested that the AFT national office send him information regarding contracts negotiated by other unions with colleges and universities, noting that the need for the information and any sample contracts was urgent.[59] The AFT office was able to provide little support, with Irvin Kuenzli noting that such contracts were exceedingly rare. Instead, he noted, most locals simply attempted to arrange a salary schedule for their faculties.[60] The only evidence of Local 440 actually negotiating points to it quickly breaking down and indicates that it was case specific, rather than for a new contract. In a speech on academic freedom in 1953,

President Johnson recalled that, despite his initial displeasure about the founding of the union, he recognized that the union was founded because his administration was not meeting the faculty's needs. He agreed to negotiate with the local, but the process ended when, according to Johnson, the faculty sided with him in a dispute between Johnson and "one of their leaders from New York" over an agenda item. He noted, "This presiding officer killed that labor union in that meeting, because the teachers of this institution did not want a labor union here to bully the administration. They wanted a labor union to represent their legitimate interests in a constructive way."[61]

Activity in the National Union

HTU members also engaged in national union efforts: they participated in legislative activities, organized African American institutions and individuals, held national vice presidencies, and became involved in the debates over communism within the union. Three weeks after HTU's founding, members gathered to greet the AFT National Legislative Committee and discuss congressional legislation affecting faculty interests. Over the ensuing months and years, members of the HTU Legislative Committee routinely attended congressional hearings, reported to the local and national, and campaigned for legislation that would benefit education at Howard, for African Americans, and more broadly.[62] In early 1936, Bunche reported to Grossman about hearings on Red Rider legislation, noting that they demonstrated the extremism and viciousness of anticommunists while highlighting the absurdity of the restrictions on the political freedoms of students and educators.[63] James A. Porter later testified before a committee of the House of Representatives in support of a bill that would have created an executive department to preserve and promote America's cultural heritage, and Wilkerson joined the National Legislative Committee, testifying before Congress regarding legislation on school funding.[64] Most importantly, HTU led the AFT's fight against a version of the Fletcher-Harrison Bill, proposed legislation that would have provided millions of dollars in federal aid for education but would have allowed states to disproportionately use the funds for White schools. As part of this campaign, the local worked with Robert C. Weaver, Advisor on Negro Affairs in the Department of the Interior, for a new version of the bill to guarantee that school appropriations would be equitable. The revised version of the bill never passed in Congress which disappointed some but was in keeping with HTU's belief that the original version without protections for African American schools would have been worse than no federal support for education.[65]

When, in 1936, the AFT began reserving one vice presidency for an African American member, Callis (1936–1937) and then Wilkerson (1937–1940) became the first two African American vice presidents in the union's history. Through these positions, Callis and Wilkerson extended the influence of Local 440, by, for example, organizing locals at other African American schools and colleges.[66] They garnered a platform and spoke for African American educators within the union, weighed in on issues involving segregation, and participated in other events involving African American institutions, such as Wilkerson's negotiation of a settlement in a tenure case at Hampton University. Hunton and others also played national roles in the struggle for academic freedom, in many ways the AFT's most pressing issue in higher education during the era.[67]

As an activist local in contentious times, HTU increasingly engaged in the struggles over communism that roiled the AFT. From its beginning, HTU was aligned with the left wing of the union, as Mary Grossman's participation in its opening meeting hints at and the local's support of the Committee of Industrial Organizations (CIO) confirms.[68] HTU sparred with Washington, DC, K-12 teachers (Local 8) over the latter's refusal to allow a former member to return to the union due to her communist sympathies, a situation which Wilkerson and Grossman tried to remedy, and otherwise sought rights and protections for leftist educators.[69] The battle over communism became *the* defining event for the AFT in the late 1930s, and, in 1939, progressive anticommunist George Counts was elected president over fellow traveler Jerome Davis largely due to this issue. When he assumed the presidency, Counts began consolidating the anticommunist elements of the union, ultimately leading to the 1941 revocation of the charters of Locals 5, 192, and 537 due to Communist Party domination.

As discord inside the national grew, Local 440 assumed an important role, including by introducing and advocating for two amendments to the AFT Constitution that spoke directly to the growing political concerns and the efforts to remove locals dominated by Communist Party members. The first was to forbid discrimination against individual members "because of race, religious faith or political activities or belief." The second was to prohibit the revocation of a charter or suspension of a local for any reason other than unpaid dues without a two-thirds vote of the convention. In a letter written to all AFT locals on behalf of HTU, Wilkerson justified the purpose of the amendments as "to merely write into the Constitution those democratic trade union practices" which already exited. He continued, "Having witnessed the disunity visited upon other internationals by violations of these democratic practices, and recognizing that even the American Federation of Teachers is not immune to the attacks of potential disrupters, we are eager to *guarantee* our Union against such unwholesome developments as have appeared all to frequently in trade-union history."[70] The campaign for these amendments was contested. HTU had to goad the national office to distribute the materials and hold the referendum, but they both passed overwhelmingly. It was based on the passage of these amendments that Murphy, in her history of teacher unionization, argued that communists felt protected even when Davis was replaced by Counts.[71] This confidence was misplaced as, in 1941, the former amendment was revised to include "except that no applicant whose political actions are subject to totalitarian control such as Fascist, Nazi, or Communist, shall be admitted to membership" and the two-thirds majority required by the latter was met.[72] HTU's efforts to insulate Locals 5, 192, and 537, and its advocacy on their behalf in the run-up to their expulsions, were to no avail.

HTU's place in the divisions over communism was complicated by disagreements within the local. As part of his larger effort to remake the AFT Executive Council, Counts convinced Bunche to run against Wilkerson for the AFT vice presidency in 1940. Hunton, then the president of HTU, challenged Bunche's candidacy and called for his removal. In special hearings at the 1940 convention, the Executive Council heard from Layla Lane, an anticommunist who had run against Wilkerson the year before, on Bunche's behalf and from Hunton as a representative of HTU. Bunche's candidacy hinged on whether his inactivity in the union during recent years and his apparent failure to pay dues should eliminate him from consideration. Lane reported that Bunche, who was not present, remembered sending a check for dues but could not recall exactly when or for how much and had no record of it. Hunton argued that the local had never received it and did not consider him a member. Following a contentious meeting and further investigation by a subcommittee of the Executive Council, Bunche's name was removed from the ballot in the moments before the election. Years later, Bunche recounted the episode as part of his refutation of charges that he had been a member of the Communist Party, noting the divisions within the local and the "unfair tactics" of Wilkerson and Hunton.[73] For Counts and the anticommunists, though, the larger victory was theirs. That evening, Lane was elected over Wilkerson as part of a sweep of Executive Council seats.[74]

The End of HTU

HTU was highly active in both local and national issues for the first five years of its existence but this energy and engagement dissipated in the early 1940s. Its fights against the revocation of the charters of Locals 5, 192, and 537 and the larger attacks on communists within the AFT, including challenging the legality of the procedures used, were among HTU's last major activities.[75] Immediately after the United States entered World War II, HTU called on the AFT to cooperate with the National Education Association and other organizations to coordinate war efforts, to campaign for increased funding to education to meet continuing and new school needs, and to reinstate Locals 5, 192, and 537.[76] In ensuing months, the local submitted its "Proposals for the Adjustment of Howard University to Meet the War Emergency" to the institution, and Wilkerson reported that HTU was developing a program to help support the war cause.[77] Although membership increased in early 1942, briefly reaching forty-nine members, there is no evidence of corresponding increases in activity or continued engagement. Membership steadily slid back into the mid-1920s by August 1943, and the union was repeatedly slow in submitting its dues to the national.[78]

The exact reasons for this decline and closing of what had been one of the more active college locals are not entirely clear, although several items are suggestive. Certainly, American entry into World War II shifted focus, caused faculty to leave their institutions for war work, and diminished faculty presence across the union. Nationally, membership in the college locals dropped from over 1,700 to under 350 between May 1939 and May 1945.[79] Also important for some of the college faculty in the AFT was the expulsion of communist locals. Several of the college locals were on the left edge of the union and joined HTU in protesting the charter revocations. The revocations may have saved the AFT, but they marginalized many higher education members and diminished their roles in the union. Closer to home, Howard similarly experienced the loss of faculty central to the union activities. Wilkerson, who had long been a driving force in HTU, announced that he was a Communist Party member and left the institution in 1943, when, according to David Levering Lewis, "his radicalism made his tenure at Howard more problematic than useful."[80] Hunton likewise left the institution in 1943 to pursue more radical political activity than his faculty position would allow.[81] Others who remained shifted their allegiances to the CIO. By 1944, when HTU closed due to a failure to pay dues and a lack of interest in returning to solvency, the local had contributed to national legislative campaigns, helped organize faculty unions at other African American institutions, achieved at least isolated victories in its work against segregation, and garnered institutional support for tenure policies. More recently, though, it had come out on the losing end in national political battles, experienced divisions within the local, failed in its effort to negotiate with the administration, and lost its most active leaders.

The CIO at Howard: The UFWA and the UPW-CIO

Even as Howard faculty founded AFT Local 440, larger changes in organized labor occurred that would affect future efforts at the institution. In 1935, United Mine Workers of America (UMWA) President John L. Lewis and other union leaders formed the Committee of Industrial Organizations in an attempt to reform the AFL, increase its activism, and further organize it along industrial rather than craft lines. Within a few years, the fissures that led to the group's formation revealed wider fractures, and, in 1938, the Committee of Industrial Organizations became the independent Congress of Industrial Organizations. The CIO changed the nature of organizing in the United States, with a "crusading zeal" and "a distinctively egalitarian approach to organizing drives and workplace protests."[82] The CIO both offered new possibilities for workers and revitalized the AFL, including around issues involving racial discrimination. The CIO explicitly sought to organize African American workers and offered both democratic rhetoric and, due to its ties to the UMWA, a history of efforts on behalf of Black workers. As Robert H. Zieger argued, "the CIO represented the first large-scale effort to bring workers of all ethnic and racial identities into a sustained, well-resourced, and politically realistic movement. CIO organizers might occasionally betray their regrettable racial views, and black workers might be skeptical, but by the late 1930s, large numbers of African American workers had joined the new CIO unions . . .."[83] Additionally, the CIO funded and supported the aforementioned NNC, an outgrowth of a conference on African Americans in the Great Depression held at Howard in 1935.

The struggles that led to the formation of the CIO as an independent organization were further relevant at Howard as they involved the efforts to unionize workers in the federal government and again implicated the divergent approaches of craft and industrial unionization. The National Federation of Federal Employees (NFFE) was formed in 1917 as an AFL affiliate and quickly became the leading organizer of federal employees.

By 1931, a long-simmering feud involving the NFFE's industrial rather than craft approach came to a head, and jurisdictional issues combined with personal animosities to lead the NFFE to withdraw from the AFL and operate independently. The AFL responded by organizing a new union, the American Federation of Governmental Employees (AFGE), causing dual unionism that weakened efforts for improved conditions. The AFGE itself struggled with internal battles and, in 1936, began suspending union lodges for their use of industrial tactics. Additional suspensions the following year brought the total number of ostracized lodges to twelve and led the CIO to charter the UFWA. With these twelve lodges as its nucleus, the UFWA expanded rapidly in the ensuing years, reaching 6,500 members in 50 locals in fall 1937 and 14,000 members in 131 locals a year later.[84] The UFWA's 1944 constitution identified its objectives as providing federal workers the same rights as those afforded in private industry and argued for collective bargaining to be extended to all public employees. Throughout its existence, the UFWA was known for its inclusion of and advocacy of rights for African American workers and its alignment with left-wing causes. Indeed, its positions often mirrored the Communist Party line. It was both the chief target of and primary opponent to the Hatch Act, which barred federal workers from political advocacy. Due to the large federal bureaucracy, the UFWA was especially active in Washington, DC.[85]

The UFWA's social, political, and employment concerns proved attractive to workers at Howard. In the same month that Local 440 closed, employees in the School of Medicine turned to the UFWA to assist them in their relations with university administration. Despite personnel changes in the school since the scuffles of the late 1930s, difficulties remained as faculty and staff in the School of Medicine believed that the administration was not accurately representing their needs to the board. In June 1944, sixty-four members of the teaching and nonteaching staffs, including forty-one physicians, formed the Howard University Branch of the UFWA under the chairmanship of physiologist Joseph L. Johnson.[86] By the end of the year, over 75 percent of the school's faculty and over 80 percent of its other employees were members of either the Teaching Shop or the Non-Teaching Shop.[87] CIO unionization quickly spread to other parts of the institution, as well. Twelve of the thirteen members of the library staff founded a shop on January 8, 1945, after a meeting with University Librarian Walter Daniel and a visit from Johnson. Daniel himself wanted to join but was ruled ineligible due to his administrative duties.[88] Indeed, the UFWA's publication *The Federal*

Record declared that "CIO-itis [was] spreading rapidly throughout Howard University."[89]

More significant than the addition of the librarians, however, was the interest that faculty outside of medicine expressed to Holmes, the former HTU founder who chaired the organizing committee of the Howard Branch of the UFWA. By the beginning of 1945, forty-five faculty members in the Undergraduate College indicated a desire to join. Hoping to capitalize on this interest, Johnson pointed to the organization in the School of Medicine and the formation of the Librarian Shop in his appeal to the faculty of the larger institution. He emphasized that the combined efforts of *all* employees at Howard with the support of the broader CIO could help improve working and economic conditions, as well as educational standards at the institution. In doing so, according to Johnson, they could benefit not only Howard but the larger society, as well.[90]

The archival evidence is fragmentary and is silent on the exact causes for the Howard Branch's early success, but the success itself is clear and may have been influenced by stagnant salaries at the institution. By October 1945, 330 of 450 Howard employees eligible for membership had joined, including over half of the faculty. At their semiannual meeting that month, the Board of Trustees responded to this strength in numbers and acknowledged "the democratic right of the teachers and non-teaching employees to join labor unions and . . . to negotiate with the University regarding the terms of employment through the agency of their union."[91] This recognition was itself a significant step forward in the unionization of college personnel and was the first time in the history of American higher education that teaching and nonteaching staff had been afforded this right together. UFWA President Eleanor Nelson attributed the agreement to both the acknowledged salary issues and a shared recognition of the "CIO's deep concern to improve and extend the best possible educational opportunities to all of America's youth."[92] The Howard Branch immediately began preparations for an official vote on representation for nonteaching staff but explicitly excluded the faculty, noting that a vote was not yet necessary for teachers.[93] On December 12, under the supervision of the National Labor Relations Board (NLRB), the nonteaching staff voted 203–0 for representation by UFWA Local 10. Over the course of the ensuing months, union representatives and Howard officials negotiated a contract that, when signed in April 1946, provided for a new salary scale, union dues check-off, and new grievance procedures before an impartial arbitrator. At its signing, Joseph

L. Johnson noted, "This contract is an expression of the desire of the employees and officers of the University to work together. We look forward to continued friendly and constructive relations."[94]

Still, indications that all was not well at the institution remained. In the weeks surrounding the signing of the contract, the *Chicago Defender* published a series of articles alleging significant unrest at Howard University. A front-page article on April 6 reported that the university's "long-smoldering feud burst into the open" with the dean of the medical school's resignation. The paper blamed the resignation on the dean's inability to bridge the divides between the "school's progressive faction and the reactionary administration" and termed the recent UFWA campaign as "a bitter struggle."[95] In the next edition of the weekly newspaper, a banner headline declared "275 Howard Professors Revolt Against Prexy." The allegation was based on an internal report prepared by the Education Committee of the Howard Branch's Teaching Shop (now Shop D) outlining concerns about the academic rigor of the institution. The report averred low retention rates, large class sizes, low faculty morale, inconsistent enforcement of rules, inadequate services for students, insufficient course offerings, and poor facilities, while offering twenty suggestions for change.[96] A week later, two pieces recounted the resignation of the acting dean of the law school, pointing to President Johnson's autocracy as the cause, and a third continued discussion of the Education Committee's report.[97] The paper alleged President Johnson "thrashed feebly about in an effort to negate" the damage of the report and focused on the source of the leak rather than addressing the concerns outlined in the report. In response, representatives of both the institution and the Education Committee condemned the *Defender*'s articles. The university secretary called the coverage "an unwarranted and vicious attack" while allowing that the institution had significant financial needs.[98] The Education Committee wrote a joint letter explaining that the report was an internal document that was presented to and amicably discussed with the university administration. They pointedly denied any revolt, noted that the administration and faculty shared the same concerns, termed the article "a glaring example of unethical and irresponsible journalism," and claimed that there had not been the "slighted degree of antagonism expressed by any of the parties concerned."[99] Still, in ensuing weeks, the *Defender* continued its attacks on Howard, frequently noting that the UFWA Howard Branch offered the possibility for change.[100]

As these events occurred at Howard, the larger UFWA experienced difficulties including lags in membership, concerns over the leadership of Eleanor Nelson, and troubles in managing the interests of its members during postwar economic reconversion. Moreover, congressional efforts to undermine the union that began with the Hatch Act continued and the union's leftist stances brought it under significant scrutiny during the postwar era. Membership including Communist Party members and sympathizers raised significant concerns among its critics. In summer 1945, the UFWA and the State, County, Municipal Workers of America (SCMWA)—a CIO union representing civic workers not employed by the federal government—began discussions about combining to form one larger union representing governmental workers across sectors in hopes of providing new strength in increased numbers. The two unions officially merged at the end of April 1946 to become the UPW-CIO, but, rather than securing the union's future, resolutions in support of the Soviet Union at the UPW-CIO's founding convention exacerbated the concerns of communist influence. Moreover, the federal workers were now a minority in the UPW-CIO; leadership was drawn from the former SCMWA; and the new union focused on the state, municipal, and county workers. A UPW-CIO plank that allowed for strikes by state and local workers further increased the difficulties for the federal employees in the union. Clarifications that the UPW-CIO remained opposed to strikes against the federal government did little to quell opposition to the union or reassure prospective federal employees that the union would serve their interests.[101] As Mary Harding noted in her history of CIO unionization in Washington, DC, "The truth of the matter was, that with the merger, the UFWA was dead."[102]

Despite these larger difficulties, the Howard Branch of the UPW-CIO continued to attract membership. While Johnson emphasized the positive opportunities offered by the Howard Branch and the amicable relations between it and the administration, others claimed that the union's very existence was evidence of discord. In a letter calling for a fundamental restructuring of the university's organization, historian Walter Dyson wrote to President Johnson and the Board of Trustees, that the unionization of faculty and staff at the institution was indicative of larger problems, including as they related to salary differentials. He argued that neither the trustees nor President Johnson understood the conditions under which they worked, in part because the administration was distant and unresponsive. This, in turn, caused suspicion and further fracturing of relationships.[103] Elsewhere, Dyson was more direct, calling for the reorganization of the board as the only remedy to an unacceptable situation.[104]

Dyson pointed to very real difficulties at the institution, as did the *Chicago Defender*, which referred to a history of "plantation-like handling" of faculty that limited the effectiveness of the institution.[105] Still, the situation was more complicated than these reports suggest. At the same time that Dyson was offering his critiques, Howard Branch leadership was working with the administration to improve salaries and provide for sick leave. On December 16, a committee approached President Johnson to request a consent election to allow for union representation of the teaching staff. The president welcomed the group and indicated his interest in the election based on the good will that had been achieved both during the negotiations for the contract with nonteaching staff and in the intervening months. Upon President Johnson's recommendation and after negotiations over voting eligibility, the Board of Trustees agreed, as well.[106] Further, Joseph L. Johnson, the founder and former leader of the Howard Branch, was one of the leading proponents of collective bargaining. In the branch's January 1947 newsletter, he passionately argued for the CIO affiliation, noting that teachers too often separated themselves from other workers and failed to see the benefits of organized labor. He called on teachers to recognize that their futures were inextricably tied to the futures of "the rank and file working man" while also highlighting the CIO's advocacy of racial justice. He continued, "Teachers cannot hold themselves aloof from these struggles of the people, neither can they be content to stand on the sidelines to cheer, jeer or silently await the outcomes. Worthy and progressive administrators are rapidly developing an allergy to the employee who holds himself aloof from his fellow workers . . . ."[107] Johnson may have counted himself among these progressive administrators. He was a longstanding union advocate but was ineligible to vote when then election was held the following month: in April 1946, President Johnson had appointed him Dean of the School of Medicine.[108]

In a February 6, 1947, election overseen by the NRLB, the faculty of Howard University voted 130–1 in favor of representation by the UPW-CIO.[109] The local attributed this overwhelming majority to the positive relations between the union and the institution, as well as its success in bargaining the earlier contract and in handling grievances. Representatives began working on a contract that, when agreed to in May, was this first collectively bargained contract for teaching faculty in American higher education. It provided for grievance procedures that included jointly selected independent arbitrators, a contractual obligation to maintain existing tenure procedures, dues check-off, and provisions for increases in faculty salaries.[110] Later that year, this last provision was enacted when the two parties agreed to a salary scale to bring salaries in line with other teachers in the District of Columbia.[111] The contract included a provision for yearly renewal unless one party requested changes to or a termination of the contract. The limited existing evidence indicates no controversy during the next two renewals, with only the addition of a provision that the institution and union to work together to provide health insurance altering the contract for the 1949–1950 academic year.[112] The evidence indicates largely positive relations, including in the aftermath of the institution's 1949 decision not to renew Associate Professor Samuel A. Corson's contract. After initially filing a grievance and investigating the situation, the union withdrew its objections and its call for the instructor to receive tenure. In a letter to the Board of Trustees, the union "express[ed] its appreciation for the earnest and sympathetic consideration given by your committee to the presentation of the case" and suggested that the institution provide the instructor a one-year terminal appointment, which the university did.[113] President Johnson later recalled that the union "had conducted itself in an entirely honorable manner, not only seeking to take no advantage of the administration in any way, but also actually astonishing me on two occasions by an unexpected sense of responsibility."[114]

These relations were not enough to forestall the demise of the Howard Branch of the UPW-CIO in 1950. Anticommunist hysteria grew in the years after World War II and unions were increasingly attacked. The 1946 Taft-Hartley Act undid some of the guarantees provided by the Wagner Act and imposed new restrictions on union political activity. Further, the law required that prior to appealing for NLRB assistance, union officers had to sign affidavits attesting that they were not members of the Communist Party, a troubling requirement that threatened to split the CIO. President Harry Truman's Federal Loyalty-Security Program, which prohibited Communist Party members or sympathizers from holding positions in the executive branch, exacerbated the difficulty for the UPW-CIO. Over the ensuing years, the Communist-led unions battled against the anticommunist unions inside the CIO while pressure was increasingly applied by reactionary governmental and external forces. In late 1949 and early 1950, the CIO expelled eleven unions for alleged Communist Party domination, claiming that they were unable to serve the needs of the workers. The UPW-CIO, the fourth of the eleven to be expelled, lost significant influence and membership amidst continuing investigations and hysteria, including a congressional investigation into the union and its leaders in 1951. The union folded as a national organization in 1953.[115]

The CIO's branding of the UPW-CIO as a Communist union led directly to its demise at Howard. At its May 1950 meeting, the Board of Trustees unanimously voted to allow the contracts for both teaching and nonteaching staff to expire that summer. President Johnson later claimed that he did not view the union local as subversive but recognized that Congress did and contended that institutional appropriations would surely have been withheld had the union remained.[116] The UPW-CIO national protested this decision, calling the institution a "citadel of intolerance," and a group of UPW-CIO members rallied on campus in July; but no evidence of faculty unrest exists.[117] Johnson noted that the faculty "cooperated with me apparently 100 percent in breaking away entirely from this union."[118] Indeed, in the weeks after the UPW-CIO's expulsion, member Anne M. Cook even refused to accept an award or to attend a reception held in her honor at the union's Interracial Nursery School due to this alleged Communist affiliation.[119] Further, Rayford Logan, who was among those who initially supported the union but was also opposed to the Communist element at the institution, wrote, "Although academic tenure remained for many years a controversy between the Administration and some Faculty members (many of whom had indefinite tenure), one issue lessened the tension."[120] Other than noting that the issue was the termination of the collectively bargained contracts, Logan offered no additional comment.

The CIO's expulsion of the UPW-CIO did not end unionization at Howard, but it set it back and fundamentally changed it with regard to faculty. In the months after Howard's termination of the UPW-CIO contracts, the CIO launched a campaign to organize workers through its new Government and Civic Employees Organizing Committee (GCEOC-CIO), including by attempting to attract UPW-CIO members. By November, the GCEOC-CIO counted the majority of nonteaching staff among its membership and appealed for either a card count or an election. Over the ensuing months, the GCEOC-CIO and Howard administrators argued over details and jurisdiction, with the CIO accusing Howard of stalling.[121] Despite the appeal to nonteaching workers, the new union did not gain traction with faculty, and fewer than two dozen were members at the end of 1950. Moreover, the delays in an election took their toll on the larger efforts at Howard. At the end of March, organizer Jean Pagano reported apathy at Howard. In a letter addressed to the CIO members at Howard, Pagano conveyed that the GCEOC-CIO was pulling out of the institution due to the delays and the lack of enthusiasm. She noted that no one had shown up at the previous three meetings and even members were unwilling to work on behalf of the union.[122] With the end of the GCEOC-CIO's efforts, unionization disappeared from Howard until the contentious struggles between AFSCME and the institution at the end of the decade.[123]

Conclusion

A 1936 letter to members of Local 440 exclaimed that teachers needed labor, that labor needed teachers, that African American laborers were especially threatened, and that "ONLY ORGANIZED EFFORT WILL FIND THE WAY OUT!"[124] Between 1918 and 1950, a series of Howard faculty shared similar perspectives and affiliated with organized labor for a variety of employment, societal, political, and economic reasons. They joined AFL-affiliated AFT locals and CIO-affiliated UFWA and UPW-CIO branches hoping to achieve change in working and living conditions in the nation's capital. Each of these unions was significant to both local and national situations, breaking new ground and helping push faculty organization in new and important directions. Even with their contributions, though, each faced difficulty and folded. This essay recovers the early history of these unions and provides insight into their purposes, activities, accomplishments, and closings. Most importantly, it locates these African American unions at the center of early efforts to organize college faculty and resurrects their too often overlooked legacies.

Unionization in higher education began at Howard University when a small group of faculty sought improvements in their working conditions in the immediate aftermath of World War I. Although it was short-lived, the pioneering union helped spread organization to other institutions in the difficult late 1910s and early 1920s. When faculty unionization returned to the AFT in the late 1920s and 1930s, societal and political issues took preeminence, and Local 440 was among the most active of the locals in both its immediate context and on the national scene. Much of the work focused on battling segregation and uniting workers across race and class lines. At the same time, members of Local 440 were interested in on-campus issues and both explored bargaining and battled for tenure rights and procedures. Although they were unsuccessful in the former, they set the stage for later bargaining efforts and achieved tenure protections that would inform the UPW-CIO contract of the late 1940s. Even before the Howard Branch could achieve this first, the UFWA united faculty with other workers, breaking down craft lines and overcoming concerns related to the professional status of faculty. These issues of professionalism, stratification, and prestige were often determinant then and are still significant impediments to faculty unionization today.

This essay provides correctives to the brief mentions of faculty unions that do exist in the literature, including rectifying the implication that Local 440 was only interested in social activism in Washington, DC, and demonstrating that faculty successfully collectively bargained almost twenty years before it is commonly believed. It also points to the complicated and occasionally conflicted nature of union membership, activity, and advocacy. So, for example, Numa P. G. Adams was an officer in Local 33 as a chemistry professor in the years just after World War I. In the late 1930s, he was the dean of the School of Medicine who was responsible for Callis' dismissal and who attempted to fire Young. At the time, Local 440 declared that Adams' actions evidenced antiunion discrimination.[125] Moreover, Joseph L. Johnson was both the founder of the Howard Branch of the UFWA and the person who the UPW-CIO charged with inappropriately dismissing one of its members, leading to a union-initiated grievance procedure.[126] Additionally, in 1936, Ralph Bunche helped found Local 440 and provided early leadership on legislative and organizational issues. By the end of the decade, however, he was on the outside looking in. Not only was he largely inactive in the union, his own local led the challenge that prevented him from assuming a larger national position. Roles, perspectives, and affiliations varied and were complex, especially in highly charged times. Moreover, among Howard faculty who emphasized class over race in their pursuit of societal change, dramatic differences in approaches and allegiances existed. For those who favored race vindication, further dissimilarities were apparent.

By emphasizing the political battles both within the unions and beyond, this essay further highlights the toll that anticommunist hysteria took on college faculty unionization. Local 33 disbanded due to Red Scare pressures and institutional fear of a congressional backlash. Members of Local 440 battled on both local and national stages as Communist Party members such as Wilkerson were in conflict with anticommunist colleagues and brothers. The splits within Local 440 both replicated and contributed to the larger AFT struggles over communism. Although not definitive, the national changes within the AFT appear to have contributed to the closing of the left-leaning local at Howard.

In its place, though, arose a branch of the UFWA, a national union more closely aligned with Communist Party orthodoxy and more progressive on racial issues. Paradoxically, though, the Howard Branch appears to have emphasized institutional issues over societal and political ones. The industrial organization and emphasis on racial equity were significant features; the contract for teaching staff was the significant accomplishment. The Howard Branch of the UPW-CIO included members such as Eugene Holmes, who would later be linked to the Communist Party; but, in its time, anticommunist administrators viewed the Howard Branch as a reasonable and legitimate bargaining partner on campus. Still, the post–World War II hysteria proved insurmountable, and the first collectively bargained faculty contract was terminated for the institution's larger political gain. Fear of communism forestalled labor gains.

Although the contributions to faculty organization at Howard are exceptional, they do highlight the larger roles of and reaction to African Americans in faculty unionization. AFT Local 33 was the first college local but was largely ignored at the time; only the addition of an AFT local at the University of Illinois a few months later attracted national attention to faculty unionization. Locally, the *Washington Post* included a three-sentence note on the founding of Local 33 but offered a lengthy editorial on Local 41, including incorrectly identifying it as the first college local, thereby further marginalizing Howard faculty.[127] The emergence of the CIO in the 1930s both pushed the AFL to reconsider race relations and offered new opportunities for African American workers, especially in the South. The AFT was already more progressive on race relations than most AFL unions and began focusing more attention on African American teachers and institutions.[128] Callis, Wilkerson, and other Howard faculty played important roles that helped spread the union to other K-12 and higher education institutions. And while eleven UPW-CIO locals included college employees, three of the four that counted faculty among their members were at HBCUs (Howard, Hampton University, and Tuskegee Institute). African American faculty at Howard and elsewhere played important, if largely ignored, roles in organizing educators, especially in the South.

Even with concerns over professional unionization, state legislation limiting public employee organization, and the United States Supreme Court's *National Labor Relations Board v. Yeshiva* ruling that private college faculty do not possess collective bargaining rights, faculty unionization has become entrenched in many states and across institutional types.[129] The most recent evidence indicates that unions represent over 40 percent of primarily instructional college faculty across sectors.[130] Almost 250,000 faculty members at over 1,000 colleges and universities are unionized, including two-thirds of all faculty at public institutions.[131] Yet despite its prevalence, too little attention is paid to faculty unionization in the scholarly literature. Additionally, even though the issues involving unionization and professionalization have deep histories that both foretold modern debates and influenced conditions of faculty employment, historical considerations are all but absent. The neglect of African American educators and their unions in the halting progression of faculty organizing has, to this point, been even more profound.

Notes

1. Robert Shaffer, "Where Are the Organized Public Employees? The Absence of Public Employee Unionism from U.S. History Textbooks, and Why it Matters," *Labor History* 43, no. 3 (2002): 315–34.
2. Jonathan Scott Holloway, *Confronting the Veil: Abraham Harris Jr., E. Franklin Frazier, and Ralph Bunche, 1919–1941* (Chapel Hill, NC: University of North Carolina Press, 2002), 31.
3. Ellen Swartz, "Stepping Outside the Master Script: Re-Connecting the History of American Education," *Journal of Negro Education* 76, no. 2 (2007): 174.
4. William Edward Eaton, *The American Federation of Teachers, 1916–1961: A History of the Movement* (Carbondale, IL: Southern Illinois University Press, 1975), 57–63, 83–85; Marjorie Murphy, *Blackboard Unions: The AFT and the NEA, 1900–1980* (Ithaca, NY: Cornell University Press, 1990), 146–49, 162–71. Other book-length histories offer even less discussion of college faculty. See, for example, Commission on Educational Reconstruction, *Organizing the Teaching Profession: The Story of the American Federation of Teachers* (Glencoe, IL: Free Press, 1955); American Federation of Teachers, *A Looseleaf History of the American Federation of Teachers* (Washington, DC: American Federation of Teachers, 1972).
5. Jeannette A. Lester, "The American Federation of Teachers in Higher Education: A History of Union Organization of Faculty Members in Colleges and Universities, 1916–1966" (EdD dissertation, University of Toledo, 1968), 52–54, 104–7. For further discussion of this oversight and one attempt to overcome it, including a treatment of Howard in the 1910s, see, Timothy Reese Cain, "The First Attempts to Unionize the Faculty," *Teachers College Record* 112, no. 3 (2010): 876–913.
6. See, for example, Judith Wagner DeCew, *Unionization in the Academy: Visions and Realities* (Lanham, MD: Rowman & Littlefield Publishers, Inc., 2003), 11–29.
7. Holloway, *Confronting the Veil*, 64–65.
8. See, for example, Bruce Nelson, *Divided We Stand: American Workers and the Struggle for Black Equality* (Princeton, NJ: Princeton University Press, 2000). Nelson's important work focused on longshoreman, steelworkers, and the construction of racial identity and cited E. Franklin Frazier, "A Negro Industrial Group," *Howard Review* 1 (1924): 196–211, and Sterling D. Spero and Abram L. Harris, *The Black Worker: The Negro and the Labor Movement* (New York: Columbia University Press, 1931). Among the useful discussions of the literature on race and labor history are: Herbert Hill, "The Problem of Race in Labor History," *Reviews in American History* 24, no. 2 (1996): 189–208; Eric Arnesen, "Up from Exclusion:

Black and White Workers and the State of Labor History," *Reviews in American History* 26, no. 1 (1998): 146–74; Robert H. Zieger, *For Jobs and Freedom: Race and Labor in America since 1865* (Lexington, KY: University Press of Kentucky, 2007), 255–66.

9.   Philo A. Hutcheson, *A Professional Professoriate: Unionization, Bureaucratization, and the AAUP* (Nashville, TN: Vanderbilt University Press, 2000); Cain, "First Attempts."

10. Wayne J. Urban, *Why Teachers Organized* (Detroit, MI: Wayne State University Press, 1982), 134–40; Murphy, *Blackboard Unions*, 83–87.

11. V. B. Turner, "The American Federation of Teachers," *Monthly Labor Review* 9, no. 2 (1919): 247–55; Lester, "American Federation of Teachers," 52; Cain, "First Attempts."

12. Babalola Cole, "Appropriation Politics and Black Schools: Howard University in the U.S. Congress, 1879–1928," *Journal of Negro Education* 46, no. 1 (1977): 7–23.

13. Rayford W. Logan, *Howard University: The First Hundred Years, 1867–1967* (New York: New York University Press, 1969), 139–84; Walter Dyson, *Howard University: The Capstone of Negro Education* (Washington, DC: The Graduate School, Howard University, 1941), 397.

14. Dyson, *Howard University*, 96.

15. Ibid., 86–87.

16. Only thirteen names appear on the application, but both an internal AFT report and Henry Callis, a future president of Local 440, noted twenty-nine founding members. "Application for Charter," box 5, folder 33 Howard University Teachers Union, AFT Collection Inventory, Part I, Series VI Old Correspondence, Archive of Labor and Urban Affairs, Walter P. Reuther Library, Wayne State University, Detroit, MI (hereafter AFT Part I, Series VI); "A Statistical History of the American Federation of Teachers, 1916–1939," box 72, folder Statistical History of the AFT, AFT President's Collection, Archive of Labor and Urban Affairs, Walter P. Reuther Library, Wayne State University, Detroit, MI; H. A. Callis, "The Negro Teacher and the A.F.T.," *Journal of Negro Education* 6, no. 2 (1937): 188–90.

17. "Constitution of the Howard University Teachers' Union," 3, folder H. U. Teachers Union Constitution, Walter Dyson Materials, HRC 2506 754-6, Howard University Archives, Moorland-Spingarn Research Center, Howard University, Washington, DC (hereafter Dyson Materials); LHS to Walter Dyson, April 15, 1919, box 5, folder 33, AFT Part I, Series VI.

18. Incomplete membership lists preclude determining whether the fifth, H. D. Hatfield, was also a member of the local.

19. Turner, "American Federation of Teachers," 248; Callis, "Negro Teacher," 189; Dyson, *Howard University*, 88, 87.

20. The resolution and other AFT documents noted a request for $1,580,000 rather than the normal $100,000, although this may have been an error considering the great disparity between the request and previous appropriations, that the amount was greater than the valuation of Howard's property and endowment combined, and that House of Representatives approved $158,000 as the appropriation, including specific uses for the funds. "Report of the Committee on Resolutions of the Fourth National Convention of the American Federation of Teachers," *American Teacher* 9, no. 1 (1920): 7–12; Richard Olney, "Address" in *The Inauguration of J. Stanley Durkee, A.M., Ph.D., as President of Howard University, November 12, 1919 and the Readjustment and Reconstruction Congress, November 13, 1919* (Washington, DC: Howard University, 1920), 37; "Howard Gets Large Sum from Congress," *Chicago Defender* (May 29, 1920).

21. Emmet J. Scott to Freeland G. Stecker, February 16, 1920, box 5, folder 33, AFT Part I, Series VI; Freeland G. Stecker to James W. Good, February 20, 1920, box 5, folder 33, AFT Part I, Series VI; Freeland G. Stecker to Francis W. Warren, February 20, 1920, box 5, folder 33, AFT Part I, Series VI.

22. Dyson, *Howard University,* 430–33; Logan, *Howard University*, 188–92; "Scores Red Book in Howard Library," *Washington Post* (January 9, 1919).

23. Callis, "Negro Teacher," 189.

24. McLeod Harvey to F. G. Stecker, June 18, 1921, box 5, folder 33, AFT Part I, Series VI.

25. Cain, "First Attempts."

26. Other reports indicate that he called Kelly Miller, a faculty member and former dean, "a contemptible pup" while Durkee acknowledged calling him "a pup." Logan, *Howard University*, 220–22, 231–42; "Durkee Resigns Presidency," *Afro-American* (June 6, 1925); Alumnus, "Alumnus Says," *Afro-American* (June 20, 1925). The sensational reports by "Alumnus" appeared throughout the spring and summer and are, according to Logan, more reliable than other discussions of the events that led to Durkee's resignation.

27. David Levering Lewis, *W. E. B. DuBois: The Fight for Equality and the American Century, 1919–1963* (New York: Henry Holt, 2000), 142–45; Robert I. McKinney, *Mordecai, The Man and His Message: The Story of Mordecai Wyatt Johnson* (Washington, DC: Howard University Press, 1997), 55–56.

28. Logan, *Howard University*; McKinney, *Mordecai*, 63–75; Cole, "Appropriation Politics"; Clifford L. Muse, Jr., "Howard University and the Federal Government During the Presidential Administrations of Herbert Hoover and Franklin D. Roosevelt, 1928–1945," *Journal of Negro History* 76, no. 1/4 (1991): 1–20. This new funding did not alleviate financial concerns, and Congressional appropriations were often short of Johnson's and Howard's hopes. Additionally, the Depression took a toll on the institution, as financial strife led to legislation rolling back salaries at and appropriations to various federally funded entities, including Howard.

29. Logan, *Howard University*, 249.

30. Logan, *Howard University*, 292–304, 333–45; Clifford Langdon Muse, Jr., "An Educational Stepchild: Howard University during the New Deal, 1933–1945" (PhD dissertation, Howard University, 1989), 55–95, 116–25.

31. Ellen W. Schrecker, *No Ivory Tower: McCarthyism and the Universities* (New York: Oxford University Press, 1986), 24–83.

32. Dyson, *Howard University*, 437–39.

33. Mordecai Johnson. "The Social Responsibility of the Administrator," in McKinney, *Mordecai*, 286–311, 310.

34. Holloway, *Confronting the Veil*, 48–49; Charles P. Henry noted that the institution was "home for the most distinguished group of black scholars ever assembled on one campus." Charles P. Henry, "Abram Harris, E. Franklin Frazier, and Ralph Bunche: The Howard School of Thought on the Problem of Race," in *The Changing Racial Regime*, ed. Matthew Holden, Jr., *National Political Science Review* 5 (Piscataway, NJ: Transaction Publishers, 1985), 36–56, 41. Howard's ability to attract such a collection of scholars was partly attributable to the difficulty African Americans faced in obtaining positions at White institutions, as well as the appeal of living in Washington, DC, relative to locales further south.

35. Holloway, *Confronting the Veil*, 4–16; Eren Miller, "Amenia Conference, 1933," in *Encyclopedia of the Harlem Renaissance*, ed. Cary D. Wintz and Paul Finkelman (New York: Routledge, 2004), 13–14.

36. Holloway, *Confronting the Veil*, 50–83; Henry, "Abram Harris, E. Franklin Frazier, and Ralph Bunche"; Clifford L. Muse, "Howard University and U.S. Foreign Affairs

during the Franklin Administration, 1933–1945," *Journal of African American History* 87 (Autumn 2002): 403–15; Erik S. Gellman, "'Death Blow to Jim Crow': The National Negro Conference, 1936–1947" (PhD dissertation, Northwestern University, 2006), 153–57.

37. Lester, "American Federation of Teachers," 90–142; Timothy Reese Cain, "For Education and Employment: The American Federation of Teachers and Academic Freedom, 1926–1941," *Perspectives on the History of Higher Education* 26 (2007): 67–102.

38. Hylan A. Lewis, "A Focused Memoir: Howard University and Frazier, 1933–1941," in *E. Franklin Frazier and the Black Bourgeoisie*, ed. James E. Teele (Columbia, MO: University of Missouri Press, 2002), 21–29, 22–23.

39. The charter application that the AFT accepted was dated January 9 and was signed by Eugene C. Holmes, Ralph J. Bunche, Hylan Lewis, James W. Butcher, Sterling A. Brown, John W. Huguley, William Alphaeus Hunton, William P. Robinson, and Harold O. Lewis. An earlier version, which was lost in the mail, included these signatures plus those of E. Franklin Frazier, Alain Locke, James V. Herring, James B. Browning, Howard N. Fitzhugh, William Leo Hansberry, Albert H. Blatt, Edwin E. Lewis, Jesse W. Lewis, and George O. Butler. Application for Charter, box 11, folder Local 440, AFT Collection Inventory, Part I, Series IV: Defunct Locals, Archive of Labor and Urban Affairs, Walter P. Reuther Library, Wayne State University, Detroit, MI (hereafter AFT Part I, Series IV); Unsigned [Eugene C. Holmes] to [Jerome] Davis, January 13, 1936, box 11, folder Local 440, AFT Part I, Series IV; Eugene Holmes and Ralph J. Bunche to Colleagues, January 15, 1936, box 25, folder 11, Ralph J. Bunche Papers, 1922–1988, SC MG 290, Schomburg Center for Research in Black Culture, New York Public Library (hereafter Bunche Papers).

40. Henry A. Callis, "President's Report," 1, Annual Meeting, April 1, 1936, box 131, folder 22, E. Franklin Frazier Papers 131, Manuscripts Division, Moorland-Spingarn Research Center, Howard University, Washington, DC (hereafter Frazier Papers).

41. "By-Laws, American Federation of Teachers, Local #440, Washington, DC," box 22, folder 1, Franklin Frazier Papers.

42. Callis, "President's Report," 3.

43. Ibid., 4–5.

44. Doxey A. Wilkerson, "William Alphaeus Hunton: A Life that Made a Difference," *Freedomways* 10, no. 3 (1970): 254–55.

45. Brenda Gayle Plummer, *Rising Wind: Black Americans and U.S. Foreign Affairs, 1935–1960* (Chapel Hill, NC: University of North Carolina Press, 1996), 64; Hylan G. Lewis to Fellow Members of Local 440, box 25, folder 11, January 21, 1939, Bunche Papers.

46. "Fight Forms against D.C. Sales Tax," *Washington Post* (March 17, 1939); "Present Status of D.C.'s Tax Legislation," *HTU News* 3, no. 3 (1939): 2.

47. See, for example, "While Rome Burns!" *H.T.U. News* 1, no. 2 (1936): 1; "The Case of the District Laundry Workers," *H.T.U. News* 2, no. 3 (1938): 2; "Wagner Act Defense Planned," *H.T.U. News* 3, no. 3 (1939): 1; H. Naylor Fitzhugh and M. D. Jenkins to "Colleague," December 15, 1938, box 25, folder 11, Bunche Papers.

48. Ralph J. Bunche to Mary Grossman, March 5, 1936, box 25, folder 11, Bunche Papers. See also, Henry A. Callis to Ralph J. Bunche, March 2, 1936, box 25, folder 11, Bunche Papers.

49. Doxey A Wilkerson to Group Theatre Acting Company, November 23, 1938, box 25, folder 11, Bunche Papers; "D.A.R. Hears Committee on Anderson Ban Protest," *Chicago Defender*, July 1, 1939; Bruce Lambert, "Doxey Wilkerson is Dead at 88; Educator and Advocate for Civil Rights," *New York Times* June 18, 1993.

50. See, for example, W. A. Hunton to Irvin R. Kuenzli, May 18, 1940, box 11, folder Local #440, AFT Part I, Series IV.
51. Lewis, "Focused Memoir," 22–23.
52. E. Franklin Frazier and W. A. Hunton to "Colleague," October 25, 1937, box 22, folder 4, Frazier Papers; "Salary and Tenure at Howard," *H.T.U. News* 2, no. 3 (1938): 1.
53. "Callis Case Before Trustees," *H.T.U. News* 3, no. 3 (1939): 1–2; W. A. Hunton, Memo from The Howard Teachers' Union to All Teachers of Howard, November 1, 1939, box 25, folder 11, Bunche Papers.
54. Ibid; "Howard University Local Wins Protection Against Dismissals," *Clip-Sheet Bulletin from the National Office of the American Federation of Teachers* 2, no. 6 (1939): 3, box 11, folder Clip Sheet Bulletins, AFT Inventory, Part I, Series III Executive Council, Archive of Labor and Urban Affairs, Walter P. Reuther Library, Wayne State University, Detroit, MI (hereafter AFT Part I, Series III).
55. "Howard's Medical School Under Fire; Head Quits," *Chicago Defender* October 21, 1939.
56. Doxey A. Wilkerson, Sterling A. Brown, Alain L. Locke, W. Robert Ming, Naomi Rushing, and J. Leon Shereshefsky to T. L. Hungate, June 1, 1939, box 11, folder Local # 440, AFT Part I, Series IV; Cain, "For Education and Employment."
57. William Alphaeus Hunton and Doxey A. Wilkerson to "Our Colleagues in the 'Callis Case,'" June 1, 1939, box 11, folder Local #440, AFT Part I, Series IV.
58. *The Callis Case: Report of an Investigation Made under the Offices of the National Academic Freedom Committee of the American Federation of Teachers into the Termination of the Contract of Dr. Henry Arthur Callis by the College of Medicine of Howard University* (New York: National Academic Freedom Committee, n.d.).
59. W. A. Hunton to Irvin R. Kuenzli, November 11, 1939, box 11, folder Local #440, AFT Part I, Series IV.
60. Irvin R. Kuenzli to W. A. Hunton, November 16, 1939, box 11, folder Local #440, AFT Part I, Series IV.
61. Johnson, "Social Responsibility of the Administrator," 292.
62. Weather prevented the delegates from showing up, so the Howard contingent discussed the issues on its own. Callis, "President's Report," 1.
63. Ralph J. Bunche to Mary Grossman, March 5, 1936, box 25, folder 11, Bunche Papers.
64. "Porter Represents A.F.T. Before Congress," *H.T.U. News* 2, no. 2 (1938): 1.
65. "Protest Harrison Bill," *HTU News* 1, no. 2 (1936): 1; Announcement, November 23, 1936, box 22, folder 8, Frazier Papers; Doxey A. Wilkerson, "Federal Aid to Education: To Perpetuate or Diminish Existing Educational Inequalities," box 22, folder 10, Frazier Papers; Doxey A. Wilkerson to The Legislative Committee, December 3, 1936, box 22, folder 8, Frazier Papers; Robert C. Weaver to E. Franklin Frazier, December 8, 1936, box 22, folder 8, Frazier Papers; C[harles] H. T[hompson], "Editorial Comment: The Harrison Fletcher Bill and Negro Separate Schools," *Journal of Negro Education* 6, no. 1 (1937): 1–6; Mary Foley Grossman, "Redefining the Relationship of the Federal Government to the Education of Racial and Other Minority Groups," *Journal of Negro Education* 7, no. 3 (1938): 450–53; Murphy, *Blackboard Unions*, 146–49.
66. See, for example, "AFT Executive Council Minutes, December 30–31, 1936," 37–39, box 21, folder Executive Council Minutes, December 30–31, 1936, AFT Inventory, Part I, Series III; "AFT Executive Council Minutes, August 21–28, 1937," 37–39, box 21, folder Executive Council Minutes, August 21–28, 1937, AFT Part I, Series III; Doxey A. Wilkerson to Irving R. Kuenzli, June 3, 1940, box 11, folder Doxey A, Wilkerson, AFT Part I, Series III. The efforts included new locals at Fisk

University, Tuskegee Institute, Hampton Institute, Lincoln University, Dillard College, and Talladega College. Although much of this organizing work was done by the vice presidents, the Howard Local as a whole played a leadership role and individual members participated in these organizing efforts, including Wilkerson's continuation of organizing as a member of the College Organizing Committee following the end of his tenure as vice president and E. Franklin Frazier's speeches and visits.

67. Doxey Wilkerson to Irvin R. Kuenzli, June 10, 1939, box 11, folder Doxey A. Wilkerson, AFT Inventory, Part I, Series III; Irvin R. Kuenzli to W. A. Hunton, January 26, 1939, box 11, folder Local # 440, AFT Inventory, Part I, Series IV.

68. The local's newsletter routinely praised the CIO both when it was an AFL committee and when it became the Congress of Industrial Organizations.

69. The division between Locals 8 and 440 also revolved around race, as Local 8 did not support Local 440's efforts to desegregate the city and resisted any potential merger due to the racism of some of its membership. "Proceedings: Executive Council Meeting Held in Conjunction with the Twenty-Second Annual Convention of the American Federation of Teachers," 16–18, 75–80, box 21, folder Executive Council Proceedings, August 15–19, 1938 (1 and 2 of 2), AFT Part I, Series III. See, also, the numerous letters and documents related to Mary Ramirez in box 11, folder Doxey A. Wilkerson, AFT Part I, Series III.

70. Doxey A. Wilkerson to All A.F.T. Locals, June 14, 1939, box 11, folder Doxey A. Wilkerson, AFT Inventory Part I, Series III (emphasis in original).

71. Murphy, *Blackboard Unions*, 166.

72. *American Teacher* 26, no. 2 (1941): 3.

73. Ralph J. Bunche, "Report Denying Communist Party Affiliation," 1954, Ralph Bunche Papers, Department of Special Collections, Charles E. Young Research Library, University of California Los Angeles. Available: http://content.cdlib.org/ark:/13030/hb967nb7pm/ (accessed September 16, 2011).

74. "Executive Council Proceeding, August 17–26, 1940," 39–65, 72–73, box 23, folder Executive Council Proceeding, August 17–26, 1940, AFT Part I, Series III.

75. "Resolution of the Howard Teachers Union to the Executive Council of the American Federation of Teachers," box 2, folder Local Resolutions and Letters re: Revocation of Charters, AFT Locals, Series XII, Archive of Labor and Urban Affairs, Walter P. Reuther Library, Wayne State University, Detroit, MI; O. Wiggins and W. A. Hunton to the Executive Council of the American Federation of Teachers, February 26, 1941, box 25, folder 11, Bunche Papers.

76. Williston H. Lofton to The Executive Council, December 19, 1941, box 11, folder Local #440, AFT Inventory Part I, Series IV, ALUA.

77. "440," *American Teacher* 26 (March 1942): 22; Doxey A. Wilkerson to Irvin R. Kuenzli, March 3, 1942, box 11, folder Local #440, AFT Part I, Series IV.

78. See the "Monthly Reports to the Secretary-Treasurer," box 11, folder Local #440, AFT Part I, Series IV; The last evidence of any activity was a January 1943 joint sponsorship of talks about the Consumer Cooperative Movement. "What's Going and Where," *Washington Post* (January 22, 1943): B10.

79. Lester, "American Federation of Teachers in Higher Education," 141.

80. Alfred E. Smith, "'Why I Joined Communist Party,' Explained by Doxey Wilkerson," *Chicago Defender* July 31, 1943; David Levering Lewis, *W. E. B. DuBois: The Fight for Equality and the American Century* (New York: Henry Holt, 2000), 527.

81. Marika Sherwood, "W. Alphaeus Hunton," in *Pan-African History: Political Figures from Africa and the Diaspora since 1787*, ed. Hakim Adi and Marika Sherwood (New York: Routledge, 2003), 89–94, 91; Wilkerson, "William Alphaeus Hunton," 255.

82. Zieger, *For Jobs and Freedom*, 106.
83. Ibid., 115. For further discussions of the CIO and African Americans, including shifts in approach, see also Hill, "The Problem of Race in Labor History"; Nelson, *Divided We Stand*; Michael K. Honey, *Southern Labor and Black Civil Rights* (Urbana, IL: University of Illinois Press, 1993).
84. Eldon L. Johnson, "General Unions in the Federal Service," *The Journal of Politics* 2, no. 1 (1940): 23–56.
85. Margaret C. Rung, "United Public Workers of America/United Federal Workers of America," in *Encyclopedia of U.S. Labor and Working-Class History*, ed. Eric Arneson (New York: Routledge, 2007), 3: 1444–46.
86. "Howard Med School Goes CIO," *Chicago Defender* (July 1, 1944).
87. Joseph L. Johnson to Colleagues, January 17, 1945, Box 2504, Dyson Materials.
88. Herbert Biblio, "Librarians and Trade Unionism: A Prologue," *Library Trends* 25, no. 2 (1976): 423–33; John J. Clopine, "A History of Library Unions in the United States," (PhD dissertation, Catholic University of America, 1951), 112–16.
89. "UFWA Growing Fast at Howard University," *Federal Record* 6, no. 9 (1944): 8.
90. Joseph L. Johnson to Colleagues, January 17, 1945, Box 2504, Dyson Materials.
91. "Howard U Agrees to Collective Bargaining," *Federal Record* 7, no. 7 (November 1945): 3.
92. Ibid.
93. The reasons for this decision are unclear, especially as the faculty expressed their concern over teaching conditions and salaries at the October Board meeting. No internal records of the Howard Branch exist to offer evidence and none of the reports explicitly noting the exclusion of faculty explains the decision. Ibid; "Howard Employees Vote 203 to 0 for a CIO Union," *Chicago Defender* (December 22, 1945).
94. "Contract Signed at Howard U." *Federal Record* 7, no. 11 (May 1946): 2.
95. "Dr. Lawlah, Dean at Howard Medical School, Resigns," *Chicago Defender* (April 6, 1946).
96. "275 Howard Professors Revolt Against Prexy," *Chicago Defender* (April 13, 1946). A shortened version of the article also appeared as "Howard U. Profs Charge College is Substandard," *New York Amsterdam News* (April 13, 1946).
97. Venice T. Spraggs, "Howard Law Professor Resigns in School Fight," *Chicago Defender* (April 20, 1946); "Resigns Howard U. Law Post," *Chicago Defender* (April 20, 1946). Two separate articles by Spraggs, one about the law school situation and one about the report appeared under one banner headline.
98. Venice T. Spraggs, "Howard Law Professor Resigns."
99. "Howard Teachers Deny 'Revolt' Charge; Say Article 'Unethical,'" *New Journal and Guide* (April 20, 1946).
100. Venice Spraggs, "Trouble Mounts in Howard U Faculty Brawl," *Chicago Defender* (April 27, 1946); Venice Spraggs, "Sub-Standard Conditions Hurt Howard University," *Chicago Defender* (May 4, 1946).
101. Mary E. Harding, "Eleanor Nelson, Oliver Palmer and the Struggle to Organize the CIO in Washington, D.C., 1937–1950" (PhD dissertation, The George Washington University, 2002), 191–214; Rung, "United Public Workers of America/United Federal Workers of America."
102. Harding, "Eleanor Nelson, Oliver Palmer and the Struggle to Organize the CIO in Washington, D. C., 1937–1950," 216.
103. Walter Dyson, "For the Consideration of the President and the Board of Trustees of Howard University," (n.d.), Box 2504, Dyson Materials.
104. Walter Dyson to Mr. Murphy, December 13, 1946, Box 2504, Dyson Materials. This letter was attached to a longer manuscript on the issue with the suggestion that it be published.

105. "Howard University," *Chicago Defender* (May 31, 1947).

106. "The President Approves," *The Light* (January 1947); "Howard Teachers in Union Election," *Chicago Defender* (January 26, 1947).

107. Joseph L. Johnson, "Professionals and Organized Labor," *The Light* (January 1947).

108. Joseph L. Johnson would hold the position until a 1955 disagreement with Mordecai Johnson over whether funds provided to the medical school could be used by the university as a whole. "Dr. Johnson, Med Dean in Howard Rift," *Chicago Defender* (May 14, 1955).

109. One hundred and forty-five members of the staff were eligible to vote. James M. Nasbit, Jr., to Mordecai Johnson, Minutes of the Executive Committee, Howard University, March 14, 1947, 1, Howard University Archives; "Professors at Howard Un. Choose UPW at Election," *Public Record* 2, no. 2 (1947): 5.

110. "Howard Teachers Join CIO Union," *Chicago Defender* (May 24, 1947); "First Contract Signed Covering College Teachers," *Public Record* 2, no. 5 (1947): 3; Minutes of the Executive Committee, Howard University, May 1, 1947, 1–5, Howard University Archives.

111. The agreement for salary increases became official in October but the June 1947 *Public Record* indicated that retroactive raises of $450 were already in place. Logan, *Howard University*, 365–66; "Region V Reports: It Pays ($$$) to belong to UPW," *Public Record* 2, no. 6 (1947): 5.

112. "Agreement between Howard University and Local 10, CIO, Covering Teachers," Minutes of the Board of Trustees, Howard University, April 16, 1949, 6, Howard University Archives.

113. "Howard Medical School Squabble Threatening," *Atlanta Daily World* (August 10, 1949); "Howard U. Terminates Dr. Corson's Contract," *Atlanta Daily World* (September 22, 1949); Minutes of the Board of Trustees, Howard University September 17, 1949, 4, Howard University Archives.

114. Johnson, "The Social Responsibility of the Administrator," 304.

115. Robert H. Zieger, *The CIO, 1935–1950* (Chapel Hill, NC: University of North Carolina Press, 1995), 253–93; Ellen W. Schrecker, *The Age of McCarthyism: A Brief History with Documents*, 2nd edn. (New York: Palgrave Macmillan, 2002), 171, 221–22; Rung, "United Public Workers," 1446; Senate Committee on the Judiciary, Subcommittee to Investigate the Administration of the Internal Security Act and Other Internal Security Laws, *Subversive Control of the United Public Workers of America* (Washington, DC: United States Government Printing Office, 1952); Rhonda Hanson, "United Public Workers: The Conscience of the Capitol," in *The Cold War Against Labor*, ed. Ann Fagan Ginger and David Christiano (Berkeley, CA: Meiklejohn Civil Liberties Institute, 1987), 1: 389–98.

116. Johnson, "Social Responsibility," 304–5.

117. "Howard, Ham'ton Hit for Ending Contract," *Atlanta Daily World* May 4, 1950; "Howard Workers Want Contract," *Pittsburgh Courier* (July 8, 1950). See also "Afro-American Scores Howard U. Labor Policy," *Public Record* 5, no. 7 (1950): 2.

118. Johnson, "Social Responsibility," 305.

119. Cook sent a telegram to the event explaining her decision. She was to be honored for leading the Howard Players on an acclaimed tour of Europe. "Head of Howard U Players Refuses to Attend 'Red' Reception," *Chicago Defender* (March 11, 1950). For a discussion of the tour, see Errol G. Hill and James V. Hatch, *A History of African American Theatre* (New York: Cambridge University Press, 2003), 266, 329, 341.

120. Kenneth Robert Janken, *Rayford W. Logan and the Dilemma of the African American Intellectual* (Amherst, MA: University of Massachusetts Press, 1993), 206; Logan, *Howard University*, 390.

121. "CIO Has a Majority!" (Flier, n.d.) and multiple issues of "CIO Organizer: A Bulletin for Howard Employees," Dyson Materials; Milton Murray to James Caldwell, July 14, 1950 and Milton Murray to Mordecai W. Johnson November 7, 1950, box 2, folder 5, American Federation of State, County and Municipal Employees: Secretary-Treasurer's Office—Government and Civic Employees Organizing Committee Collection, Archive of Labor and Urban Affairs, Walter P. Reuther Library, Wayne State University, Detroit, MI (hereafter AFSCME Secretary-Treasurer's Office GCEOC Collection).

122. Jean Pagano, Report to Milton Murray (January 29, 1951); Jean Pagano, Report to Milton Murray (March 27, 1951) and Jean Pagano to All CIO Members, box 4, folder 4, AFSCME Secretary-Treasurer's Office GCEOC Collection.

123. These difficulties involved allegations that the institution delayed negotiations with the union for two years and that administrators refused to sign agreements once they were reached. They were given added significance because they complicated the proposed transfer of Freedman's Hospital to the institution and revealed deep concerns over the administration's attitude toward organized labor. President Johnson pointed to the experiences with the UFWA and UPWA in his attempts to counter the notion that the institution was antiunion. As part of the dispute, James B. Carey, president of the International Union of Electrical Workers (AFL-CIO) and former Secretary-Treasurer of the CIO, termed the institution's stance "indefensible" and resigned his position on Howard University's Board of Trustees in February 1959. "Labor Leader Quits As Howard Trustee," *Washington Post* (February 2, 1959). See box 50, folder 3 and box 12, folder 1, American Federation of State, County and Municipal Employees: President's Office—Arnold S. Zander Collection, Archive of Labor and Urban Affairs, Walter P. Reuther Library, Wayne State University, Detroit, MI; box 25, folder 1, AFSCME Secretary-Treasurer's Office GCEOC Collection; and the records of the Freedman's Hospital merger in box 9, AFSCME Secretary-Treasurer's Office GCEOC Collection.

124. H. Naylor Fitzhugh to Fellow Worker, May 11, 1936, box 22, folder 4, Frazier Papers.

125. Doxey A. Wilkerson, Sterling A. Brown, Alain L. Locke, W. Robert Ming, Naomi Rushing, and J. Leon Shereshefsky to T. L. Hungate, June 1, 1939, box 11, folder Local # 440, AFT Part I, Series IV.

126. As is noted above, the union later withdrew its complaint and praised the thoroughness and equity with which the institution investigated the matter.

127. "Local News Briefs," *Washington Post* (November 30, 1918); "The Teachers' Union," *Washington Post* (April 28, 1919).

128. Rolland Dewing, "The American Federation of Teachers and Desegregation," *Journal of Negro Education* 42, no. 1 (1973): 79–92.

129. *National Labor Relations Board v. Yeshiva*, 444 U.S. 672 (1980).

130. Ernst Benjamin, "Faculty Bargaining," in *Academic Collective Bargaining*, ed. Ernst Benjamin and Michael Mauer (Washington, DC: Modern Language Association of America and the American Association of University Professors, 2006), 23–51.

131. Marc Bousquet, *How the University Works: Higher Education and the Low-Wage Nation* (New York: New York University Press, 2008), 96–97.

Competing Visions of Higher Education: The College of Liberal Arts Faculty and the Administration of Howard University, 1939–1960

Louis Ray

Limited finances framed a debate at Howard University during the 1930s regarding how to gain the maximum value from the university in terms of its production of leaders. Prominent faculty sought to focus on: (1) undergraduate education, (2) reduced tuition, and (3) higher academic and admissions standards. On the other hand, with the exception of teacher education, Howard's administration gave funding priority to professional education in order to provide the advanced training that Afro-America needed, yet so few HBCUs provided.

With the onset of the depression, it appeared in the 1930s that the task before African-American higher education was no longer that of strengthening the faculty and growing the physical plant.[1] Instead, the challenge was one of survival. In the 1930s, debates over tuition costs and organizational priorities were sources of friction among faculty and administrators at Howard University, the largest historically black college and university during the segregation period.

As the depression deepened, proponents of competing visions of black higher education at Howard University renewed their debate about how to allocate the university's scarce resources.[2] This case study examines a debate at Howard that not only featured competing goals but also highlighted a push by the faculty for a larger voice in policymaking.

Perspectives on the History of Higher Education 29 (2012): 151-172
© 2012. ISBN: 978-1-4128-4771-1

Among the questions the faculty debated were: Should Howard University specialize in providing quality undergraduate instruction (making graduate and professional training the province of mainstream higher education)? How many resources should go into making education at Howard affordable? How selective should its admissions standards be? What criteria should Howard use when setting its tuition?

From the early surveys of black higher education such as those conducted by Du Bois in 1910 and Thomas Jesse Jones in 1917, Howard University ranked among the strongest black colleges.[3] In 1933, Howard's student enrollment exceeded the combined enrollments of Fisk University, Atlanta University, Morehouse College, and Spelman College—its closest rivals.[4] Therefore, the debate at Howard had implications for the management of black higher education nationally, especially its regionally accredited colleges.

Not all observers viewed Howard University as the epitome of higher educational opportunity. Charles H. Thompson, then a professor of education at Howard and editor of the *Journal of Negro Education* (hereafter referred to as the *Journal*) was skeptical. In July 1933, Thompson alluded to mainstream criticism of the qualifications of the teaching staffs of the black colleges.

According to Thompson, in *The American Race Problem* sociologist E. B. Reuter claimed, "The total number of really educated Negroes in the country is not sufficient to make a faculty for one first-class college."[5] Reuter's remarks challenged the commitment of private foundations such as the General Education Board to ensuring equal higher educational opportunity albeit within the framework of segregation. Thompson wrote that Reuter's comment set off a furor in black education circles in 1927; yet he acknowledged there was some truth to Reuter's observation. Critical assessments such as Reuter's spurred, wrote Thompson, "considerable effort . . . by administrators of Negro colleges, with the aid of fellowships from two or three philanthropic organizations, to remedy this situation by sending promising young Negro students to our large graduate schools."[6]

In providing these fellowships, historian Wayne J. Urban argued private foundations such as the Rosenwald Fund and the General Education Board sought to develop a network of black academics.[7] Returning south, these scholars worked to raise the caliber of instruction at the black colleges during the 1930s, 1940s, and 1950s. While acknowledging that modest progress had occurred since the launching of the initiative, in July 1933, Thompson concluded:

If it were true, in 1927, that there was not a sufficient number of 'really educated' Negroes to man *one* first-class college, it is true today [July 1933] that there is not a sufficient number to man more than two or three first-class colleges, and they would have to be very small. This observation is strikingly illustrated by the fact, from the point of view of degrees alone, one-third of the 220 faculty members in colleges rated as 'A' by the Southern Association have *only* bachelors' degrees; and fewer than one-tenth have doctor's degrees. If this is the case in the best Negro colleges, involving biracial faculties, one can easily surmise what the average must be.[8]

As early as 1933, various stakeholders in black higher education argued for narrowing the mission and scope of the black colleges because of the limitations imposed by, for example, small numbers of highly qualified teachers. Some believed that the resources of black higher education were too paltry to provide quality undergraduate, graduate, and professional education. A wiser choice, they argued, would be to invest available resources in undergraduate education. This, they believed, was the quickest route to strengthening black higher education, generally.

As this essay shows, the faculty of the College of Liberal Arts at Howard argued that undergraduate education was a university's first priority. In April 1939, in his editorial response to the *Gaines* (1938) decision, Thompson assessed the states of Virginia and Texas' efforts to add graduate programs onto the "Negro state college." He wrote, "It does not take any great amount of investigation to arrive at the only sound conclusion possible in such instances, that the lack of personnel and library resources in such institutions raises the question as to whether even first-class *college* work can be done, to say nothing about *graduate* work."[9]

Thompson's July 1933 observations did not apply directly to Howard because the Middle States Association and not the Southern Association accredited the university. Nevertheless, his comments underscored Thompson's concern with defining the mission of black higher education in ways that acknowledged the limitations set, for example, by its teaching staffs. In his *Journal* editorials during the 1930s, Thompson also argued that the development of black higher education be driven by clearly defined educational goals and the findings of valid, empirical research.[10]

In July 1933, Thompson discussed data collected by Fred McCuistion, executive agent, Association of Colleges and Secondary Schools of the Southern States. McCuistion chaired the committee responsible for evaluating the black colleges seeking accreditation from the Southern Association. According to the best available data in 1932, "17,333, or approximately 77 per cent, of Negro college students, as listed by Mr. McCuistion, are enrolled in institutions which are below the standard of a real college as determined by regional accrediting agencies," wrote Thompson.[11]

Only 5,276 black college students in 1932 attended a regionally accredited black college.[12] The logical implications of Thompson's argument was that only 5,276 blacks college students in 1932 received the caliber of undergraduate education that prepared them to pursue graduate or professional study or leadership positions. Did regionally accredited black colleges, including Howard, have an obligation to educate the most promising black students? This question vexed Thompson and other black educators during segregation. As the largest college in black higher education, did Howard University have an obligation to demonstrate leadership on this issue was a question faculty leaders at the university wrestled with in the winter of 1939.

Charles H. Thompson

Historians Adam Fairclough and Francine Rusan Wilson described Thompson as politically left of center. Fairclough portrayed Thompson in the early 1930s as one of the "young black radicals."[13] Thompson earned this appellation through his uncompromising opposition to racial segregation and discrimination.[14] Over the years, his unflagging advocacy of desegregated public education proved to be more enduring than even that of a stalwart such as Du Bois.

On campus, historian Francine Rusan Wilson placed Thompson among: "The group of faculty often called the Howard radicals [who] included E. Franklin Frazier, Ralph J. Bunche, Emmett E. Dorsey and Charles H. Thompson."[15] Thompson was a progressive who believed in the potential of social engineering. He also believed that the rigorous application of the scientific method could reduce discrimination and enhance educational and social outcomes.[16]

A 1917 graduate of Virginia Union University, in 1925 he earned notoriety as the first African American to earn the PhD in education. He completed the doctorate in educational psychology at Chicago in a department led by Charles H. Judd. From 1922 to 1924, he was the director of instruction at the State Normal School, Montgomery, Alabama. During 1925–1926, he was an instructor of psychology and social science at Sumner High School and Junior College in Kansas City, Kansas. Thompson entered Howard University as an associate professor in 1926. So productive was he in terms of service, teaching, and research he earned promotion to full professor an astounding three years later in 1929.[17]

Shortly before his promotion to professor, in November 1928, he published in the *Annals of the American Academy of Political and Social Science* alongside race relations heavyweights such as Du Bois, Ernest W. Burgess, George E. Haynes, E. Franklin Frazier, Charles S. Johnson, Alain Locke, Kelly Miller, R. R. Moton, Robert E. Park, E. B. Reuter, and Monroe Work.[18]

In his article "The Educational Achievements of Negro Children," Thompson focused on what he characterized as erroneous assumptions that persuaded mainstream scholars to conclude that African Americans were mentally inferior to whites. He respectfully, but directly, challenged this thesis. Thompson wrote, "It is our aim, in the first place, therefore, to point out the fact that not only is the interpretation of the results of comparative racial measurements as indicative of an inherent racial inferiority or superiority logically untenable, but that, in many instances, it is specifically refuted by the facts."[19] He continued:

> . . . it is perfectly easy to comprehend why our present experimentation with mental and scholastic tests has been predicated upon the assumption of an inherent mental inferiority of the Negro race. While this hypothesis is easy to comprehend, it has been unfortunate in that the interpretation of the results of comparative racial measurements has been, in too many cases, so conditioned by this premise that more logical interpretations have been overlooked or ruthlessly discounted.[20]

His thirty-one-year editorship of the *Journal of Negro Education* began in April 1932. Within one year of publication, educators deemed the *Journal* of sufficient value to warrant its inclusion in *Education Index*.[21] As editor of the *Journal*, Thompson earned a reputation as a fierce critic of lower standards for black education and an even more formidable opponent of segregation and discrimination.

Describing the function the *Journal* served, historian Adam Fairclough wrote: "the *Journal* also provided a forum for intellectuals, civil rights leaders, and teachers to address all the major issues affecting black education." According to Fairclough, the *Journal* played a salutary role in reducing the divisions separating northern and southern black teachers and those working in private and public schools. Thompson designed the *Journal* to facilitate candid, critical discussions. Fairclough elaborated, "Thompson believed the vulnerability of public school teachers made journals like the *Bulletin*, the major organ of the NATSC [National Association of Teachers in Colored Schools] insufficiently forthright, especially when it came to criticizing segregation. Thompson kept the *Journal* open to all comers, but he was keen to promote criticism of Jim Crow."[22]

Charles Thompson's foray into administration at Howard in 1931 began at roughly the same time as he assumed his editorial duties. For one year, he served as acting dean of the College of Education. His first major administrative assignment was as dean of the College of Liberal Arts from 1938 to 1943. Thompson also served as the Graduate School dean at Howard from 1944 to 1961.[23]

As a scholarly journal editor and dean at Howard, he was a respected, highly visible educational insider during the period under discussion. Renowned for his scholarship and integrity, Thompson was adroit enough politically to sustain a forty-year career in oftentimes-tumultuous black Washington, DC. Howard University also was no stranger to controversy as historians Rayford W. Logan, Constance M. Green, and biographer Richard I. McKinney attest.[24] Historian John Hope Franklin described his travails as a rising scholar at Howard University and identified Thompson as one of the most competent, affable, and accessible senior administrators at the university. Franklin also described Thompson as a strong champion of young faculty.[25]

In spring 1980, Faustine C. Jones, *Journal*'s interim editor, summed up Thompson's career in her eulogy, "In Memoriam: Dean Charles H. Thompson (1896–1980)." Jones chose the phrase "an educational giant" to capture Thompson's significance at Howard University and beyond. During his long career, Jones argued that Thompson was "an educator's educator" who gained notoriety "as a sage ... and hard task-master." He excelled as a mentor, Jones observed, "Ever so many of Dr. Thompson's students over that forty-year period of service at Howard University regarded him as a father figure and mentor, for his role with them exceeded by far that prescribed by the common dictates of academic instruction. He was their guiding light, ever available to them."[26] Quoting a July 18, 1946 letter from Edwin Embree, president of the Rosenwald Fund, historians Patrick J. Gilpin and Marybeth Gasman portrayed Thompson in the postwar years as "a mature, able man of high academic standing ... [who was not] involved in any of the acute rivalries."[27]

The conflict this essay examines over how best to fulfill the purpose of black higher education at Howard pitted leading black intellectuals against the university administration. Both sides of the controversy enlisted scholars who were active in the African-American civil rights movement. The debate featured faculty leaders of the College of Liberal Arts against its president, the fiery-tempered, former pastor Mordecai Wyatt Johnson.

According to historian Rayford Logan, during Johnson's presidency faculty enjoyed "two kinds of academic freedom—one somewhat specious, the other, genuine." While prominent faculty members were free to express their views on external events, Logan contended that, "The Faculty had a limited voice in running the university." Some of Johnson's critics, Logan continued, alleged that Johnson created "a Senate, Council of the Senate and Steering Committee to answer the criticism of the Middle States Association concerning the Faculty's limited voice."[28] In winter 1939, Thompson and the department chairs of the College of Liberal Arts made a bid to play a major role in university governance on issues that troubled them.

Mordecai Wyatt Johnson at Howard University

Elected to the presidency in 1926, Johnson was Howard University's first African-American president. Historian Rayford Logan, a staunch critic of Johnson, described Johnson as a light complexioned or "voluntary Negro" with a flair for micromanagement. Johnson experienced what Logan described as "Messianic Moments."[29] An inspired Johnson "would tell the late E. Franklin Frazier the kind of sociology to write or the late Abram Harris the kind of economics to study," asserted Logan.[30] According to Logan, for years Johnson battled zoologist E. E. Just over control of the research grants Just obtained from private foundations.[31]

When Johnson accepted the presidency in 1926, faculty morale at Howard was low because of high teaching loads, low salaries, and substandard facilities. Johnson realized that the federal government was the only source of funding capable of putting the university on a sound footing. Within two years of taking office, Johnson developed and implemented a plan for obtaining federal financing for Howard.[32]

In the fall of 1960, Thompson recalled, "During the first year and a half of his administration, Dr. Johnson made a thorough study of the needs and prospects of Howard University. He concluded that the federal government had a moral obligation to the Negro minority which could only be met by the development of the University into a first-class institution, and that Howard University should be made in fact, as well as in name, 'the Capstone of Negro Education.'"[33] "Dr. Johnson was unusually successfully in selling his program for Howard University to the Federal government," Thompson continued.[34]

In his salute to Johnson, Thompson also highlighted the rationale underlying the Twenty-Year Plan Johnson negotiated with federal officials. The development of Howard University would offset, in part, the lack of higher educational opportunities for African Americans in the segregated South.[35] To demonstrate its continuing relevance and to sustain federal funding, it was imperative to grow Howard University. Therefore, the thinking underlying the Twenty-Year Plan explicitly linked growing enrollments to increases in the university budget.

According to Johnson's biographer Richard I. McKinney, Johnson succeeded in gaining federal support for the university with the aid of philanthropist Julius Rosenwald.[36] McKinney described Rosenwald and Abraham Flexner of the General Education Board as among Johnson's early sponsors. A turning point for the university occurred on December 13, 1928, when President Herbert Hoover signed H. R. 8466 a bill amending the Howard University charter to authorize annual federal appropriations to the university. Logan attributed the growth of Howard University into the strongest university in segregated black higher education to this charter amendment.[37]

Historian Michael R. Winston attributed the increased flow of federal funds to the university to President Franklin D. Roosevelt's decision to transform Howard University into "a vital symbol of Negro progress." According to Winston, on October 26, 1936, "Roosevelt himself dedicated the new chemistry building at Howard University." This development represented "the first time that a Negro institution received more than a million dollars for a science facility." For many years, Winston continued, "the science facilities at Howard University were the best available to Negro scientists in universities."[38] During this period, the faculty at Howard included some of the leading intellectuals of Afro-America. They included Percy R. Barnes, PhD (chemistry), Ralph J. Bunche, PhD (political science), Charles E. Burch, PhD (English), Charles Hamilton Houston, JD (law), E. Franklin Frazier, PhD (sociology), Abram L. Harris, PhD (economics), Ernest E. Just, PhD (zoology), Alain L. Locke, PhD (philosophy), Rayford W. Logan, PhD (history), Benjamin E. Mays, PhD (religion), Francis C. Sumner, PhD (psychology), Charles H. Thompson, PhD (education), and Charles H. Wesley, PhD (history).[39]

After securing the amendment to the university charter, Johnson worked out the details of a Twenty-Year Plan with federal officials. The Twenty-Year Plan projected the growth of the university between 1930 and 1950 including its enrollment goals. After the elapse of ten years, in late 1938 the time had come to assess Howard University's performance in terms of the Twenty-Year Plan's goals.

Though the College of Liberal Arts accounted for more than 70 percent of the university's enrollment during the 1930s, Johnson championed and invested heavily in small professional programs (medicine, dentistry, engineering, law, pharmacy, and religion) accounting for less than 10 percent of the university's enrollment.[40] Howard's professional schools were major gateways to the professions for African Americans during segregation. In fact, the decision to refuse admission to part-time students by closing the night school of the Howard School of Law was controversial in 1929. Johnson was the object of animosity for raising standards in order to gain accreditation for the law school.[41]

Among the assignments awaiting Thompson as incoming dean in November 1938, was preparing a progress report on the first ten years of implementing the Twenty-Year Plan at the College. Compounding the need to report on the first ten years of implementing the Twenty-Year Plan was the need to respond to the Supreme Court's historic December 12, 1938 *Gaines* ruling. These concerns sparked the flurry of research and committee meetings at Howard that resulted in Thompson's *Revision of the Twenty Year Plan.*[42]

In February 1939, Thompson acknowledged that he and the College of Liberal Arts faculty faced deadline pressures. He wrote: "The brief time at our disposal in which to accomplish so fundamental a task ... necessitates a much more general treatment than desirable. However, the broad outlines indicated here are valid in general, necessitating only *more* detailed facts than we have been able to assemble to date."[43]

As he acknowledged on the title page, he prepared the report, *Revision of the Twenty-Year Plan with Especial Reference to the College of Liberal Arts*, in "consultation and cooperation with" the College's Council of Department Heads. The twenty-member Council was interracial and interdisciplinary representing the College's top leadership. By consulting and developing the report in cooperation with the department chairpersons, Thompson modeled the democratic approach to governance he advised policymakers in black education to adopt in his *Journal* editorials during the 1930s.[44]

While agreeing that the *Gaines* decision "was far-reaching, in its theoretical implications," Thompson argued that *Gaines* would do little to alter the landscape of black higher education in the South by 1950.[45] All *Gaines* required, he implied, was for black public colleges in the segregated states to offer the same type and quality of higher education as the white state university. This would not propel the growth of black public higher education in the segregated South, he reasoned:

> We need only keep in mind the fact that there are not more than one or two first-class colleges in the South for white students, to estimate what practical effect this decision might have on Negro higher education in the South. What is more important, the decision, while it has implications for college education, is specifically concerned with the *lack* of professional education for Negroes.[46]

Despite their illegality, some of the more progressive segregated states continued to opt for out-of-state scholarships, Thompson wrote in April 1939. Therefore, gaining the optimum value from the limited resources available to black education remained a pressing concern for scholar/activists such as Thompson. It is profitable to view the *Revision*, through the lens of black scholars' insistence upon wresting the maximum value from black higher education. It is also profitable to view the *Revision* as an act of self-determination in which scholars at Howard insisted on having a voice in shaping the policies that affected their wellbeing and that of Afro-America.

Rising Tuition and Falling Enrollment at the College

According to the Twenty-Year Plan's projections, enrollment at the College of Liberal Arts was to reach 1,600 students in 1935–36 and 2,200 students by 1940–41. The Graduate School at Howard was to grow from 190 to 600 students. As modest as the numbers are by today's standards, Thompson wrote the College of Liberal Arts at Howard failed to reach the enrollment goals set for 1935–36 and probably would fail to meet those set for 1940–41.[47]

Instead, student attrition worsened around the time the Twenty-Year Plan won approval. He wrote: "our enrollment began to drop sharply in 1929–30."[48] Enrollment at the College of Liberal Arts was in a freefall dropping 11.3 percent in 1929–30. It fell 13.2 percent in 1930–31. Rebounding, enrollment rose 8.1 percent in 1931–32 only to plummet 20.9 percent in 1932–33.[49] In the *Revision*, Thompson sought to ferret out what factors accounted for the College's steep enrollment declines between 1929–30 and 1932–33.

The steep drop in enrollment at Howard in 1929–30 was an anomaly. To illustrate this point, Thompson selected a comparison group of "37 public and 32 private colleges and universities." These institutions experienced no serious losses of students during the first two years of the depression. It was only during 1932–33 that significant numbers of students withdrew. Surprisingly, Thompson reported, enrollment at the black land-grant colleges grew by more than 28 percent during the first two years of the depression. Only once (1932–1933) in the five-year period ending in 1933–34, did enrollment dip at the black land-grant colleges by a modest 3.4 percent. Enrollment at the College the same year plummeted 20.9 percent.[50]

After eliminating several comparatively minor reasons, Thompson wrote that he was "practically certain" that the nearly 21 percent decline in enrollment at the College was in response to the 25 percent rise in tuition. The university planned to phase in this tuition rise over three years beginning in 1929–30. He questioned the rationale for raising tuition:

> Just why this policy was instituted at this point is not at all clear, since tuition at Howard was already higher than in any other Negro college or many white State universities, and since Government appropriations had been insured by legislation and there had been a small but definite increase in such support from year to year and the immediate prospects indicated a considerable increase from this source.[51]

According to the university treasurer, in 1939, student accounts at the College were $50,000 in arrears—nearly 59 percent of the College faculty's annual salary. Moreover, the university treasurer reported "every year some 150 or 200 students are suspended for non-payment of fees although many of them manage somehow to get reinstated." By 1939, it was clear that raising tuition did not stabilize the College's finances.[52]

Tuition at the College of Liberal Arts in 1939 was set at $150 annually. In contrast, he asserted, the average in-state tuition for the collegiate divisions of public universities in the United States hovered around $79 annually. In the *Revision*, Thompson reported data showing the average out-of-state tuition charged by public colleges in the United States was $128 annually. The College's high tuition created a competitive disadvantage that was difficult to overcome or justify.[53]

"There are some 20 Northern State colleges and universities . . . where a Negro student from any State would pay less tuition and other fees than at Howard University." According to Thompson, the universities charging lower tuition included "the *University of Colorado, State University of Iowa, University of Kansas, University of Michigan, University of Nebraska, and the University of Minnesota.*"[54] The data suggested the College's tuition rate was a major barrier to the achievement of the Twenty-Year Plan's enrollment goals.

To make matters worse, the data suggested that the university relied upon a crude method for basing enrollment projections and ignored existing evidence. Within the first five pages of the *Revision*, Thompson made the startling observation:

> First, it should be pointed out that the bases employed in predicting the [Twenty-Year Plan enrollment goals] were fallacious, both for the University as a whole, as well as for the separate divisions. The prediction of the enrollments for the College and Graduate School, as well as for other divisions, was made by extending a line-graph, based upon five year intervals from 1900 to 1930 inclusive, to 1935–36 and 1940–41. The use of a five-year interval masked the very important fact (or it was ignored) that enrollment began to drop sharply in 1929–30.[55]

Reporting enrollment annually rather than every five years would have revealed the negative correlation between rising tuition and falling enrollment, he continued.

In a footnote, he wrote that information about declining enrollment was known before a consultant prepared the report used for setting the university's enrollment targets under the Twenty-Year Plan. Thompson contended: "This fact was known . . . and could and should have been taken into account in attempting to predict enrollment."[56] When measured in terms of full-time attendance, the 945 students enrolled at the College in 1937–38 fell short of the 1,044 students enrolled in 1928–29.[57] As late as 1937–38, enrollment at the College had not recovered for the losses associated with the imposition of significantly higher tuition rates.

Scholarships, Admissions Standards and Faculty Hiring

According to Thompson, the university "radically revised" its policy for awarding scholarships in 1932–33.[58] Some faculty (including Thompson) argued for reducing tuition; others at the university argued for creating scholarships derived from the "surplus" generated by the tuition paid by affluent students. The proponents of creating scholarships won over those favoring a reduction of tuition. While this approach might sound appealing, Thompson noted, "The difficulty with the whole plan has been, however, that we have not been able to provide enough scholarships on this basis."[59]

The shortfall in scholarship aid proved to be persistent. The College awarded 241 undergraduate scholarships in 1938–39 totaling $35,270. The Committee on Scholarship and Student Aid reported that 95 percent or 1,140 of the 1,200 applicants for admission annually demonstrated financial need. For every applicant who did not need support to attend the College, nineteen applicants did.[60]

Typically, the College awarded 250 scholarships annually to new and continuing students that were large enough to support attendance at Howard. Twice that number of qualified students decided against enrolling each year for financial reasons. If more money was available for scholarships, the Committee estimated the College could admit on merit an additional 400 qualified applicants annually. In other words, it could expand its enrollment of first-year students by 260 percent.[61] Existing policy discouraged talented, low-income students from enrolling contrary to the rationale of the Twenty-Year Plan.

Thompson estimated that it would require 691 additional scholarships to meet the enrollment projections in force under the Twenty-Year Plan. The cost of reaching the goals set for 1950–51, he declared, would be an amount he regarded as prohibitive—$114,960 annually.[62] In addition, Thompson estimated the College would need to add twenty-one faculty members to the eighty-one currently working in 1939 to teach the additional students the projections required the College to admit. The cost of hiring twenty-one faculty members (including ten at the rank of professor) would cost another $83,589 for salaries and research expenses alone.[63]

In the throes of the depression, Thompson argued it was unlikely the Roosevelt administration would approve a $200,000 budget increase for the College.[64] In contrast, the typical black college's budget was less than $83,000 annually in the 1933. Almost one-quarter of black colleges in the 1933 subsisted on less than $25,000 a year.[65] The most realistic path forward for the College, he argued, involved raising admission standards, negotiating for a more equitable funding formula, and lowering the cost of attendance by reducing tuition.

University Finances

Some of the toughest criticism Thompson leveled in the *Revision* involved university finances and budget decisions. His discussion highlighted the fact that equity issues on campus complicated those associated with the higher education discrimination practiced by the segregated states. He began the section of the report entitled "Distribution of Funds Within the University" with the candid observation, "One of the outstanding difficulties in the administration of the Twenty-Year Plan, as far as the College has been concerned, has been the inexplicable (and obviously uneven) distribution of funds among the several divisions of the University."[66]

Despite growing enrollment, funding for the College in 1938–39 was 18.2 percent below its 1931–32 budget levels, he reported. While enrollment in engineering, music, medicine, and religion was static, their budgets registered growth ranging from 25.7 percent (engineering) to 49.4 percent (religion). Moreover, Thompson argued the expenses of operating professional programs at Howard exceeded those of similar programs at Harvard, Stanford, Michigan, Illinois, Iowa, Ohio State, or Pennsylvania. The costs of operating professional programs at Howard was twice as expensive, and in a few cases three times as costly, as similar programs at some of the nation's top universities.[67]

The data compelled Thompson to conclude: "If the College of Liberal Arts is to achieve its objectives in the next ten-year period, it will have to receive a greater share of University funds than formerly; certainly, it will have to be treated at least as well as liberal arts colleges in other universities in relation to their professional divisions."[68]

Recommendations

In the *Revision of the Twenty-Year Plan*, Thompson argued that the university administration based at least three major policy decisions on fallacious assumptions. The thinking underlying the decisions regarding tuition, scholarship aid, and enrollment targets, he implied, undercut the university's mission. For example, the decision to raise tuition beyond the ability of most African Americans to pay was tantamount to pricing the College out of existence. More important, the decision to raise tuition failed to recognize the relationship among higher tuition rates, declining enrollment rates, and lower admissions standards. It failed to recognize that the university's clientele were primarily low-income people who were typically the last hired and the first fired.

Thompson argued that the rise in tuition undercut the purpose of the Twenty-Year Plan of offsetting higher educational discrimination in the South. As the scholarship data showed, high tuition rates dampened the demand for higher education among African Americans and placed the university on the defensive as purportedly failing to meet challenging enrollment targets. A more proactive approach, Thompson insisted, would have been to persuade the federal government, and by implication the segregated states, to pay the same per capita costs for educating African-American students as they paid for educating white students. Support at that level, Thompson argued, would come closer to meeting the minimum requirements set by the separate but equal doctrine enunciated in *Plessy v. Ferguson*. Comparable support was necessary to slow the expanding gap in higher education opportunity in the South. Instead, the university shifted the onus in the form of high tuition rates onto those who least could afford to pay them, African-American students and families.[69]

Arguing that the cost of tuition at public universities nationally ranged between 30 percent and 35 percent of the cost of instruction, Thompson advocated dropping tuition fees at the College from $150 annually to as close to $72.50 annually was politically feasible. Recognizing that a 50 percent drop in tuition was untenable, he argued tuition at the College of Liberal Arts should be set no higher than $100 annually or at about 40 percent of the cost of instruction.[70]

Accompanying the 33 percent reduction in tuition fees would be more selective admission standards phased in over three years. In 1939, Thompson estimated at least one-third of the students enrolled in the College of Liberal Arts were "definitely sub-collegiate." He considered it "wasteful to dissipate our resources upon these students."[71] He declared:

> In spite of the fact that we know that at least one-third of our students are sub-collegiate, yet initial results from a study of distribution of grades in the College disclose that we are giving as many "A's" and "B's" to our students as are given to students in Harvard College in the same general fields. This obviously can mean but one thing, namely, that we are up-grading poor students and thereby degrading real college standards. We can continue this practice only at the peril of our academic life.[72]

The first priority of the university, he argued, was to provide quality undergraduate education. A quality undergraduate education would prepare gifted students for graduate and professional education and for the demands of leadership.

Thompson asked Johnson to renegotiate with federal officials the enrollment projections of the Twenty-Year Plan. In his opinion:

> the most reasonable procedure would involve setting up an enrollment limit which we have a reasonable chance of obtaining funds to teach properly; and which would allow us to set up more highly selective admission requirements as early as possible.[73]

Lower tuition rates also were to be a negotiation objective.

For Thompson, it was reasonable to forecast that federal support might grow slowly until by 1950–51 the College had enough qualified teachers to educate 1,000 undergraduates and 250 graduate students. He and the College's department chairs asked the university to reduce the size of the 5,000-student university Johnson championed by 75 percent.[74]

By 1950–51, the College of Liberal Arts should have the resources to provide a first-class education to 1,000 students selected on merit,

Thompson predicted. Even with growth, its teaching and other resources would not allow it to educate 1,200 students entering at many different skill levels. If the College was indeed the "core of the university," then smaller student to teacher ratios were imperative to undo the damage of Howard students' substandard elementary and secondary training in segregated schools.

While the preparatory, cultural, and vocational aims of collegiate education at Howard were similar to those of mainstream American colleges, he argued the College of Liberal Arts differed in two important respects. First, its principal rationale was the "Development of Honest and Intelligent Leadership for a Disadvantaged Racial Minority." Equally important, Thompson argued for collegiate education designed to promote the "Development of the Ability and Disposition to Safeguard One's Mental and Physical Health."[75] Without apology, he recognized the hazards racism posed for African Americans' mental and physical health, and by implication, their potential for service and leadership.

Johnson's Response

Rather than entering into a direct confrontation with prominent members of the faculty, Johnson appeared to adopt several of their recommendations as a means of deflecting criticism. According to historian Rayford Logan, Johnson combined his enrollment goals with several goals Thompson and the Council of Department Heads advocated. Johnson recommended on October 28, 1941, strengthening "professional and graduate work, based upon a college of liberal arts of limited enrollment but of a very high quality of instruction and student body."[76]

According to Logan, during the early 1940s, Johnson also agreed to request the federal government to fund 68.6 percent of the university's current expenses. Consistent with a recommendation in the *Revision*, he agreed to request federal support comparable to "the percentage of support available from all governmental sources in publicly supported institutions during 1937–38 . . ."[77] He also agreed to phase-in standardized entrance examinations for students graduating from unaccredited high schools.

Johnson also appeared to support Thompson's proposal for creating national scholarships capable of making Howard accessible to more gifted, low-income students, wrote Logan. In 1941, Mordecai Johnson and the Howard trustees approved the creation of merit-based, national scholarships using funds from the federal government, "private philanthropy and other friends of the University."[78]

Most important, Johnson requested authorization from the university trustees to renegotiate student fees with federal officials with the aim of significantly lowering them.[79] He also asked the trustees for approval to hire staff with expertise in marketing, publicity, and fundraising. This action appeared to be in response to criticism in the *Revision* questioning the decision to fire the person responsible for university fundraising. The *Revision* also noted that the university failed to respond to what Thompson characterized as an "unrelenting and disparaging newspaper campaign against Howard University and the Administration . . . waged by the *Afro-American*" during the late 1920s.[80]

Based upon Johnson's recommendation, on October 27, 1942, the Howard trustees approved in principle tenure and retirement benefits for the faculty. Their action occurred less than one year after Thompson's call for explicit tenure, promotion, and retirement benefit policies for the black colleges in the editorial columns of the *Journal*. Thompson argued in April 1941 that it was a common practice for the presidents of the African-American colleges to dismiss faculty without holding a hearing before their peers or providing them with an explanation for their dismissal. An adept politician in response to public criticism from well-positioned stakeholders, Johnson made concessions while maintaining a steel grip on university policy.[81]

During the early 1940s, Johnson forcibly advanced his agenda for expanding the university physical plant, budget, and enrollment delivering his reply in bricks and mortar, contracts, jobs, and construction crews. According to Logan, as part of the second phase of the Twenty-Year Program, Johnson recommended adding "buildings involving 14 projects at a cost of $6,000,000" in federal funds.[82]

Such a large expansion of facilities required an equally large number of students to fill the new dormitories and classrooms. The College was a prime candidate for expansion. As Thompson ably argued in the *Revision*, the cost of operating professional programs at Howard were twice and sometimes three times as high as the cost of operating similar professional programs at eight research universities. On the one hand, Johnson made meaningful concessions to his critics. On the other hand, he aggressively pursued university expansion focused on the College of Liberal Arts despite faculty opposition.[83]

According to historian Michael R. Winston, Thompson realized he could not remain a dean at Howard if he continued to oppose the president.[84] Realizing that he could not battle Johnson indefinitely, Thompson decided to sidestep pressures to grow the College by relinquishing his deanship in 1943. According to Winston, Thompson asked Johnson to appoint him as dean of the much smaller Graduate School. Valuing Thompson's expertise, Johnson complied in 1944.

When summing up Johnson's major contributions, in fall 1960, Thompson addressed his remarks specifically to Johnson's successor, incoming president James Madison Nabrit, Jr. In a career lasting thirty-four years, Thompson argued Johnson had made the "physical, organizational and financial" dimensions of Howard into those of a first-class university. "The main tasks left to his successor," he averred, "is to do for instruction and research what Dr. Johnson did for the physical, organizational and financial aspects of the University".[85]

According to Thompson, a rigorous inspection would find most of the university's colleges and programs operated at "only a little more than the minimum point of adequacy." Then, he revived arguments similar to those he advanced in the *Revision of the Twenty-Year Plan*. For Howard to become a truly first-rate university in 1960, Thompson urged the incoming president take the following actions. First, he needed to raise and invest large sums in expanding its faculty and raising the standard of instruction. By implication, he should employ those higher standards when making tenure and promotion decisions.[86]

Thompson reminded Nabrit of the need for making significantly larger investments "specifically earmarked" for research, scholarly activities, librarians, and library resources. He also called upon the "teachers-scholars already on the staff" to fulfill their responsibilities to their profession and community by increasing their production of quality research. Most important, he reminded his audience that students were central to the university's mission—calling for significantly larger investments in merit-based student financial aid.[87]

Thompson believed quality education was the key to African American and American progress. In 1939, he and the College department chairs sought to persuade the university's leadership to make tuition affordable and to focus on recruiting and educating the caliber of students capable of addressing the needs of Afro-America. They believed strengthening undergraduate education was the key to increasing the production of black college graduates at Howard and nationally. This approach also would increase the numbers of black students qualified to enter and complete graduate and professional degrees successfully. They also demonstrated that the erroneous assumptions underlying the decisions to revamp scholarships, raise tuition, set funding formulas, and allocate budgets within Howard, might promote its ruin if left unchecked.

The literature often focuses on educational inequality and educational discrimination. To a lesser extent it focuses on internal campus conflicts over equity-related issues that had implications for the larger debate. A resource university leaders tended to overlooked, Thompson and the department chairs argued, was the perspectives and skills of the faculty. In early 1939, the faculty of the College of Liberal Arts at Howard seized a mundane progress report to insert their voice and perspectives into university policy. The *Revision* demonstrated that rather than stymieing progress, widening governance beyond the president and the trustees could help prepare Howard for the uncertain world both sides of the controversy knew existed on the other side of the veil beyond segregation.

Notes

1. Charles H. Thompson, "The Socioeconomic Status of Negro College Students," *Journal of Negro Education* 2, no. 1 (January 1933): 26–27. This article was the product of research conducted by a faculty committee at Howard comprised of G. M. Lightfoot (chair), H. H. Donald, C. H. Parker and Thompson.
2. Charles H. Thompson, "Revision of the Twenty-Year Plan with Especial Reference to the College of Liberal Arts," (Washington, DC: Howard University, February 20, 1939), 4–23 passim, School of Education papers, Howard University Archives.
3. James. D. Anderson, *The Education of Blacks in the South, 1860–1935* (Chapel Hill, NC: The University of North Carolina Press, 1988), 251.
4. Charles H. Thompson, "Introduction: The Problem of Negro Higher Education," *Journal of Negro Education* 2, no. 3 (July 1933): 262–63.
5. Ibid., 266.
6. Ibid., 266–67.
7. Wayne J. Urban, *Black Scholar: Horace Mann Bond, 1904–1972* (Athens, GA: University of Georgia Press, 1992).
8. Charles H. Thompson, "Introduction: The Problem of Negro Higher Education," *Journal of Negro Education* 2, no. 3 (July 1933): 267.
9. Charles H. Thompson, "The Missouri Decision and the Future of Negro Education," *Journal of Negro Education* 8, no. 2 (April 1939): 136 (Italics in original).
10. Charles H. Thompson, "Are There Too Many Negro Colleges?" *Journal of Negro Education* 3, no. 2 (April 1934): 159–67.
11. Charles H. Thompson, "Introduction: The Problem of Negro Higher Education," *Journal of Negro Education* 2, no. 3 (July 1933): 262.
12. Ibid.
13. Adam Fairclough, *A Class of Their Own: Black Teachers in the Segregated South* (Cambridge, MA: The Belknap Press of Harvard University Press, 2007), 335.
14. Charles H. Thompson, "Introduction: The Problem of Negro Higher Education," *Journal of Negro Education* 2, no. 3 (July 1933): 257.
15. Francille Rusan Wilson, *The Segregated Scholars: Black Social Scientists and the Creation of Black Labor Studies, 1890–1950* (Charlottesville, VA: University of Virginia Press, 2006), 171.

16. Charles H. Thompson, "Some Initial Observations on the Carnegie Corporation's Study of the Negro in America," *Journal of Negro Education* 13, no. 2 (April 1944): 133–38.

17. Charles H. Thompson, "Questionnaire Completed and Returned to Who's Who in American Education," December 26, 1957, School of Education papers, Howard University Archives.

18. Donald Young, ed. "The American Negro," special issue, *The Annals of the American Academy of Political and Social Science* 140 (November 1928): iii–v.

19. Charles H. Thompson, "The Educational Achievement of Negro Children," in *The American Negro*, ed. Donald Young, special issue, *The Annals of the American Academy of Political and Social Science* 140 (November 1928): 193.

20. Ibid.

21. Charles H. Thompson to Johanna Kramm, letter, May 4, 1932, School of Education papers, Howard University Archives.

22. Adam Fairclough, *A Class of Their Own: Black Teachers in the Segregated South,* 335.

23. Charles H. Thompson, "Questionnaire Completed and Returned to Who's Who in American Education," December 26, 1957, School of Education papers, Howard University Archives.

24. Constance McLaughlin Green, *The Secret City: A History of Race Relations in the Nation's Capital* (Princeton, NJ: Princeton University Press, 1961), 212, 214; Rayford W. Logan, *Howard University: The First Hundred Years, 1867–1967* (New York: New York University Press, 1969), 249–346; Richard I. McKinney, *Mordecai, The Man and His Message: The Story of Mordecai Wyatt Johnson* (Washington, DC: Howard University Press, 1997), 77–98; Raymond Wolters, *The New Negro on Campus: Black College Rebellions in the 1920s* (Princeton, NJ: Princeton University Press, 1975), 99.

25. John Hope Franklin, interview by Louis Ray, 1996.

26. Faustine C. Jones, "In Memoriam: Dean Charles H. Thompson (1896–1980)," *Journal of Negro Education* 49, no. 2 (Spring 1944): 113–14.

27. Edwin Embree to L. Hollingsworth Wood, letter, July 18, 1946, quoted in Patrick J. Gilpin and Marybeth Gasman, *Charles S. Johnson: Leadership beyond the Veil in the Age of Jim Crow* (Albany, NY: State University of New York Press, 2003), 219.

28. Logan, *Howard University*, 250–51.

29. Ibid., 249.

30. Ibid.

31. Ibid., 348–50.

32. Michael R. Winston, "Johnson, Mordecai Wyatt." *Encyclopedia of African-American Education* (Westport, CT: Greenwood Press, 1996), 234–36.

33. Charles H. Thompson, "Howard University Changes Leadership," *Journal of Negro Education* 29, no. 4 (Fall 1960): 409.

34. Ibid., 409.

35. Ibid.

36. McKinney, *Mordecai, The Man and His Message*, 65, 68–69.

37. Logan, *Howard University*, 258–65.

38. Michael R. Winston, "Through the Back Door: Academic Racism and the Negro Scholar in Historical Perspective," *Daedalus: The Journal of the American Academy of Arts and Sciences* (Summer 1971): 704–5.

39. Walter Dyson, *Howard University, the Capstone of Negro Education, a History: 1867–1940.* (Washington, DC: The Graduate School of Howard University, 1941), 191–92.

40. Thompson, *Revision of the Twenty-Year Plan with Especial Reference to the College of Liberal Arts* (Washington, DC: Howard University, February 20, 1939), 28–34, School of Education Papers, Howard University Archives.
41. Logan, *Howard University*, 266.
42. Thompson, "Howard University Changes Leadership," 409; Thompson, *Revision of the Twenty-Year Plan*, 4.
43. Ibid, 1.
44. See for example, Charles H. Thompson, "A 'New Deal' in the Administration of Negro Colleges?" *Journal of Negro Education* 6, no. 4 (October 1937): 590.
45. Thompson, *Revision of the Twenty-Year Plan*, 3.
46. Ibid., 2–3. (Underlining is in the original.)
47. Ibid., 4.
48. Ibid., 5.
49. Ibid., 11.
50. Ibid., 5–11 passim.
51. Ibid., 11.
52. Ibid., 11, 17.
53. Ibid., 17.
54. Ibid., 17. (Underlining is in the original.)
55. Ibid., 5.
56. Ibid., 11.
57. Ibid., 13.
58. For research that appears to have been specifically conducted in response to the decision to alter scholarship policy, see Charles H. Thompson, "The Socioeconomic Status of Negro College Students," *Journal of Negro Education* 2, no. 1 (January 1933): 26–27.
59. Thompson, *Revision of the Twenty-Year Plan*, 16.
60. Ibid., 14–15.
61. Ibid., 15.
62. Ibid.
63. Ibid., 21.
64. Ibid., 23.
65. Ibid., 21–23; Thompson, "Are There Too Many Negro Colleges?" *Journal of Negro Education* 3, no. 2 (April 1934): 160.
66. Thompson, *Revision of the Twenty-Year Plan*, 28.
67. Ibid., 32–33.
68. Ibid., 33–34.
69. Ibid., 10, 12–17.
70. Ibid., 18, 20.
71. Ibid., 24.
72. Ibid., 25.
73. Ibid.
74. Ibid., 23–28; Logan, 356–64; Thompson, "Howard University Changes Leadership," 410.
75. Thompson, *Revision of the Twenty-Year Plan*, 35.
76. Logan, *Howard University*, 359.
77. Ibid.
78. Ibid.
79. Ibid., 356–64.
80. Thompson, *Revision of the Twenty-Year Plan*, 10. (Underlining in the original.)
81. Ibid., 356–65; Charles H. Thompson, "Rank, Tenure and Retirement of Teachers in Negro Colleges," *Journal of Negro Education* 10, (April 1941): 139–50.

82. Logan, *Howard University*, 355.
83. Ibid., 356–64.
84. Michael R. Winston, interview by Louis Ray, Silver Spring, MD, April 17, 1996.
85. Thompson, "Howard University Changes Leadership," 410–11.
86. Ibid., 410.
87. Ibid., 410–11.

The First Black Talent Identification Program: The National Scholarship Service and Fund for Negro Students, 1947–1968

Linda M. Perkins

The National Scholarship Service and Fund for Negro Students was the first national talent identification organization dedicated to recruiting Black students (initially from the South) to predominately or all white colleges and universities. Founded in 1947, the organization found itself in competition with historically Black colleges for "talented Negro students."

While there has been significant attention given to the efforts of public colleges and universities and their efforts to attract student of color, little attention has been given to the enormous influence of key private talent identification programs in recruiting such students. Public institutions of higher education initiated minority recruitment programs in great numbers after the 1964 Civil Rights Bill and the 1965 Higher Education Act, and more forcefully after the assassination of Dr. Martin Luther King, Jr., in 1968. These programs were established in conjunction with the TRIO programs founded by the federal government that provided funds for Project Upward Bound, Talent Search and Student Services Equal Opportunity Programs (EOP) on public campuses were created and offered students in these programs a myriad of academic support services including special counseling, tutoring, remedial, and enrichment courses. In her case study of the first decade (1965–1975)

Perspectives on the History of Higher Education 29 (2012): 173-197
© 2012. ISBN: 978-1-4128-4771-1

of the University of Illinois-Champaign-Urbana EOP program, Joy Ann Williamson provides an excellent documentation of the issues and challenges of these programs.[1]

While most of the minority recruitment activities on public institutions grew out of the Black power student protest movement as well as Civil Rights legislation, this essay shall discuss the National Scholarship Service and Fund for Negro Students (NSSFNS) founded in 1947 as the first talent identification program in the nation to identify and place Black students in predominately White institutions of higher education.

There had been attempts to integrate White institutions prior to the founding of NSSFNS. The National Association for the Advancement of Colored People (NAACP) began litigation in the 1930s to gain entrance for Black students into White public institutions. These efforts culminated in the victory of the 1954 landmark *Brown v. Board* case that ended legalized racial segregation. While the NAACP was working on the integration of public education institutions, another organization, the NSSFNS, a nonprofit talent identification organization, was quietly integrating and placing Black students in some of the leading White private colleges and New England preparatory schools. This essay will discuss the early history of NSSFNS from its founding in 1947 until the late 1960s when White institutions began to establish their own minority recruitment offices and admissions programs. This study also discusses the shift in the philosophy of NSSFNS in 1968 when the leadership changed from the White leadership that had controlled the organization for twenty years to a more Afrocentric, nationalist Black president. Finally, this essay will discuss the clash of this organization with the presidents of the private Historically Black Colleges who in 1944 established the United Negro College Fund (UNCF).[2]

NSSFNS was the first national organization dedicated to the identification of talented Black students. This group was highly successful in identifying and placing thousands of "talented qualified Negro youth" prior to the establishment of affirmative action programs and prior to the *Brown v. Board* decision.

Founded in 1947 by Felice Nierenberg Schwartz, a wealthy White Smith College student during the WWII years, Schwartz was very concerned that there were only six Black women students out of a student body of 2,000 at the elite Seven Sister colleges.[3] The head of the religion department of Smith College, Ralph Harlow, challenged his students to live out their religious beliefs and not simply study them. This mandate had a profound impact on Schwartz. She recalled that Harlow would come to class "just dripping with clippings" of moral and ethical issues of the day. Concerned about the absence of Black students in White colleges, as a student, Schwartz began a writing campaign to White colleges to inquire if they had Black students and if not, why and would they admit them if they were qualified. Most replied that they rarely received applications from Black students and would not discriminate against them if they did apply.[4] It became Schwartz's goal to flood these institutions with applications from Black students.

When Schwartz graduated from Smith in 1945, she returned to her home in New York City to work at the NAACP to advance this project. After nine months with the organization and frustrated with the lack of support from them, she severed her relationship with them and started the NSSFNS. The project moved into a Black church in Harlem, The Church of the Master, that was headed by a prominent activist African American minister, James Robinson. Before becoming an officer of NSSFNS, Robinson had been instrumental in integrating White institutions such as Vassar and Barnard Colleges. He spoke regularly on White campuses and urged White students to become more vocal and active in getting their campuses integrated. He also helped to integrate White hospitals and summer camps.[5]

Schwartz put together an impressive and influential Board of Directors and officers of the newly formed group. Harry Carman, Dean of Columbia University, served as chairman and Henry Van Dusen, president of neighboring Union Theological Seminary, jointly wrote a letter to 146 college presidents asking them to serve on an advisory board to this group. According to Schwartz, all 146 responded and accepted.[6]

The wealthy and well-connected Schwartz was keenly aware of the power of having influential (as well as committed) people working with her. Her Board and officers were both Black and White, male and female, and religiously diverse. Among those chosen were Robert C. Weaver, a labor and housing specialist, officer of the John Hay Whitney Foundation, and later the first secretary of HUD (1966–68) as well as the first African American to hold the post; Kenneth B. Clark, the distinguished African American psychologist whose research on the impact of segregation of Black child was cited in the landmark *Brown v. Board* case and who served as an officer and researcher for the organization; Jane Bolin (Wellesley'28), the first Black woman to graduate from Yale Law School ('31), the first Black woman admitted to the New York Bar, and in 1939, the first Black woman appointed as a judge in the United States; Channing Tobias, Chairman of the NAACP; Attorney Susan Brandeis, daughter of Supreme Court Justice Louis Brandeis; Frank Bowles, Director of the College Entrance Examination Board (CEEB); John Monro, Director of Financial Aid, Harvard University; Henry C. Luce, the influential editor-in-chief of Time, Inc.; and Lyle Spencer, the head of Science Research Associates, an authority on educational tests and guidance programs whose firm produced the exams for the National Merit Scholarship Corporation.[7]

Schwartz, along with student volunteers from the National Student Association, sent out 18,000 letters to Black high schools in the South and to all the high schools in the North stating that if there were any "Negro students who are interested in going to college, please have them contact her office."[8] Schwartz utilized her student connections by visiting college campuses and having student newspapers write editorials decrying the lack of Black students on campus. She also kept alive the issue of the integration of the campuses.[9] Schwartz and her volunteers spent the first year of the organization cataloging the $14 million dollars in scholarship monies that existed.[10]

With her active Board, within two years, Schwartz had a paid staff and three sources of scholarships: the Seven Sister Fund, the Embree Memorial Scholarships, and the Jean Tennyson Fund. The 1950 Annual Report noted that they had counseled 764 students. Two hundred eighteen students applied to nearly 200 White colleges (they referred to them as interracial colleges). One hundred ninety-seven of these students were accepted to 161 different colleges. Eighty-two of these students were awarded scholarships by these colleges. In addition to referring students to colleges, the organization also had a Prep School program in which they sought southern Black students to recruit to these schools. Thirteen students were placed with scholarship aid at Phillip Exeter, Mount Herman, and Northfield School for Girls, the Putney School, the New Lincoln School, and the Slovak School for Girls.[11] The organization proudly noted that their efforts continued an "erosion, helping to break down segregated education; in the South by bringing qualified students north." They noted that most institutions "are glad to have us bring these students to their attention; some are willing, a few are reluctant".[12]

Years prior to the establishment of NSSFNS, Black scholar and activist, W. E. B. Du Bois as editor of the *Crisis Magazine*, the journal of the NAACP, surveyed White institutions each year to ascertain the number and treatment of Black students within their institutions. In 1913, the *Crisis* began publishing an annual issue on Blacks and higher education. By the 1920s, member of the NAACP began speaking on White college campuses to engender support for racial integration and equality from the students. Du Bois as well as the Reverend James Robinson were frequent speakers on White college campuses.[13] Du Bois and Robinson challenged what they viewed as the racist admissions practices of many of these institutions.[14]

NSSFNS tactics and views were quite different. Schwartz stated that she did not approach these institutions from the standpoint that they were discriminatory. The premise of NSSFNS was not built on saying to colleges, "you're discriminating; why don't you do something about it?" but rather, "here are a large number of qualified Negro students applying to you, I'm sure you will welcome this because you said so." The results were spectacular.[15]

In 1949, the organization received a $10,000 grant from the General Education Board (GEB), originally established by John D. Rockefeller and a huge supporter of selected Black colleges in the South. John D. Rockefeller, Jr., served as the Chair of the Board of the UNCF. The GEB grant was to support staff to compile and publish information regarding scholarships available through individuals, institutions and foundations[16] When the publication was released and the organization did not list Lincoln University, a historically all-male Black college, the African American president, Horace Mann Bond, wrote a letter of protest and outrage to Robert D. Calkins, the vice president and director of the GEB. Bond noted that the NSSFNS stated that they provided information and counsel to Black students on "interracial" colleges. He pointed out that NSSFNS publications defined an interracial college as a "non-segregated college, open to all students regardless of race, in the non-segregated Northern and Western states."[17] Bond continued that the "interracial" institutions listed for the state of Pennsylvania had virtually all White faculties, staffs, and presidents and yet were perceived as "healthy" places for Black students:

> But, if at Lincoln, 40% of your Board is Negro and 60% White; if your President is a Negro; if 60% of your faculty is Negro and 40% White, and if 97% of your alumni is Negro and 3% White; if 75% of your maintenance and clerical staff is White; and 25% Negro; if 98% of your student body is Negro and 2% White; then you cannot rate as an "interracial" institution and must be excluded from recommendation to Negro students as a proper institution in which their studies may be conducted; and your institution is an "unhealthy" place for a Negro student.[18]

Bond stated that the omission from this publication as a "recommended" institution for Black students not only damaged the reputation of Lincoln University but also endangered its financial status.

Calkins responded apologetically and stated, "there was no indication that the problem you mentioned would arise at the time our grant was made." He continued, "once a grant is made, we think it quite unwise to us to try to interfere". He concluded, "I am deeply sorry that events in this instance have seemed to you to be prejudicial to Lincoln University. Beyond that, all I can say is that the matter is one between your institution and the National Scholarship Service and Fund for Negro Students, and I hope that the matter will be amicably settled."[19] This incident simply fueled the outrage on the part of many of the presidents of UNCF colleges.

The Southern Project and the Politics of Race

By 1953, NSSFNC received an important grant from the Fund for the Advancement of Education, an arm of the Ford foundation of $170,000 for what NSSFNS called the Southern Project. This project was focused at Black students in the South. The aims of the Southern Project were to recruit Black students to White institutions outside the South and also attempt to persuade private southern White colleges to consider admitting Black students.[20]

Ford reluctantly provided funds to NSSFNS.[21] NSSFNS was fiercely integrationist and refused to advise students about Black colleges. Most of the major foundations such as the GEB of the Rockefeller Foundation and Ford itself supported Black colleges. Thus, to support an effort of a northern White organization to go south to attract the brightest and best Black students north created a problem for the foundation. Already, as noted by Bond's letter, their efforts were impacting Black colleges outside of the South. In addition, the UNCF was established several years prior to NSSFNS (1944).[22] The leading presidents of these institutions were well known to the foundation officials such as Ford and Rockefeller.

When NSSFNS sought GEB funds in 1949, the proposal noted that they were seeking to inform Black students in the northern and western states about college opportunities in those regions. When the organization returned to GEB for additional funds for additional staff, travel expenses, and publication, their proposal was rejected. In a memo to the file, the foundation officer noted:

> He [the program officer] feels the agency [NSSFNS] has done a good job in compiling information with regards a permanent basis, as the information that it has gathered may be turned over to the American Council of Education for publication and the US Office of Education is considering using the information and keeping it

up to date through its publications. {We} feel that it is logical for the U.S. Office of Education to make such information available. However, until this is done the agency is performing a useful and needed function. The GEB grant was made to enable the agency to increase its field staff to permit it to contact more educational institutions in the Midwest and Far West. Supplementary aid, such as the GEB has given, for this purpose is justified and worthwhile for the time being at least.

A request from the agency to the GEB in relation to the scholarship aid for Negroes which it is proposing agencies for this purpose.[23]

The memorandum concluded by stating that Richard L. Plaut, the Executive Vice President of NSSFNF was so persistent in attempting to convince the officers of the GEB of the merits of the proposal that he was perceived as "tactless."[24]

Not obtaining the GEB grant was a major disappointment to the officers of NSSFNS. However, the establishment of the Southern Project in 1953 generated enormous excitement and hope for the organization. This was short-lived because the grant created enormous concern to the presidents of the private Black colleges who comprised the UNCF. Robert Weaver, who was on both NSSFNS and UNCF boards, visited Ford and told the officials that there was no conflict between funding NSSFNS and UNCF. The foundation records noted that "Weaver said that the United Negro College Fund is helping the colleges which will educate the vast majority of Negroes, while the Scholarship fund is working with a relatively small number of superior students, helping them to get a better education than they otherwise would, and making an attack on the problem of segregated education by helping place good students in so-called White institutions."[25] The memo to the files noted that Weaver was told that the foundation needed advice on the "whole question of education for Negroes from the presidents of Negro colleges to help formulate its policy in this area."[26]

It appears that the foundation officials felt the NSSFNS officials were naïve about what they hoped to achieve. In addition to recruiting Black students to northern prep schools and colleges, they also wanted to recruit White students to the leading Black colleges to establish a "two-way" rather than a one-way pattern of integration. The foundation quietly polled several Black college presidents to seek their opinions and a couple stated they were not supportive of such an effort.[27] Another outside consultant asked to assess NSSFNS stated that he believed the group was "interested in getting a potential Negro leader type into a name institution and not in helping to raise the general level of Negro education." He continued, "Their approach is not without value, but is a specialized type of approach. I found nothing of positive value and received no suggestions, which I found new or novel. My interest is more in means of raising the level of Negro education in the South and of improving the opportunities offered to larger number of able Negroes."[28]

This assessment was incorrect. NSSFNS was interested in improving the level and aspirations of all talented Black students. With their Ford grant, two African American male professors from Black colleges, Dr. Paul F. Lawrence of Howard University and Donald Wyatt from Fisk University, were hired as codirectors of the Southern field services. Seventy-eight Black high schools in forty-five southern cities and towns were visited seven times each by the two men. Counselors were provided training regarding the expectations and requirements of White institutions. Deadlines for applications and exam requirements were explained.

Principals of the high schools visited were asked to select the top ten percent of their senior classes for an orientation about college opportunities and also to have them take the SAT exam. NSSFNS worked closely with the College Board and as noted earlier, had a representative on their board as well as Lyle Spencer whose company produced the National Merit Scholarship Qualifying Exam on the Board.[29] While NSSFNS was aware that Black students scored very low on such exams, they also understood that the institutions that they were recommending that these students apply to required this examination. However, throughout the years, NSSFNS sought to analyze and explain the biases and limitations of the exams in assessing Black students. The fact that NSSFNS utilized the exams at all became a source of criticism when the leadership changed in 1968.

In the two years of this project, more than 3,000 students from seventy-eight Black high schools were selected to be considered for NSSFNS referrals. In the first year of the project, only 49 percent of the recommended students met the qualification of NSSFNS and the second year 59 percent. NSSFNS did not believe these numbers were high since the students represented the top students from their high schools. Of the group who were considered qualified for admission to a CEEB school, only 33 percent completed the applications. From the initial 3,100 students, 520 students enrolled in White colleges. Although this number represented more Black students than the number who had enrolled in the past ten years from the South, NSSFNS was concerned with the number of "qualified" students who chose not to apply to White institutions.[30] In NSSFNS's assessment, this is because of: (1) reluctance on the part of both students and parents to venture out of a life-long segregated environment; (2) fear of not being able to meet the scholastic standards and the financial costs of interracial colleges; and (3) the influence of parents, principals, teachers, and counselors in favor of the predominately Negro college near home, often their alma mater.[31]

All of these reasons seem plausible and probable. Another reason is the lack of desire to confront potential racism in these institutions. NSSFNS tended to emphasize that much of the difficulty of African American students entering White institutions had more to do with the shortcomings of the students as opposed to attitudes and policies of the institutions. For example, in their report of the Southern Project, it stated:

> The number of currently qualified Negro college candidates in the South has been estimated, as was the extent of their financial needs for higher education. Estimates were also made of the potential talent. A far more important by-product, however, has been the identification and analysis of the factors holding down an even modest development of the potential: the motivational, preparational, cultural, and economic handicaps. A good deal was also learned about how to overcome them."[32]

Another report of NSSFNS reiterates this point and noted that less than 3 percent of all Black high school graduates in the southern states were found to be likely candidates for an interracial college. This relatively poor showing was explained as the result of reduced academic motivation because of economic and cultural deprivation in the home and due to the ill effects of segregation on the development of scholastic aptitude.[33]

In 1955, after eight years of existence, NSSFNS had placed more than 4,000 students in over 300 predominately White colleges. However, it was most proud of the Southern Project. A study of the group entitled *Blueprint for Talent Searching: America's Hidden Manpower* (1957) outlined the organization's approach to identifying talented youth.

Community involvement was a large aspect of the project's earlier identification of students. The senior year was viewed as much too late to work with students who had not had the necessary prerequisite courses or who had planned to enter college the fall after graduation. Feature articles on the study were covered in the *New York Times, Time Magazine, Newsweek, US and World Report*, and many other papers and publications throughout the nation. Headlines in southern and northern papers such as the *Charlotte, North Carolina News*, and the *New York Journal American* read, "Project finds Dixie Negroes Gain in College" and "Dixie's Negro: A Wasted Resource?" Other papers headlined, "Poor Segregated Students Catch Up Fast in College."[34]

One of the most celebrated students from the project was Nathanial Lamar from Atlanta, Georgia. Through NSSFNS, he attended elite Phillips Exeter Academy preparatory boarding school in New Hampshire. From there he attended Harvard College where he graduated with highest honors. He won a Henry Fellowship at Harvard, which took him to Cambridge University in England. Lamar returned to Harvard and earned a Master's in English Literature.[35] However, his father was a physician and his family a solid member of the Black elite of the city. Thus, Lamar, while helped significantly by NSSFNS, would have certainly attended college without their assistance. However, he probably would not have attended Exeter, Harvard, and Cambridge without their assistance.

And, Lamar represented the type of talented student who was now lost to the historically Black college.

As the news spread and the NSSFNS hired a public relations firm, their press releases emphasized the poor students who had been assisted by the organization. In one release in 1959, it stated, "a few weeks ago an 18 year old Negro boy named Tommy Boardwalk, president of the senior class at Harrison High School in Blytheville, Arkansas, received his diploma. The son of a tenant farmer whose yearly income for a family of five is somewhat less than $2,000, Tommy now has something besides farming to look forward to. Next fall he will be a freshman at Blackburn College in Carlinville, Illinois." Ronald Robinson, from Cleveland, Ohio, also eighteen and Black who was VP of his Student Government, president of his dramatic clubs, and who lives with his mother and three brothers and sister on an income of $1,700 will be going to Oberlin College, where he will specialize in languages. Another student from Peekskill, New York, twenty-one who support an invalid mother and father will enroll in Ohio's Antioch College and major in science. They are two of seventy-five Black students who may never had attended college except with the encouragement, custom-tailored counseling, and financial help of an agency called the NSSFNS.[36]

In 1963, another study of the students of the Southern Project was released by NSSFNS. Entitled, *The Negro Student at Integrated Colleges*, this study was conducted by psychologist and NSSFNS board member Kenneth B. Clark and his colleague at City College, Lawrence Plotkin. This study was a follow-up study of the NSSFNS classes of 1952–1956. The findings indicated that despite the lower test scores of the students, they overwhelmingly were successful. More than 80 percent graduated and less than 20 percent dropped out. This study also noted that the graduation rates of these students were significantly higher than the national average, which was closer to 60 percent. Dropout rates at various types of colleges (Big Ten, black colleges, public institutions, private institutions) ranged from 65 to 40 percent. The student's dropout rate in the NSSFNS groups was one quarter that of the reported White rate.[37] The grades of the students were average with one-third obtaining a grade point average of a B– or better. About 50 percent or more earned a C+ or worse.[38]

One article noted, "the largest movement of Negro students from segregated high school in the South to non-segregated colleges—in the South as well as the North—ever to take place in any one year was reported today by the NSSFNS." This talent search, aimed at uncovering qualified Negro college candidates, also produced statistical affirmation of the recent Supreme Court ruling that a "separate" school system was not inherently "equal." The fact that only half of those students who were identified as being in the top ten percent of their senior classes qualified for college admissions based on the CEEB SAT exam confirmed in their minds the inferiority of the schools.[39]

However, Richard Plaut, the president of NSSFNS, was very clear about the impact of the exams on the black students in the South. In a memo to Kenneth Clark, he stated that there was a big misconception by noneducators on the terms of aptitude versus achievement in testing. He said, of the students tested in the Southern Project, only thirty-six of the high schools administer any type of objective test and only seven out of the thirty-six administer what would be considered an "achievement test." Thus, the overwhelming number of Black students who took the SAT had never had such an exam before. He noted that the only objective test known to be used in Black high schools were a standardized test called the Intercollegiate Testing Program used for Black colleges. Plaut felt the comparison of Black students to the national norm was not a fair assessment. He stated that, these tests are constructed specifically to predict success in college and, therefore, reflect to a large degree cultural influences at home, as well as preparational differences in school. He felt that the Black students' scores should be compared with the White students in the same cities.[40]

Students who participated in the Southern Project took a modified SAT exam free of charge. NSSFNS was puzzled and concerned about the wide range of test scores for students whose grades were very similar (ranged from the 1st to the 99th percentile) of the national norms.

Researchers believed that "motivational and cultural factors accounted for the differences in scores." Despite the low scores, the organization was pleased with their follow-up results which indicated that these students did better than their scores predicted.

The students who participated in the Southern Project were the subjects of numerous research projects. NSSFNS kept excellent records on these students and did several follow-up studies. One of the surprise findings by the Scholarship Fund was that students from lower-income families did better in college (as based on their grades) than those of middle-income level. Another finding that stunned the officials at NSSFNS was the fact that Black students from the South did better in interracial colleges than those from the North. A study by Kenneth Clark noted, "students born in the South tend to achieve higher college grades than those born elsewhere. This seems to refute the preconception that Negroes receive better secondary preparation in Northern high school, students from Southern secondary schools have higher college grades than those from high schools in New York, Pennsylvania and New Jersey."[41]

While Kenneth Clark believed that high motivation accounted for much of the success of these students, dedicated teachers and counselors also made a big difference. A *New York Post Magazine* article in 1964 interviewed three Black students attending Columbia University who were from southern cities. One was from Phoenix City, Alabama, the others were from Roanoke, Virginia and Charleston, South Carolina. James Dawson, a math major from Charleston noted that one of his teachers, Mrs. Margaret Broadnax, tried her best to get 300 of the 369 students to attend college. He stated she was disappointed that only 200 of the students continued to college. The student from Roanoke, Thomas Dudley, an engineering major was transferred from an integrated Catholic school to a Black high school. He said while the academics at the Catholic school were superior, he commented that he would not be at Columbia had he graduated from the Catholic School. "The Sisters were fine and good teachers, but they could never impart the drive to Negro children to get ahead that is really ingrained in our Negro teachers and counselors."[42]

Commenting on the regional differences in the performance of southern Black students, Thomas said, he thought that northern Blacks take for granted much that is foreign to southern Blacks. He said, "there is not a museum in Roanoke—even for White people. Here, I can visit three of the world's greatest museums in a ten-block area of 5th Avenue."[43]

With the increased militancy and activism of the Black Power and Civil Rights movement of the 1960s, coupled with the March on Washington and the passage of the Civil Rights Bills ensuring equal rights to African Americans in all aspects of American life, White colleges were under increased pressure to move from token Black student representation to a more representative number. This resulted in many institutions attempting to recruit such students on their own. In addition, other programs were being developed. For example, the National Urban League established a program entitled "Tomorrow's Scientists and Technicians in 1958" in which NSSFNS felt was in competition with their talent search programs.

In 1964, the National Merit Scholarship Corporation initiated a special National Achievement Scholarship Award (NAS) for Black students. The scholarship was initially funded by the Ford Foundation in which the NSSFNS viewed as a slight. However, the NAS were awarded to Black students to attend the college of their choice—not just White institutions. In a letter of thanks for the establishment of this scholarship, Benjamin E. Mays, the president of the all-male Morehouse College wrote the Ford Foundation and noted, "it is gratifying to know that the students will be permitted to choose their college."[44] After the civil rights movement of the 1960s, an explosion of so-called "talent search" groups emerged and significant government and foundation monies were invested in increasing black student enrollments in White institutions.

As colleges sought to dramatically increase their minority student bodies, the response of the press in criticism was swift. In a prelude to later anti-Affirmative action suits, *US News and World Report* ran a feature story in May of 1964, entitled, "Getting Negroes Into College-some Schools give Them a Break." The author wrote: "Is there equal opportunity for White and Negro students in college admissions? Not always, finds this newspaper survey." He cited cases in colleges and universities where usual requirements are being eased—in favor of underprivileged Negroes. "They are being accepted on skimpier educational backgrounds and on poorer performance in test than schools traditionally require. In some case, Negro students are being recruited, offered special assistance to get them onto campuses. This search is giving a break to some Negroes."[45] Similarly, the *Boston Globe* published an article entitled, "Colleges Seek Negroes." "The girl came home to her father in tears. She is the only girl in her public school senior class who has her heart set on Wellesley, and it looks as if she is good enough to make it. That day, she told her father, she had found out that a Negro girl in her class also wanted to go to Wellesley and that she was sure that the Negro girl would get in instead. She probably will too. For there is a kind of reverse discrimination operating in the nation's colleges this year. The Ivy Leagues and other popular colleges are sending their representatives to schools they have never visited before. To read the promotion literature, it sounds as if a predominately Negro school in New York's Harlem will get more college recruiters than city high schools that have a high majority of White pupils."[46] Clearly from the tone and statements of both of these articles, the presumption that elite White schools were reserved for White only reflected the attitudes that many Black students confronted on these campuses. The example of the White girl who had a Black classmate did not indicate that the Black girl was not "qualified" only that she was Black and would be thus, preferred.

While many attempts were made by colleges to recruit African American students, NSSFNS had developed a skilled and well-trained staff of college counselors and field representatives who were knowledgeable of the various types of colleges and students who would be a good match for one another. Gail Horne, Radcliffe graduate of 1960 and the daughter of the entertainer Lena Horne, worked as a counselor at NSSFNS in the 1960s. She wrote in her family memoir, *The Hornes*, "I went to work for the National Scholarship Service and Fund for Negro Students—known as NSSFNS, and pronounced Nessfeness. NSSFNS sent me to Columbia University for postgraduate psychology courses. I became a counselor for black students seeking scholarships to predominately White colleges. Using test scores, grades, and recommendations, I advised students on college applications and became their advocate with college admissions directors. The work was always interesting and sometimes exciting."[47]

NSSFNS Collides with the Black Power Movement

By the twentieth year of NSSFNS, Richard Plaut who had served throughout the years as executive vice president and president of the organization approached retirement and a search by the Board for a new president ensued. In light of the changing times, a committee was established to review the mission and goals of the organization. The Board was polled on two questions: does NSSFNS want to continue doing what it does but on a larger scale, and does NSSFNS want to view itself as a pioneering service organization with strongly innovative approaches?[48] Some members felt that NSSFNS had been overtaken in recent years by a number of organizations that were doing the same thing with substantially more money. Some viewed the organization's strength in research a plus. Now that talent search organizations had become a growth industry, some Board members believed that the organization needed to work with more "riskier" students to be competitive and also begin to include different types of schools, including community colleges among their clientele. Some felt that the group should not work exclusively with Black students but expand to include all disadvantage students. The Board members were also polled as to whether race should be a factor in the selection of their new president. Most felt all things being equal, yes. Most responded that a Black president was needed for these times.[49] Richard Plaut, the current president, felt that because NSS-FNS had a White president and a White chair of the board, these factors were now an "embarrassment."[50] He said that NSSFNS was thought of as the "White" agency. He said that after twenty years of developing Black youth and talent, it would be pathetic if the organization could not find a well-qualified Black president.[51]

In the summer of 1968, Hugh W. Lane, a psychologist and director of the National Achievement Scholarship of the National Merit Scholarship Corporation was appointed the first Black president of NSSFNS. Lane sought to redirect the organization in a variety of ways. First he stated, while the group was not a Civil Rights organization, he felt it must have more relevance to the tension and turmoil of the Black community. He felt it was necessary to interact with a broader cross-section of Black people and be responsive to the Black agenda. He stated that the organization should change the rhetoric on its publications from that of a college referral service for "qualified" Negro students to simply stating it is a black talent registry. To state "qualified" implied to Lane that there were a limited number of talented Black students and that NSSFNS would find them and "refer to them to a limited set of colleges."[52] He noted that one of the criticisms of NSSFNS is that it focused primarily on Eastern colleges (which actually was not true). He proposed that the organization collect information on all Black students in American high schools. They should be referred to four year, two year, and for those not college eligible, counseled for employment opportunities. He proposed a computerized data bank that could process as many as 250,000-student profile as opposed to the 20,000 students that NSSFNS was currently counseling.[53] An Atlanta office was opened since Lane felt that most of the students that needed assistance were in the South. Samuel H. Johnson, a specialist in minority youth education, was appointed head of that office.[54]

In a proposal to the Ford Foundation for $300,000, which was funded, for a computerized system to reach all black high school students, Lane outlined in his proposal the new NSSFNS and indicated all of the ills that he perceived of the organization that he inherited. He noted that the old NSSFNS worked with only the top 2–3 percent of Black students. The new NSSFNS would work with ALL Black students. He noted with the new Black pride and Black power movements, "NSSFNS found itself—quite unintentionally—the object of considerable hostility coming particularly from the leaders, graduates, and supporters of the traditionally Black colleges. Their most widespread complaint was that NSSFNS supported a limited concept of racial integration that was injurious to the well being of Black institutions of higher education. With considerable evidence to support them, they argued that NSSFNS should pursue a more even-handed policy of racial integration of the schools that would also encourage talented White youth to attend some of the stronger traditionally black colleges." Obviously, Lane did not know the history of the organization because the two-way integration project of the 1950s sought to accomplish this objective. This proposal was not funded by any foundation and received little interest from Black college presidents. Indeed, one consultant to the Ford Foundation who reviewed the proposal wrote: "this project appears to me to be a somewhat unrealistic hot-house endeavor which would result in placing a few perhaps neurotic White students in Negro colleges. A real question is why White students should seek to go to Negro colleges today."[55] Lane also noted that "more militant opponents of NSSFNS went further to claim that the organization was merely a "tool of White interests" seeking to destroy the traditionally Black colleges. He said that under his administration, the organization had eradicated the image of being anti-Black college. He hired as his executive director, David Kent, Jr., former director of admissions of Lincoln University in Pennsylvania, a historically Black college.[56]

Lane also announced to the Board that he, along with other talent search directors, endorsed resolutions that were presented at a National Conference of College Admissions Counselors in 1969. In a tone typical of the 1960s, among the eleven resolutions that the group passed were: all member institutions should have a minimum of 10 percent minority student undergraduate population, half of which should be of "high risk." They stated that aptitude tests scores as a major factor in admissions decisions should be eliminated. In addition, the group proposed that minority students' admissions should be determined by a special committee with

Black and Brown students and faculty comprising these committees. The document continued that minority students should be given two years to adjust to the university environment and support services should be made available to these students.[57] In a published speech, Lane noted that he felt colleges should move toward open admissions rather than selective admissions.[58] These views were antithetical to the mission and goals of the original NSSFNS and certainly to those of Kenneth Clark.

Blacks had always been a part of the decision-making operation of NSSFNS. This was an interracial endeavor from the beginning. As noted, the Reverend James Robinson was the vice president from the inception. Numerous Blacks served on the board of directors throughout the history of the organization. In addition, many Blacks served as counselors. All were graduates of White institutions, which probably did not please Lane. Julius Robinson, an African American and a Dartmouth alumnus, served as vice president of the organization until 1964. He was Kenneth Clark's choice for the presidency of NSSFSN. Clark informed the board that Robinson was his "only choice."[59] And, in 1967, William J. Trent, Jr. became the first African American Chairman of the Board after the death of Harry Carman.

Needless to say, the Board changed dramatically under the new leadership. Lane felt the Board should add Black celebrities and nominated the entertainer James Brown, basketball player Walt Frazier, and singer Dionne Warrick to the Board. Frazier and Warrick were elected members of the Board. It does appear that Clark attended any of the meetings during Lane's presidency. During this period, of the many notices that Clark was sent, on one, William Trent scribbled a handwritten message at the bottom: "come to the meeting, dammit!"[60]

In 1970, Clark resigned from the Board of NSSFNS after more than twenty years of service. When his letter from the nominating committee came requesting his desire to remain a Board member, the letter also noted that they wanted members who were willing to "participate actively." Clark in a note to his secretary wrote "no," underlined it, and noted for her to write a "kind note" of regrets.[61]

The Ford Foundation poured millions of dollars into NSSFNS under the new leadership. This is something they had not done since the 1950s when they provided a two-year grant for the Southern Project. While the old NSSFNS existed off of various small grants, college chest funds and individual donations, the major foundations such as Ford and Rockefeller provided little assistance, presumably as not to offend the presidents of the Black colleges.

Despite this support from Ford and other federal agencies, by 1973, NSSFNS ran into financial difficulties and was unable to meet its payroll. Creditors sued the organization and by May of 1974, Hugh Lane was no longer employed by NSSFNS.[62] David Kent took over and worked with the Ford Foundation to alleviate the financial problems of the organization. Ford was quite sympathetic and notes to the files indicated that they did not believe the organization should suffer because of "sudden expansion and poor administration under Lane." In a final grant evaluation, the program officer Fred Crossland noted:

> Over the years, FF has made grants (including this one) totaling more than $1 million to NSSFNS. Indeed, a small grant was made subsequent to the one here being evaluated. It all was money well spent, because NSSFNS has focused and continues to focus on an important problem that needs doing. It might well be argued that much of NSSFNS's financial difficulty is the result of its successes during its thirty-year life; it was the lonely voice in its early years as it sought to expand higher education opportunities for black Americans. Although by no means have all legitimate goals been fully achieved, we have moved a considerable distance in the right direction and NSSFNS no longer is alone in its advocacy.[63]

NSSFNS New York office subsequently closed with the Atlanta office remaining. This office, despite the same name, did not reflect the mission and goals of its founders. The organization became like many other such groups that competed to identify Black students. They tried to become all things to all Black students and hence lost their distinctiveness.

The Black College Dilemma

Founded because of religious convictions and a belief that segregation should be eradicated from our society, Felice Schwartz believed that education would be a primary vehicle in this crusade. She established a stellar, diverse, devoted, and active group of people to help her carry out this goal. Through personal contacts and individual counseling, she opened the doors of campuses and secondary prep schools to thousands of "qualified Negro youth," regardless of their socioeconomic background. By the 1960s, in the era of Black power, NSSFNS with its wealthy New York eastside White officers and Blacks who seemed to be from another era as well, the organization was ironically criticized for attempting to raise Black students' aspirations and opportunities for a northern "White" education. To suggest that Black students attend the same institutions as the White elite was viewed as suspect and a tool of the oppressor. Even the terms, "talented, qualified Negroes" which was stated with pride by the organization were now viewed as racist. NSSFNS attempted to demonstrate to the nation that despite the separate and profoundly unequal education that most Blacks received, this did not mean that there was not "talent" among this group. The students' poor tests scores could be explained and often did not reflect their true capabilities. NSSFNS did extensive research on these students as a means to track and document their progress and their problems. The new president, Hugh Lane, was a product of the new "in your face" protest tradition. Clearly, the Black college presidents who were concerned about this organization were probably more focused on the financial loss that NSSFNS may pose to their institutions rather than those reasons espoused by Lane. Many Black college presidents and faculty actually sent their children to White colleges. Frederick Patterson, the founding president of UNCF and president of Tuskegee Institute, noted in his autobiography that his son, Frederick, III, "completed his BA in cultural and intellectual history and philosophy at Empire State College of the State University of New York."[64]

The NSSFNS' efforts also collided with those of the presidents of the UNCF in decades earlier. Kenneth B. Clark was a very devoted Howard University graduate and was a staunch supporter of UNCF, and William Trent served as executive director of UNCF as well as chairman of the Board of NSSFNS. These men were interested in the higher education of Black students in all types of institutions. In contrast, many of the Black college presidents attempted (and succeeded) in preventing the funding and growth of NSSFNS, thus preventing educational opportunities for many Black students outside of the Black college option.

One of the future presidents of UNCF, Vernon Jordan was a product of the Southern Project of NSSFNS. Jordan recalled that during the fall of 1952:

> Paul Lawrence, a representative from the National Service and Scholarship Fund for Negro Students, came to my school to encourage the best students to think of applying to White colleges in the North. Traditionally Black colleges were great, he said, but it was important for us to know there were other choices we could make.[65]

Until this presentation, Jordan stated that he and his two best friends had planned to attend Howard University. However, Lawrence's visit changed his thinking. He wrote: "Lawrence was a very tall, imposing man. I remember being quite impressed by him, and what he had to say. His message was something of an eye-opener to me."[66]

Although Jordan did apply to Howard, he stated he also applied to numerous White institutions as well. To his surprise, his Black teachers were not enthusiastic about him applying to White colleges and were reluctant to write references for him. He stated that his Black teachers, like many other Black people, felt that Blacks who went (or desired) to attend White institutions thought themselves better than other Blacks. Jordan stated, they said: "If Morehouse was good enough for me . . . If Morris Brown was good enough for me . . . There was a tension with them . . . there was this notion that my decision to apply to a White school was a judgment of them, and of the schools they attended."[67]

This view bothered Jordan and he said:

> For my part, it really was just about trying something different. Someone had made me aware of an alternative I hadn't known about. I saw it as a great challenge; to do something neither I nor anybody else expected me to do. This was in no way a statement of how I viewed my teachers. I admired them very much, but it didn't mean I had to follow the same path in life that they had followed.[68]

Jordan graduated from DePauw University in Greencastle, Indiana, in 1957, and continued his studies at Howard University Law School where he graduated in 1960.

Unfortunately, while there were many Black students who had attended "interracial" institutions long before the founding of NSSFNS, going back to the early nineteenth century, these students were overwhelming from the Black middle and upper classes (particularly if they attended private colleges).[69] Most poor Black students had no knowledge or access to such institutions. NSSFNS, made no social class distinctions when recruiting Black students. In fact, as noted earlier, their research studies indicated that the poorer Black students performed better academically than those of a higher social–economic background.[70]

The resistance to the efforts of NSSFNS on the part of Black college presidents as well as many of the Black teachers who discouraged their students from taking advantage of the opportunities of NSSFNS can be interpreted as self-interest, class bias, jealously, and racial self-hatred. Vernon Jordan noted that the basic objection of his teachers to his application to White institutions was that he would think himself better than them. He also noted that their objection was also social class based. He said:

> I noticed there was a hint of surprise among some of my teachers and others back home in Atlanta that I could afford to go away to school, especially a White school. That sort of thing was rare, and strictly for upper-class blacks. In their eyes, my family didn't belong in that category. I was the son of a cook and a postal worker.[71]

This narrow and short-sided view of higher education for Black youth resulted in thousands of them being denied the opportunity to consider other higher educational options beyond the Black college. While every southern college-bound Black student had no desire to attend a college outside their community and race, many never had the option.

The efforts of NSSFNS were thwarted and after the two-year Southern Project of 1953–55, they never received additional funding to continue the program. NSSFNS was pioneering and ahead of its time in being able to provide individual counseling to students and to provide them with information about a vast array of college options. The organization ensured that students found the right "fit" in their placements and provided them financial and psychological support in their college endeavors. Students recruited through NSSFNS had personal contacts with the counselors and advisors. Also, they had hundreds of examples of students who had been a part of the NSSFNS experience.

Thousands of Black students did benefit from the efforts of NSSFNS including some of the top leaders of the race. The program had a high success rate with low attrition. In addition to Vernon Jordan, Ronald Brown, who served as secretary of commerce in the first Clinton Presidential Administration (1993–1996) and the first Black chairman of the Democratic National Committee (1988–1993), graduated from Middlebury College in 1962 through the efforts of NSSFNS and later from law school at St. John's University in 1970. Attorney and United States Representative Eleanor Holmes Norton graduated from Antioch College in 1960 as a NSSFNS recruit and later from Yale Law School. Judge Almalya Kearse graduated from Wellesley in 1959 and later from the University of Michigan Law School. The list of recipients of NSSFNS reads like a who's who of Black America.[72]

While the historically Black colleges continued to also produce graduates of distinction, the deliberate reduction of opportunities for Black students in the south remains a gross injustice to them. The primary recipients of NSSFNS were middle-class Black students primarily from the north and the Washington, DC, area. The Black students of the South were socialized to believe that they should stay in their place, at home, and not look beyond Black colleges for a higher education. Ironically, with the demise of NSSFNS, White colleges after the 1960s began to actively recruit Black students nationally into their institutions. Many Black students did take advantage of these opportunities which has resulted in some Black colleges experiencing greater competition for students today.[73]

Reflecting on the founding of NSSFNS and its subsequent fate, Felice Schwartz, stated in a 1971 interview her shock at the treatment she received by many Black educators and Civil Rights leaders:

> One of the hardest things to survive was the experience with the NAACP, because I did think black was beautiful and I thought that all blacks were wonderful. And, I had to find out the truth, which was that there were good and bad blacks, which again when you're twenty is hard to fact that reality when you've idealized it. And, I guess the other hard thing was that my biggest opposition came from the presidents of Negro colleges. Understandably when you look at it retrospectively, because if we were successful, we would pull off the cream of the Negro population. Now, today, there are many black youngsters who go to college who are average. There are some who are less than average, but, of course, we had to refer the cream of the students, so that we were robbing the black colleges of some of the really good students and it was shattering to get letters from these leading black educators that showed bitterness about this movement. But, as I say, I understand it now, but I didn't at the time.[74]

The quest to identify and recruit "talented" Black students continues. Both HBCUs as well as predominately White institutions remain important in the education of Black youth.

Notes

1. Joy Ann Williamson, *Black Power on Campus: The University of Illinois, 1965–1975* (Urbana and Chicago, IL: University of Illinois Press, 2003). The early years of these programs experienced significant retention problems as well as student adjustment to a White campus culture. In addition, many faculty members believed these programs recruited students who were less capable than regular admit students.
2. The primary sources for this study come from the Archives of the Ford Foundation, which provided NSSFNS an important grant for the program discussed in this essay. Significant sources are from the Papers of Kenneth B. Clark, the Black psychologist who served as an officer and Board member of NSSFNS for the entire period discussed in this study, and the oral history of Felice Schwartz, the founder of NSSFNS and from press releases and studies of the students recruited by NSSFNS.
3. Transcribed alumna interview with Felice Schwartz, Smith College 1971, Smith College Archives, Northampton, MA.
4. Ibid.
5. Ibid.
6. Schwartz interview, Smith College Archives, 1971.
7. See roster of Officers and Board Members (referred to as Directors) on the NSSFNS Annual Reports, *Kenneth Clark Papers.*
8. Ibid.
9. See for example the editorial entitled, "Real Results" in *The Cornell Daily Sun,* May 24, 1950.
10. Schwartz interview, Smith College, 1971.
11. The Annual Report of NSSFNS, 1950 in *Kenneth Clark Papers.*
12. Chairman's Report of NSSFNS, October 1950 in *Kenneth Clark Papers.*
13. June Jackson Christmas, "A Historical Overview: The Black Experience at Vassar," *Vassar Quarterly* (Spring 1988): 4–5.

14. For information on Robinson see biographical folder in *James Robinson Papers*, Amistad Research Center, New Orleans, Louisiana; W. E. B. Du Bois, "Postscript," *Crisis* (August 1932): 266.
15. Schwartz's Interview, Smith College, 1971.
16. Memorandum to the files from Doris Goss, Reference, the National Scholarship Service and Fund for Negro Students, March 21, 1950 in *Rockefeller Family Archives*, RB2 (MR), Educational Interests, 114.1, Miscellaneous, National Scholarship Fund and Service for Negro Students, Box 4, folder, 24; For information on John D. Rockefeller's role in the United Negro College Fund, see Marybeth Gasman's, *Envisioning Black Colleges: A History of the United Negro College Fund* (Baltimore, MA: The John Hopkins University Press, 2007).
17. Horace Mann Bond, President of Lincoln University, Lincoln University, Pennsylvania, April 3, 1951 to Robert D. Calkins, Vice President and Director of the General Education Board, New York, New York, in the *General Education Board Papers*, Box 257, folder 2663 at the Rockefeller Archive Center, New York.
18. Ibid.
19. Robert D. Calkins, General Education Board, New York, New York, April 9, 1951 to President Horace Mann Bond, Lincoln University, Pennsylvania, in *General Education Board Papers*, Box 257, folder 2663, Rockefeller Archive Center, New York.
20. The Southern Project Report, 1953–1955, NSSFNS, New York, New York, in *Kenneth Clark Papers,* Box 111, folder 12.
21. Ibid.
22. See Gasman, *Envisioning Black Colleges.*
23. Memorandum to the File, Doris Goss, March 21, 1950, *Rockefeller Family Archives.*
24. Ibid.
25. Memorandum to the Files from Elizabeth Paschall, The Fund for the Advancement of Education, Ford Foundation Archives, New York City.
26. Ibid.
27. Memorandum to the Files from Elizabeth Paschall, The Fund for the Advancement of Education, the Ford Foundation Archives.
28. John Stalmaker to Clarence Faust, Pasadena, California, September 18, 1952, Ford Foundation Archives.
29. See the Southern Project Report, *Blueprint for Talent Searching: America's Hidden Manpower* (NSSFNS, 1957).
30. Ibid.
31. Southern Project Report, 6, NSSFNS.
32. Ibid., 2.
33. NSSFNS Press Release, November 24, 1954.
34. Southern Project, *New York Times* December 26, 1955; "Dixie's Negro: Wasted Resource?" *Charlotte News (NC)* January 3, 1956; "Wasted Talent" *Time Magazine* (November 21, 1960).
35. "For the Talented," *Newsweek* (July 25, 1955).
36. Press Release, NSSFNS, November 1959 in *Kenneth Clark Papers*, Box 72, folder 1.
37. Kenneth B. Clark and Lawrence Plotkin, *The Negro Student at Integrated Colleges* (National Scholarship Service and Fund for Negro Students, 1963).
38. Ibid.
39. See NSSFNS press release, November 24, 1954 in *Kenneth Clark Papers*, Box 72, folder 1.

40. Memo from Richard Plaut, President of NSSFNS to Dr. Kenneth Clark, City College, October 9, 1963, *Kenneth Clark Papers*, Box 71, folder 7.
41. Quoted in "Scholarships for Negroes: A Program that Works" in *New York Post, Sunday Magazine* (April 19, 1964): 6.
42. Ibid.
43. Ibid.
44. Benjamin E. Mays to Henry Heald, The Ford Foundation, July 15, 1964.
45. "Getting Negroes into College: Some Give Them a Break," *US News and World Report* 56, no. 21 (May 25, 1964): 82.
46. "College Seeks Black Students" in the *Boston Globe* (Boston, MA) (November 24, 1968): B 61.
47. Gail Lumet Buckley, *The Hornes: An American Family* (New York: Applause Books, 2002), 240.
48. Minutes of the Special Meeting of the Board of Directors of the NSSFNS, December 9, 1967, New York, New York, in *Kenneth Clark Papers*, Box 71, folder 4.
49. Ibid.
50. Ibid.
51. Ibid.
52. Ibid.
53. Statement of the President of NSSFNS to the NSSFNS Board, entitled, "To Provoke Discussion", July 14–15, 1968, New York, *Kenneth Clark Papers*.
54. See NSFFNF Press Release, "Sam Johnson Joins NSSFNS in Atlanta," August 29, 1968, in *Kenneth Clark Papers*, Box 385, folder 7.
55. John M. Stalnaker to Clarence Faust, The Fund for the Advancement of Education, September 3, 1952, Box 235, recruitment folder.
56. President's Report, 19.
57. Resolutions, prepared by Wisconsin ACAC Delegates to the Assembly, October 11, 1969, *Kenneth B. Clark Papers*, Box 385, folder 7.
58. Hugh W. Lane, "Admissions Procedures in Transition: Some Interrelations," speech delivered by Lane on January 13, 1970 to The Association of American College, Houston, Texas, in *Kenneth Clark Papers*.
59. Diana Hansard, Secretary to Dr. Kenneth B. Clark to J. Oscar Lee, Chairman, Special Committee, NSSFNS, November 16, 1966, Box 71, folder 3 in the *Kenneth B. Clark Papers*, Library of Congress.
60. Trent to Clark on notice of NSSFNS Board of Directors Meeting, September 1970, *Kenneth Clark Papers*, Box 386, folder 1.
61. John H. Mortimer, October 8, 1970 to Kenneth B. Clark; *Kenneth B. Clark Papers*, Box 386, folder 1; Kenneth B. Clark to John H. Mortimer, October 23, 1970, *Kenneth B. Clark Papers*, Box 386, folder 1.
62. Lane tragically died in 1976 at the age of fifty. See obituary in *Jet Magazine* (November 18, 1976): 55.
63. Inter-Office Memorandum from Fred Crossland, December 18, 1975, Ford Foundation Archives.
64. Marita Graham Goodson, *Chronicles of Faith: The Autobiography of Frederick D. Patterson* (Tuscaloosa and London: University of Alabama Press, 1991), 151.
65. Vernon E. Jordan, Jr. with Annette Gordon-Reed, *Vernon Can Read! A Memoir* (New York: Public Affairs, 2001), 60.
66. Ibid., 61.
67. Ibid.
68. Ibid., 62.
69. For a discussion of the higher education of the Black middle and upper class, see Linda M. Perkins' "The African American Female Elite: The Early History of

African American Women in the Seven Sister College, 1880–1960" in *Harvard Educational Review* 67, no. 4 (Winter 1997); also Adelaide M. Cromwell, *The Other Brahmins: Boston's Black Upper Class, 1750–1950* (Fayetteville, AK: University of Arkansas Press, 1994) and Willard Gatewood's, *Aristocrats of Color: The Black Elite, 1880–1920* (Fayetteville, AK: University of Arkansas Press, 1990).

70. *The Southern Project, 1953–1955 Report: 26.*
71. Jordan, *Vernon Can Read*: 78.
72. Personal Interview with Lois Dickson Rice, November 16, 2003, Washington, DC. Rice is a 1954 Radcliffe graduate and was a recruit of NSSFNS. Rice served on the National Board of NSSFNS. A distinguished educator, Rice served as the vice president of the College Board. She is a distinguished Fellow of the Brookings Institution.
73. See Eric Kelderman, "Black Colleges See a Need to Improve Their Image" in the *Chronicle of Higher Education*, June 27, 2010. According to this article, only 12 percent of Black students attend Black colleges.
74. Interview with Felice Schwartz, Smith College, 1971, transcript at Smith College Special Collection, Northampton, MA.

List of Contributors

Lauren Kientz Anderson received her PhD from Michigan State University in 2010 and is currently a postdoctoral scholar at the University of Kentucky. She studies African American intellectual history and is a regular contributor to the blog of the Society of U.S. Intellectual History.

Richard M. Breaux is an assistant professor of ethnic studies and history at Colorado State University. His articles have appeared in the *Journal of African American History*, *History of Education Quarterly*, and the *Journal of African American Studies*.

Timothy Reese Cain is an assistant professor in the Department of Education Policy, Organization & Leadership at the University of Illinois at Urbana-Champaign. His research examines historical issues involving academic freedom, tenure, student speech, and faculty unionization. He would like to thank the Illinois Campus Research Board for its support of this research and Kathleen A. Murphey for her helpful comments on a version of this paper presented at the 2009 annual meeting of the American Education Research Association.

Michael Fultz is a professor in the Department of Educational Policy Studies at the University of Wisconsin-Madison. His research interests focus on issues concerning African American teachers from the 1860s through the 1970s.

Marybeth Gasman is a professor of higher education at the University of Pennsylvania. An historian of higher education, her work explores issues pertaining to philanthropy and historically black colleges, black leadership, contemporary fundraising issues at black colleges, and African-American giving. She is the author, coauthor, or editor of fifteen books related to these topics, including *Envisioning Black Colleges*, *Understanding Minority Serving Institutions*, *The U.S. History of Higher*

Education: Methods for Uncovering the Past, The Morehouse Mystique: Becoming a Doctor at the Nation's Newest Black Medical School, and *Booker T. Washington Rediscovered.*

Roger L. Geiger is distinguished professor of higher education at Pennsylvania State University and editor of *Perspectives on the History of Higher Education.*

Linda M. Perkins is an associate university professor and director of Applied Women's Studies and the Africana Studies Certificate Program at Claremont Graduate University. Her areas of research are the history of Black women's higher education and the history of talent identification programs.

Louis Ray is an assistant professor at Fairleigh Dickinson University's Peter Sammartino School of Education. He holds memberships in the American Educational Research Association, the Association for the Study of African American Life and History, and the History of Education Society.